Evaluation of Seafood Freshness Quality

FOOD SCIENCE AND TECHNOLOGY

Series Editor

Y. H. Hui, PhD
American Food and Nutrition Center
P.O. Box 34
Cutten, CA 95534

Other Books in the Series

F. W. Schenck and R. E. Hebeda (editors)
Starch Hydrolysis Products: Worldwide Technology Production and Applications

Y. H. Hui (editor)
Dairy Science and Technology Handbook, Volumes 1–3

John Prentice
Dairy Rheology

D. R. Tainter and A. T. Grenis
Spices and Seasonings: A Food Technology Handbook

M. Caric
Concentrated and Dried Dairy Products

Forthcoming Books in the Series

T. Cogan and J.-P. Accolas (editors)
Dairy Starter Cultures

Y.-W. Huang, et al. (editors)
Seafood Science and Technology, Volumes 1–3

Y. H. Hui and G. G. Khachatourians (editors)
Food Biotechnology: Microorganisms

B. H. Lee
Fundamentals of Food Biotechnology

S. Nakai and H. W. Modler (editors)
Food Proteins: Properties and Applications, Volumes 1 & 2

Evaluation of Seafood Freshness Quality

J. R. Botta

VCH

J. R. Botta
14 Marigold Place
St. John's, Newfoundland
Canada A1A 3T6

This book is printed on acid-free paper. ∞

Library of Congress Cataloging-in-Publication Data

Botta, J. Richard
      Evaluation of seafood freshness quality / by J. R. Botta.
          p.   cm.—(Food science and technology)
      Includes bibliographical references and index.
      ISBN 1–56081–612–0 (alk. paper) : $100.00
      1. Fish as food—Analysis.   2. Seafood—Quality control.
   3. Fishery products—Spoilage.   I. Title.   II. Series: Food science
   and technology (VCH Publishers)
   TX556.5.B68   1995
   664'.9497—dc 20   94–40213
                                                              CIP

Printed in the United States of America

ISBN 1–56081–612–0 VCH Publishers, Inc.

Printing History:
10 9 8 7 6 5 4 3 2 1

Published jointly by

VCH Publishers, Inc.   VCH Verlagsgesellschaft mbH   VCH Publishers (UK) Ltd.
220 East 23rd Street   P.O. Box 10 11 61   8 Wellington Court
New York, New York 10010   69451 Weinheim, Germany   Cambridge CB1 1HZ
                                                                   United Kingdom

Preface

People involved in the seafood industry frequently want to evaluate the freshness quality of a specific seafood product using scientifically sound procedures, but do not do so. This is not because scientifically sound procedures do not exist. During the past 60 years a tremendous amount of scientific research concerning the measurement of seafood quality has been conducted and published.

Two major factors have resulted in people either not evaluating freshness quality or evaluating it using methods that are not scientifically sound. Scientific research concerning freshness quality is often published in "academic" journals, and therefore do not reach the people who would regularly apply the information. In addition, the large number of different methods that are available has caused confusion, particularly when the reported usefulness of individual methods is observed to vary with the author. For example, promoters of using chemical methods to determine freshness quality often state that chemical methods are superior to sensory methods because, unlike sensory methods, chemical methods are objective methods of evaluating freshness quality. Although some sensory methods are indeed subjective methods, other sensory methods are actually objective methods that directly evaluate the freshness quality of a sample. Consequently promoters of sensory methods often state that sensory methods are superior to chemical methods because, unlike chemical methods, sensory methods are both objective and direct methods of measuring freshness quality.

Thus a practical overview of the different methods that may be used to evaluate freshness quality of seafood is needed. Such an overview would allow seafood processors, purchasers, and/or regulators to compare their specific needs for measuring freshness quality with the strengths and the weaknesses of various scientifically sound methods, enabling them to select a method that (for their specific situation) has maximum benefits and minimum weaknesses. This book is my attempt to fulfill this practical need. Since the topic of evaluating freshness quality is very broad, it was decided to include references, as this allows the reader to obtain additional information about any topic discussed. It is hoped that this book will encourage the use of scientifically sound methods, whenever seafood freshness quality is evaluated.

I gratefully acknowledge the extensive cooperation, involving assistance and/or suggestions, that I received from many of my colleagues.

J. R. Botta
St. John's, Newfoundland
April 1995

Contents

1

Introduction

1.1 What Is Quality?

The term quality is often misunderstood. This is because there can be no single, brief and consistent definition of a concept. Because quality is not a specific object (e.g., a ball) or a clearly defined actuality (e.g., sunrise), its definition depends upon what impresses a person and ultimately, upon that person's conclusion, concerning those impressions. Thus, different people frequently have different definitions of the term quality.

A review of some of the more common definitions of quality (Table 1.1) reveals two major points. First, quality involves all of the attributes, characteristics, and features of a product that the buyer, purchaser, consumer, or user of the product expects. Consequently quality as related to seafood involves availability, safety (chemical and microbiological), convenience, freshness, integrity, and nutritional value.[1,2] Second, a product with excellent quality is a product that clearly meets the buyer's or user's highest expectations, whereas a product with unsatisfactory quality is a product that does not meet the buyer's or user's minimum expectations. Therefore, this book defines quality as "the degree of excellence to which a product meets all of the attributes, characteristics, and features of the product that the buyer and user of the product and regulatory agencies expect." This definition clearly signifies that (1) quality is a concept rather than a specific object or a single actuality with one consistent definition; (2) quality depends on both the particular product being produced and the reason it is being produced; and (3) quality depends on the buyer and user of the product and the agency that regulates the product. Acceptance of this definition makes it mandatory for the producer to clearly identify, in writing,[3] all the expectations that each buyer, user, and regulatory agency has for every product. If this is not done the

Table 1.1. DEFINITIONS OF QUALITY

Reference	Definition
1	"Quality is the extent to which a product fulfills consumer needs and wants."
30	"The degree to which the user's expectations for wholesomeness, integrity and freshness of seafood have been met."
36	"All those attributes which consciously or unconsciously the fish eater or buyer considers should be present."
40	"The composite of various attributes and properties of the product that influence its acceptability to the buyer or consumer."
41	"To most people it is the integration of the biological factors determining safety and nutritional values and the physical factors (ie., size and weight uniformity, color and blemished surfaces) used in a grading system."
46	"The characteristic which imparts to a product or a service the ability to satisfy certain minimum demands and expectations of the consumer or purchaser."
47	"An aesthetic standard for a product usually set by experienced users."
47	"The composite of the characteristics that differentiate among individual units of product and have significance in determining the degree of acceptability of that unit by the user."
48	"Quality means conformance to requirements."
49	"Sensory quality is that complex set of sensory characteristics, including appearance, aroma, taste, and texture, that is maximally acceptable to a specific audience of consumers, those who are regular users of the product category, or those who, by some clear definition, comprise the target market."
50	"Quality means pleasing consumers, not just protecting them from annoyances."
51	"It is the combination of attributes or characteristics of a product that have significance in determining the degree of acceptability to a user."
52	"Quality is the degree of excellence or fitness of purpose."
52	"Quality is the sum of those attributes that govern its acceptability to the buyer or consumer."

potential benefits of measuring quality would be lost. Because there are so many different types of quality, it is beyond the scope of this book to discuss each of these in the same detail with which freshness quality will be discussed. As a result other kinds of quality will be discussed only briefly, with references provided to enable readers to study these types of seafood quality in additional detail.

1.1.1 Seafood Safety

The most important type of seafood quality is seafood safety. All else is irrelevant if, upon being consumed or used, the seafood is not wholesome (Glossary) and causes illness. This is why consumers demand that food be safe; thus consumers will not negotiate with food producers about this aspect of food quality.[1] It is difficult to take preventive action against unsafe food as safety cannot be easily identified.[2] Determining if a seafood is safe is often complicated and/or expensive; consumers are, therefore, forced to rely on governmental or independent agencies to ensure that the seafood offered for sale is indeed safe. There are many different issues concerning safety (Glossary) of seafood. However, a seafood is generally made unsafe due to (1) the presence of microorganisms (Glossary) that may occur naturally in the seafood or may be transmitted to the seafood after it is caught or (2) contamination (Glossary) of the seafood with chemicals.

For further information concerning seafood microbiological safety, such as parasites (Glossary) and viruses (Glossary), naturally occurring pathogens (Glossary), pathogens transmitted to seafood after it is caught, natural seafood toxins (Glossary), scombroid poisoning (Glossary), and safety of canned seafood the reader is referred references 4–7. Until recently the microbiological safety of seafood was assured by laboratory testing of the final seafood products.[8] However, it has recently been realized that final product testing was very costly and of limited value.[8] A new system based on assessment of microbiological hazards associated with the product, determination of critical control points, and establishment of procedures to monitor these critical control points has been observed to be much less costly and much more effective in ensuring the microbial safety of seafood. This new system, called the Hazard Analysis Critical Control Point (HACCP) system, is being adopted throughout the world.[8,9] Although HACCP was originally developed to ensure the safety of foods, it has been adapted for other uses. For example, the Canadian Government and the Canadian Seafood Industry now utilize HACCP not only to ensure that seafood products are safe, but also to ensure that the products are of acceptable freshness quality and to prevent economic fraud.[10,11] For additional information concerning microbial safety and the HACCP system the reader is referred references 8 and 11–19.

A seafood is made chemically unsafe by becoming contaminated, prior to being caught in the ocean, with metals (arsenic, cadmium, lead, mercury, and selenium) or organic compounds (polychlorinated biphenyls, dioxins, and chlorinated hydrocarbon pesticides).[20] Even if a seafood is not chemically contaminated when it is caught it may, while it is being processed, become contaminated with nitrosamines, products of chlorination, bromination, and iodization, sulfites, and residues of ozonation.[20] In addition, aquaculture of seafood can result in the seafood becoming chemically contaminated with antibiotics, nitrofurans, and sulfonamides.[20] For additional information concerning the different kinds of chemical contamination of seafood and methods of assessing if a seafood is chemically unsafe refer to references 20–22.

1.1.2 Seafood Nutritional Quality

Food is necessary for humans to live and grow and keep well.[23] Consequently the nutritional quality (Glossary) of a food is very important. The nutritional importance of seafood has increased substantially because of the now scientifically recognized beneficial effects of eating seafood fats and oils.[24–27] Seafood is also an important source of high-quality, highly digestible protein and a respectable source of essential minerals.[24,28] The nutritional quality of seafood is affected by body part of the seafood being consumed, method of handling, method of processing (including cooking at home), season of harvest, sex of the animal, and species.[24,28] References 23–28 provide further information concerning seafood nutritional quality.

1.1.3 Availability, Convenience, and Integrity

Availability (like freshness quality, nutritional quality, and seafood safety) is a traditional aspect of seafood quality[1,29] because excellent freshness quality, excellent nutritional quality, and excellent seafood safety are irrelevant if the seafood product is not available.

Convenience (Glossary) and integrity (Glossary) have become important kinds of seafood quality.[1,2,29-31]

The importance of convenience as a kind of seafood quality has developed because of three major factors. First, the modern consumer is greatly affected by the widespread effects of time pressure.[1,32] Second, many consumers do not frequently eat seafood and therefore lack confidence in preparing seafood at home.[33] Third, frequently only one person in the family "likes" seafood, which means that there is a demand for seafood that can be prepared in small quantities.[34] Thus, depending upon the consumer, convenience of seafood includes a variety of items such as (1) a simple packaging system that allows the consumer to rapidly and easily purchase, store, and unpack the product,[1,2] (2) an appropriately sized package for the consumer's particular requirements,[32,34] (3) simple quick recipes that allow the consumer to easily and rapidly prepare the product with confidence,[32,34] and (4) achievement of all of this without sacrificing freshness quality.[2]

Regardless of whether the seafood product lacks integrity because it does not live up to the producer's claims (on the package or in advertisements) or it is inferior to the last time that product was consumed, failure to meet the buyer's or consumer's expectations is extremely important.[1,2,30,35] In fact, a seafood product is not accepted by the buyer or consumer until the quality of the product equals the buyer's or consumer's perception of quality.[2] Similarly, whether the consumer feels the seafood product is overpriced is also important.

1.2 What Is Freshness Quality?

Because the term freshness, like the term quality, refers to a concept not a distinct object or a specified actuality, it is also frequently misunderstood. Thus, people often have different definitions of the term freshness. A examination of some of the various definitions of fresh seafood (Table 1.2) indicates that freshness is defined in terms of time (e.g., time since the seafood was caught, delivered to the store, etc.), how the seafood was processed (e.g., not canned, not cooked, not cured, and not frozen), and the characteristics of the seafood (e.g., appearance, odor, flavor, and texture) of the seafood. Changes in these characteristics can be brought about by a combination of different (e.g., biological, chemical, microbiological, and/or physical) processes.

Freshness, defined only in term of time, without defining how the seafood must be handled and/or stored, can be very confusing to any buyer or user since the manner in which any specific seafood item is handled and/or stored can greatly affect the acceptability of that item. Consequently the practical usefulness of the term "fresh," when defined only in terms of time, is often limited. Similarly freshness, defined only

Table 1.2.   DEFINITIONS OF FRESH SEAFOOD

Reference	Definition
7	"The term fresh indicates that the fish is not and has never been frozen, cooked, cured or otherwise preserved, and that it exhibits a clean, natural odor and physical characteristics representative of the species in good condition."
30	"Freshness reflects the degree to which microbiological spoilage or chemical deterioration has occurred."
40	"Fresh seafood is not easy to define. Loss of freshness followed by spoilage is a complex combination of microbiological, chemical and physical processes."
52	"A seafood that has the characteristics of a newly harvested seafood, it is not the opposite of stale."
53	"A seafood that is the opposite of stale."
53	"A seafood that has not been frozen."
54	"A seafood is fresh from the point of death of the animal until the first detectable signs of spoilage."
55	"Fresh means natural raw fillets or minced fish which has not been changed to any other state by freezing, cooking, curing, etc."
56	"Fresh designates the time the seafood is removed from the water and spoiled marks the state in which definite deterioration has taken place rendering the seafood inedible."
57	"Consumers consider the first point of freshness to be the time the seafood arrives at the store."
58	"Freshness is the degree of microbiological spoilage or chemical degradation to which the raw product has progressed."

in terms of how the seafood was handled and/or processed can also be confusing to the buyer or user. An ungutted Atlantic cod stored in ice for 10 days would be classified as being "fresh," with its appropriate connotations. In contrast, an Atlantic cod bled, , gutted, washed, and iced as soon as it was brought onboard the fishing vessel, but frozen as soon as rigor mortis was resolved, would be classified as "not fresh" with opposite connotations. Thus it has been suggested that the term "chilled" be used to replace this type of "fresh."[33] However, "freshness" defined in term of specific characteristics (appearance, odor, flavor, and texture) is usually much more consistent and less confusing.[33]

In addition, the term "quality" has been previously defined (in this book) as involving a degree of excellence of attributes, characteristics, and features. Therefore "freshness quality" has been defined as the degree of excellence to which a seafood meets the characteristics concerning appearance, flavor, odor, and/or texture that the buyer, user, and regulatory agency normally associates with a particular seafood when it is caught at the best time of year, caught in the best location, caught by the best method, and handled and/or processed in the best manner. Since "what is best" depends upon the particular buyer or consumer, so does the exact definition of freshness quality. Consequently, to benefit from the potential advantages of measuring freshness quality, the producer must first identify, in writing,[33] the characteristics (concerning appearance, flavor, odor, and/or texture) that the buyer and user desires, expects, or wants. The important effect of both the time of year and location of catching on the intrinsic freshness quality (Glossary) must not be overlooked.[36,37] For example, the freshness quality of fillets from Atlantic cod tainted with dimethyl sulfide (Blackberry odor), fillets from jellied flounder, or the flesh of Pacific salmon caught near their spawning streams is clearly believed (by a large number of seafood buyers or users) to be quite low, as these conditions negatively affect at least some of the seafood's sensory characteristics.

1.2.1 Why Does Freshness Quality Need to Be Evaluated?

As previously stated, there are many types of seafood quality. Freshness quality is considered to be an extremely important factor in determining overall quality of a particular seafood item.[38–40]

Although seafood safety is indisputably the most important type of seafood quality, the buyer or user is generally not capable of readily determining the safety of a particular seafood item.[2] The buyer or user is thus forced to assume that the agencies responsible for the safety of seafood have successfully fulfilled their obligations and that the particular seafood item being purchased and/or used is indeed safe. Therefore, the importance of seafood safety in determining if a particular seafood item is purchased or used is not great. Similarly, although the nutritional quality of seafood has been primarily responsible for the recent substantial increase in seafood consumption,[24,41–43] determination of nutritional quality is also often complicated and/or expensive. Since the nutritional quality of seafood cannot normally be readily determined by the buyer or user, its importance in determining if a specific seafood item (not seafood in general) has been purchased has been limited. However now that the "new" U.S. food labeling regulations[44] have been implemented, this will probably change. Depending on the particular seafood item being purchased (e.g., chilled, frozen, or canned), the buyer may or may not be able to readily determine the freshness quality of that seafood item. However, the freshness quality (appearance, flavor, odor, and/or texture) of each seafood item is, consciously or unconsciously, determined by each user as each seafood item is being consumed.[40,45] The degree to which the freshness quality of that seafood item meets the buyer's or user's expectations concerning freshness quality will greatly affect whether that seafood item will be purchased or used, particularly if that seafood item will be purchased again.[1,2,30,40] Therefore, whenever a seafood product is available for purchasing, freshness quality, convenience, and integrity are controlling factors that determine if that seafood product will be purchased more than once.

1.3 Objective of This Book

Whenever the buyer's or user's expectations concerning seafood freshness quality have been established, it is obviously very desirable for the producer to ensure that these expectations have indeed been met.[3] Similarly, it is frequently very desirable for a buyer or a regulatory agency to ensure that established expectations have been met.[3]

During the past decades there has been a large number of developments in the technological measurement of seafood freshness quality. The practical usefulness of these different methods varies greatly. Only by utilizing proven practical, but technologically sound methods can the producer, buyer, or regulatory agency consistently and accurately determine the "level" of appearance, flavor, odor, and/or texture that, when compared to the appropriate established, written,[3] expectations, dependably confirms the actual freshness quality. Such a process may be of great use during either product/process development or during commercial production.

The objective of this book is to clearly describe these different technological methods, indicating the major advantages and/or disadvantages of each, and, if possible, to suggest when that particular method should be used to measure freshness quality of seafood.

The number of methods that may be used is extremely large. In general, the major practical methods of determining seafood freshness quality involve chemical analysis, physical instruments and/or principles of physics, sensory evaluation procedures to grade selected samples, and sensory evaluation techniques to assess sensory attributes of selected samples. A separate chapter will be devoted to the discussion of each of these different types of methods. The order in which the chapters are arranged and the topics within individual chapters are presented is not related to the usefulness of the methods in determining freshness quality of seafood. Some references will be made to evaluation of freshwater species, even though they are not harvested from the "sea," because such results may be of use in the evaluation of marine species.

2

Chemical Methods of Evaluating Freshness Quality

2.1 Introduction

Chemical methods involve chemically analyzing a sample to determine the concentration of a specific chemical(s) within the sample. This observed concentration is used to indirectly measure (predict) the level of a specific sensory attribute, which allows for the immediate determination of freshness quality once the predicted level of the sensory attribute is compared to that specified in the appropriate product standards. Such methods have been used to measure the freshness quality of seafood for over 100 years.[59]

Chemical methods of measuring freshness quality have been considered to be objective (Glossary) methods and therefore superior (less variable) to methods involving sensory evaluation.[60–63] Although affective methods of sensory evaluation (Glossary) are subjective (Glossary), discriminative (Glossary) and descriptive (Glossary) methods, including grading, of sensory evaluation are objective.[63–67] Thus arbitrarily classifying all chemical methods of evaluating freshness quality as being objective and all sensory methods as being subjective is now widely recognized as wrong.[63,68,69] In addition, even when chemical methods of measuring freshness quality are observed to be less variable than sensory methods,[60–62] it does not mean that these chemical methods are thereby more accurate (Glossary).[70] Reduced variability means that chemical methods are more precise (i.e., exact), not necessarily more accurate.[70] The tremendous practical importance of understanding the difference between results that are precise and results that are accurate is clearly demonstrated by the example given by Powers[70] ("the archer or marksman may group shots close together, thus being precise, but the shots may be at the rim of the target instead of at the bull's-eye," thus being inaccurate).

Unlike freshness quality grading (Chapter 4) or some types of attribute assessment (Chapter 5), chemical methods of evaluating freshness quality indirectly measure the level of a sensory attribute. For example, Piggott[71] states "A gas chromatogram, even with 250 peaks on it, unequivocally identified, does not provide any information about the flavor, but only about the volatiles. These are not the same." Only when it has been clearly established that the concentration of a particular chemical is closely related to the level of a specific sensory attribute can the concentration of that chemical be realistically used to estimate the level of the specified sensory attribute. This estimated level is then compared to the product standard, and the freshness quality concerning that specific attribute is indirectly determined. Consequently, to ensure that the results of a chemical test are indeed "hitting the bull's-eye" both the type of product being analyzed and the chemical method being used must be identical to those used when the aforementioned relationship was clearly established. Similarly, when such a relationship is investigated, the sensory evaluations must be conducted using scientifically sound procedures. Whenever these conditions have been met, chemical methods are capable of being readily used to evaluate freshness quality and therefore should be used.[70,72] One additional characteristic of the major chemical methods of evaluating freshness quality is that these methods primarily estimate only the freshness quality aspects involving flavor and odor (not appearance and texture).

2.2 Chemical Methods That May Measure Freshness Quality

The selection of appropriate objective chemical methods of measuring freshness quality (determined by appropriate objective sensory evaluation procedures) is extremely difficult unless all of the reasons why the freshness quality of that particular product needs to be determined are clearly defined in writing.[3] Critically comparing the factors that affect the relevance of each method being considered with each written reason will help maximize the benefits and minimize the limitations of the chemical method(s) that is ultimately selected.

2.2.1 Major Chemical Methods

2.2.1.1 Total Volatile Basic Nitrogen (TVB-N)

2.2.1.1.1 Stage of Spoilage of Samples

During the postmortem storage of a wide variety of seafood, microbiological spoilage causes the formation of volatile bases (primarily ammonia, dimethyamine, and trimethylamine), which have often been determined to measure indirectly the freshness quality of such seafood.[63,73–78]

This method is not capable of identifying the early stages of deterioration of freshness quality.[63,73–75] Thus, unlike the results of the Tasmanian Food Research Unit (TFRU) freshness quality grading system (Chapter 4), total volatile basic nitrogen (TVB-N) values are not linearly related to the length of time (days) the species being evaluated was stored in ice and it cannot be used to predict the storage life of that species. However TVB-N values do identify the latter stages of spoilage and, therefore, in principle, can be routinely used as a standard method to determine if chilled, frozen, dried, and canned seafood is spoiled (i.e., not suitable for conventional markets).[36,63,73–75]

2.2.1.1.2 Method of Analysis

The large number of different methods that are presently available to determine TVB-N makes it difficult to implement TVB-N as a standard index of freshness quality,[74,76,77] as the method used to determine TVB-N has been shown to greatly affect the observed TVB-N value (Fig. 2.1). Whenever TVB-N values are used to determine if groundfish are marketable, one must be sure that the limit (e.g., 35 mg TVB-N per 100 g of fish muscle) defined in the product standard is indeed appropriate for the method being used.

Collaborative studies concerning the determination of TVB-N have also revealed that even when a single method of determination is used, significantly different results may occur among different laboratories.[73] These differences are believed to be caused by small differences in the types of apparatus used or differences in the procedures used during the analyses.[76]

Consequently, the Western European Fish Technologists' Association (WEFTA) has recommended that a standard procedure, with each step of the analysis clearly specified, be used.[73] When compared to other chemical methods, this recommended method (Table 2.1) is quick (17 min), simple to use, and inexpensive, but it is accurate, if the detailed procedures are clearly followed.[73] Both the speed and the low cost are major advantages of using TVB-N value, rather than other chemical methods of evaluating freshness quality.[63] Whenever there is doubt concerning the results of this rapid method, a more detailed method (Table 2.1) (which unfortunately is both slower and more expensive) is recommended.[73]

2.2.1.2 Trimethylamine (TMA) and Related Compounds

The total volatile bases developed during the storage of unfrozen fish consist primarily of ammonia and trimethylamine (TMA).[78] The suitability of using TMA content itself as a chemical method of evaluating freshness quality of seafood has been investigated extensively.[60,79,80] Depending on the species (see individual sections on groundfish, pelagic species, and shellfish) evaluated, it has been observed to be a useful measure of freshness quality (particularly flavor and odor aspects) of a variety of seafood,[79] but this usefulness depends upon the time of year and/or the location of catching, stage of spoilage, type of processing, and/or storage, and method of analysis.

2.2.1.2.1 Time of Year and Location of Catch

The actual TMA content of different species has been observed to be affected by both the time of year and the location of catching.[79] Thus even when a TMA (as a method

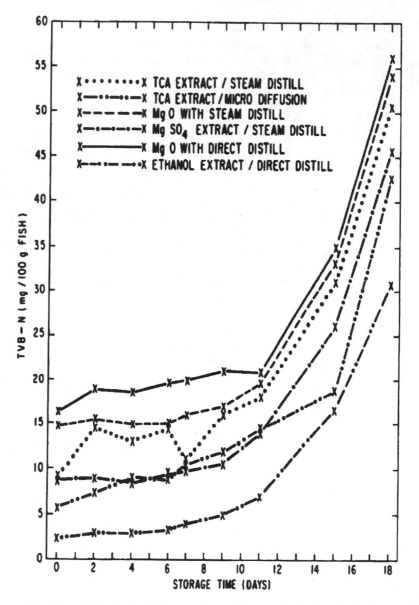

Figure 2.1. Effect of method of determination on the magnitude of total volatile basic nitrogen (TVB-N) in chilled stored Atlantic cod (*Gadus morhua*). Printed with permission from Canada Department of Fisheries and Oceans, Inspection Branch, St. John's, NF, Canada.

of evaluating freshness quality) has previously shown to be appropriate for the species that is to be chemically analyzed, it is very important to ensure that neither of these factors has negated this relationship between TMA concentration and the level of the sensory characteristics of interest.

Table 2.1. DETAILED STANDARD METHOD OF ANALYSIS FOR THE DETERMINATION OF TOTAL VOLATILE BASIC NITROGEN (TVB-N).[a,b,c]

---

1. *Principle*

The volatile basic nitrogen content is liberated by addition of magnesium oxide (MgO), a weak alkali, to the thoroughly homogenized fish, followed by steam distillation. The volatile bases are absorbed in boric acid solution, and determined by titration with 0.1 N acid. Alternatively, an extract of fish with 0.6 N perchloric acid is used for confirmation in cases of doubt. Because this is a standard method, the defined working and distillation conditions must be well adhered to, in order to keep deamination at a constant level.

2. *Equipment*

2.1. Balance, accuracy 0.05 g or better.

2.2. Steam distillation unit such as

    a. Antona apparatus consisting of 2-liter round-bottom flask with glass side arm and stopcock (steam generator), reaction vessel insert, connecting tube and coil condenser with extended outlet or an appropriate projection from the condenser, electric heating mantle for the 2-liter round-bottom flask, receiver support (height adjustable);

    b. Buchi distillation unit model 315-special with insulating mantle for the reaction vessels, control valve for steam regulation, and special condenser; or

    c. A related unit with adjustable reduced steam flow.

2.3. Mincer, homogenizer/blender (e.g., top-drive blender).

2.4. Weighing dishes, preferably with spout (approximately 50 ml content).

2.5. Powder funnel, diameter at top 10 cm, at bottom 2 cm.

2.6. 300-ml broad-necked Erlenmeyer flask, graduated, as distillate receiver.

2.7. 10- or 25-ml buret for the 0.1 N acid.

2.8. Funnel, diameter 15 cm, with fast filtering fluted filter papers (for alternate method only).

2.9. 25-ml pipettes (for alternate method only).

3. *Reagents*

3.1. Water, distilled or deionized.

3.2. Magnesium oxide, reagent grade.

3.3. Silicone antifoam emulsion.

3.4. Approximately 3% aqueous boric acid solution.

3.5. 0.1 N hydrochloric acid or sulfuric acid.

3.6. Tashiro-indicator mixture (methyl red and methylene blue).

3.7. Perchloric acid, 0.6 N (6%) (for alternate method only).

4. *Preparation of the distillation unit*

4.1. Before analyzing samples, carry out a blind distillation of 200 ml water into the receiver (put 50 ml water into the reaction vessel and 100 ml water into the receiver), to avoid TVB-N losses in the first distillates.

4.2. Adjust the distillate flow to 10 ml/min; check the distillate amount occasionally.

4.3. Pipette approximately 10 ml of the boric acid solution into the graduated Erlenmyer flask (receiver), add 8 drops of the Tashiro indicator, and fill up with distilled water to 100 ml. Place the flask on the receiver support, so that the outlet of the condenser is immersed.

5. *Preparation of samples*

5.1. Take a fish flesh sample of at least 100 g (preferably a total fillet) and homogenize with a mincer and/or blender. Investigate immediately, within 1 hr in chilled storage, otherwise quick freeze the minced sample (e.g., in a closed container/plastic bag) and store at −18°C or lower for a limited period.

(Continued)

Table 2.1. (*Continued*)

5.2. From frozen fish, e.g., fillet blocks, cut a 100–200 g sample of approximately 2 cm thickness, place it in a water-tight plastic bag, and thaw, e.g., by immersing the bag in a gently stirred water bath at about 20°C but not more than 25°C; thawing takes approximately 15 min. Homogenize the total sample including thaw drip.

6. Separation of TVB-N

6.1. *Directly from fish flesh*

Weigh 10.0 ± 0.1 g of the homogenized fish flesh sample into a suitably sized flat dish. After the addition of a small amount of water, disperse the sample with a glass rod. Transfer it by means of a powder funnel quantitatively into the reaction vessel. Rinse with a small amount of water to ensure that as far as possible the sample lies on the bottom of the vessel. Shake to ensure proper dispersion and avoid clotting during distillation.

6.2. *From extracts (for alternate method only)*
     a. Weigh 20.0 ± 0.1 g of the homogenized fish flesh sample into a suitable beaker, add 80 ml 0.6 *M* perchloric acid, homogenize for 1–2 min by use of a homogenizer, then filter through fluted filter paper. (The extract can be stored at 2–6°C up to 7 days.)
     b. Pipette 25 ml of the extract into the reaction vessel.

6.3. Add to the sample in the reaction vessel 2–3 g magnesium oxide (e.g., with a measuring spoon) and 2–3 drops of silicone antifoam emulsion.

6.4. Insert the reaction vessel immediately into the preheated steam generator and connect with the bridge to the condenser at once.

6.5. Antona unit: bring the water in the round-bottom flask (approximately 1 liter) to the boiling point with the stopcock open to reduce dilution by condensation, which would retard the process of separation: close the cock when boiling starts.

6.6. Distill for 10 min with the outlet tube from the condenser immersed, and 2 min with it above the surface. (Lower the support with the receiver.)

6.7. When distillation is completed
     a. Open the cock in the steam generator (Antona unit) or switch off the distillation (Buchi unit);
     b. Rinse the condenser outlet with a small amount of distilled water and then remove the receiver for titration.

6.8. Preparation of the units for the following sample.
     a. Remove the reaction vessel while it is still hot, empty and rinse the reaction vessel well with water, and rinse condenser and connecting tube of the Antona unit a little. It is advantageous to operate two reaction vessels alternatively for preparation and distillation.
     b. Antona unit: after each distillation, with glass stopcock open, fill the steam generator with hot water and preheat near to the boiling point before the next reaction vessel is inserted. Grease the joints well to avoid sticking.

7. Determination of TVB-N

7.1. Titration. Titrate the distillate containing the volatile basic nitrogen against the 0.1 *N* acid (from a buret) until the neutral point is reached (the color changes from green to red–violet and is gray at the neutral point).

7.2. Calculation. Volume (ml) 0.1 *N* acid $\times$ 14 = mg TVB-N/100 g or, expressed more exactly, ml 0.1 *N* $\times$ 1.4 $\times$ 100/sample mass in g (if 25 ml extract is used, sample mass in calculation is 25% of original mass extracted).

---

[a] Method recommended by WEFTA. (Western European Fish Technologists' Association)

[b] Reprinted with permission from Antonacopoulos and Vyncke.[73]

[c] Steps 2.8, 2.9, 3.7, and 6.2 are not normally included in the analysis of TVB-N value. These steps are used only with the alternate procedure.

2.2.1.2.2 Stage of Spoilage of Samples

When used with "appropriate" species, TMA is primarily suitable for evaluating samples of medium to poor freshness quality as it usually does not indicate a change in freshness quality until the fish have been stored in ice for approximately 6 days.[40] This is moderately superior to that of TVB-N, which usually does not change until the fish have been stored in ice for approximately 10 days,[81] but it does mean that TMA content cannot be used to predict the "future" freshness quality of the samples being examined. However, diethylamine (DMA) content of iced cod and haddock has been observed to increase at a constant rate, even during the first few days of iced storage, and, therefore, is a superior chemical index of freshness quality.[81] This agrees with the statement of Martin et al.[82] that analysis of DMA is most useful during the early stages of spoilage, but that analysis of TMA is most valuable during the latter stages of spoilage.

2.2.1.2.3 Type of Processing and Storage

Although TMA content has been observed to be a useful indicator of freshness quality when "appropriate" intact fish or fillets are chilled, it has been observed to be unreliable when these same species are minced or canned (thermally processed).[79]

Similarly, whenever preservatives such as ethylenediaminetetraacetic acid (EDTA) are used the content of TMA is not a useful index of freshness quality, even with "appropriate" species.[83] This is because these preservatives inhibit the growth of TMA-producing bacteria such as *Pseudomonas putrefactions*, thereby keeping TMA production low, while allowing spoilage to occur.[83]

Trimethylamine content has usually been observed to not be a dependable method of evaluating freshness quality whenever "appropriate" species have been stored frozen.[79] This is because under such circumstances DMA and formaldehyde, rather than only TMA itself, are also produced.[84–86] Thus DMA has been suggested to be a useful indicator of freshness quality of "appropriate" species that have been stored frozen. It has also been suggested[87] that both TMA and DMA be measured so that the deterioration of freshness quality that occurred prior to freezing (measured by TMA) and the deterioration of freshness quality that occurred during frozen storage (measured by DMA) could be evaluated. However, the usefulness of measuring DMA content of groundfish that have been stored frozen is limited to gadoid species, as other species do not develop adequate amounts of DMA during frozen storage.[79] In addition, the absence of air has been observed to affect the degradation of trimethylamine oxide (TMAO) to DMA and formaldehyde during chilled storage (not frozen storage) of red hake.[88]

2.2.1.2.4 Method of Analysis

The long-term extensive investigation of TMA as a chemical method of measuring freshness quality has resulted in a large number of different analytical methods that may be used to determine its concentration in seafood.[79] Since then even more methods have been developed, some of which are briefly described in Table 2.2. Therefore whenever a product standard stipulates a specific TMA value it is extremely important to ensure that this specified value is actually appropriate for the method of analysis that is to be used. For example, the TMA content determined by the picrate salt method (Table 2.2) has been reported to be 35% higher than those determined by high-performance liquid chromatography (HPLC).[89] Most of these methods (Table 2.2) are not portable, as laboratory facilities are required, they entail at least 25–30 min, and they involve destructive sampling, which is a distinct disadvantage when compared to freshness quality grading.[90] One partial exception to these criticisms is the method that uses a diagnostic strip to measure TMA content of the press juice,[91] as it is portable and simple to use, requires only 5 min, and is relatively nondestructive because only 5–10 g of the muscle (not the entire fillet) needs to be pressed (destroyed) (Table 2.2). Another partial exception is the method involving headspace analysis method,[92,93] which does not require destructive sampling, measures both TMA and DMA, and entails only 10–15 min, but is not portable as expensive laboratory equipment is required (Table 2.2). Although they require expensive laboratory equipment and involve destructive sampling the methods involving either gas chromatography (GC) or HPLC analysis also measure both TMA and DMA.

The picrate salt formation method has historically been one of the widely used procedures to determine TMA.[79] However when compared to the other methods described in Table 2.2, its measurement of TMA is not specific (other amines present in the fish muscle may alter the observed TMA values, making these values incorrect),[89] requires laboratory facilities, involves destructive sampling, and is the most time consuming.

2.2.1.3 Nucleotide Degradation Products

Once a fish dies, the chemical composition of adenosine triphosphate (ATP) (Glossary) is broken down into numerous other chemical products (Table 2.3). Using the concentration of some of these breakdown products to estimate freshness quality has been investigated extensively.[60,61,82,94]

2.2.1.3.1 Degree of Spoilage of Samples

The degradation of ATP to inosine monophosphate (IMP) (Table 2.3) has been reported to be caused entirely by enzymes naturally present in groundfish tissue (i.e., "autolysis") and to normally occur within 1 day,[95,96] although the actual of speed of ATP degradation is known to be influenced by factors such as the amount of struggling prior to death, not bleeding the fish, rough handling, and temperature at which the fish is stored.[97] The subsequent breakdown of IMP to hypoxanthine (Table 2.3) is slow and caused by both autolytic and microbial enzymes.[98] Thus measuring the concentration of nucleotide degradation products is believed to be an index of both autolytic and microbial changes and is, therefore, capable of measuring changes in freshness quality that occur during the early stages[82,95] as well as during later stages of chilled storage. This is something that chemical tests such as TMA and TVB-N (that measure only microbial changes) are incapable of measuring and is one reason

Table 2.2.   VARIOUS PUBLISHED METHODS USED TO DETERMINE THE
TRIMETHYLAMINE (TMA), DIMETHYLAMINE (DMA), AND
FORMALDEHYDE CONTENT OF SEAFOODS[a]

Trimethylene (TMA) Content

1. Analysis of pressed juice or neutralized perchloric acid extract using a diagnostic test strip for semi-quantitative analysis.[91] Using a modified plugged syringe and a small sample (<10 g) of a fillet, the pressed juice is diluted and reacted with a diagnostic strip, and the color visually compared with a set of TMA standards. This method is rapid (approximately 5 min), relatively nondestructive, and does not require sophisticated equipment, but has not been widely used because of the absence of a commercial source of TMA dehydrogenase necessary to make the diagnostic strips.[60]

2. Enzymatic analysis of a neutralized perchloric acid extract using TMA dehydrogenase.[180] Extracts are prepared, utilizing entire fillets, a food processor to mince the fillet, perchloric acid, and a blender. Aliquots of the filtered extract are reacted with a TMA dehydrogenase mixture for 20 min at 30°C and the resulting color measured using a spectrophotometer or by visually comparing the color to that of TMA standards. Although this method is very specific, the lack of a commercial source of TMA dehydrogenase is a very severe limitation.[60]

3. Gas chromatographic (GC) analysis.[88] An extract of the sample is prepared by blending the sample with perchloric acid for 2 min. The filtered extract is reacted with benzene and sodium hydroxide for 10 min at 60°C and mechanically rotated for 10 min, after which a small aliquot is injected into a GC column. The concentrations of DMA and TMA are quantitatively determined within 5 min of this injection. Alternate GC methods (such as that described by Perez-Martin et al.[192]) that also simultaneously determine the concentration of both DMA and TMA may be used.

4. TMA headspace analysis.[92,93] The fillet or a subsample is placed inside a sealed container, allowed to sit for 5–10 min for the vapors to equilibrate, and a headspace sample of vapors is collected using an absorber tube, which is then attached to an GC column. Within an additional 5 min the concentrations of both DMA and TMA are quantitatively determined.

5. High performance liquid chromatographic (HPLC) analysis.[89] A 50 g portion of a complete fillet that had been previously minced is blended with perchloric acid for 2 min, reacted with 30% potassium hydroxide, filtered, and subjected to microfiltration, and a small aliquot is injected into an HPLC column. The HPLC analysis requires an additional 15–20 min.

6. Picrate salt formation method of Dyer[193] as modified by Tozawa et al.[194] to ensure that only TMA, rather than TMA and DMA, is measured. A 10–20 g portion of a fillet, which had been previously minced, is reacted with water and trichloroacetic acid (TCA) for a period of at least 30 min. and filtered. An aliquot of this extract is reacted with 25% potassium hydroxide and toluene, heated at 30°C for 5 min, thoroughly shaken, and allowed to stand for 10 min, after which the toluene layer is removed. An aliquot of the water-free toluene extract is reacted with a picric acid solution and the resulting color is quantitatively measured using a colorimeter or a spectrophotometer.

Dimethylamine (DMA) Content

1. Copper dimethyldithiocarbamate method of Dyer and Mounsey.[195] A 10–20 g sample of fish muscle, which had been previously minced, is reacted with water and TCA for at least 30 min prior to being filtered. Alternatively, a TCA extract may be prepared by blending (for 2 min) the fish sample with perchloric acid.[88,89] A measured aliquot of this extract is reacted with a copper-ammonia reagent and a solution of carbon disulfide in benzene, heated at 40–50°C for 5 min, shaken rapidly for 5 min, and reacted with acetic acid, after which the benzene layer is decanted and subsequently dried by shaking it with anhydrous sodium sulfate. The yellowish color of dimethyldithiocarbamate is quantitatively measured using either a colorimeter or a spectrophotometer.

2. The DMA concentration in seafood may also be determined using methods that simultaneously measure both DMA and TMA. Such methods are GC analysis of a perchloric acid extract,[88,192] HPLC

(*Continued*)

Table 2.2. *(Continued)*

analysis of a perchloric acid extract,[89] and GC analysis of headspace.[92] Each of these methods has been briefly outlined above (TMA content).

3. The DMA concentration in some species, such as Argentine hake (*Merluccius hubbsi*), may be indirectly (but accurately) determined by measuring formaldehyde content.[196] Although accurate, the steam distillation procedure that was used is reported to be a simpler method than the solvent extraction method of Dyer and Mounsey.[195,196]

Formaldehyde Content

1. Spectrophotometric analysis of a steam distillate.[196] A mixture of fish muscle, phosphoric acid, and water is steam distilled until a predetermined volume of distillate is collected. An aliquot of distillate is reacted with a chromotropic acid reagent by vigorously shaking the mixture, heated at 100°C for 30 min; the absorbance (at 570 nm) of the solution is determined by using a spectrophotometer.[196]

2. Spectrophotometric analysis of a TCA extract of the fish muscle.[197] A predetermined aliquot of this extract is diluted with a predetermined volume of water, the pH adjusted to 6.0, by adding the necessary volume of acetic acid, and further diluted to a specified total volume. A predetermined aliquot of this diluted and adjusted extract is reacted with an equal volume of the Nash color reagent, heated at 60°C (in a water bath) for 5 min, and cooled under running tap water; the absorbance (at 415 nm) is determined using a spectrophotometer.[197]

3. Enzymatic analysis of a TCA extract of the fish muscle.[198] The pH of a specified volume of this extract is adjusted to 7.0 using 30% potassium hydroxide. A 0.5 ml sample of this neutralized extract is reacted, for 30 min, with a solution containing phosphate buffer, formaldehyde dehydrogenase, and β-nicotinamide adenine dinucleotide. The concentration of formaldehyde is determined by comparing the absorbance at 340 nm of this solution before it is reacted with the TCA extract to its absorbance after the 30 min reaction.[198]

[a] The "description" of each method presented in this table is a general outline not a detailed description. Whenever one of these methods is to be used to analyze a sample, it is extremely important that the exact procedures, described in the original appropriate reference(s), be accurately followed.

why nucleotide degradation products have been so extensively investigated.[99] In addition, unlike TMA, the concentration of these degradation products may be used to measure the freshness quality of freshwater fish.[82] Using the concentration of these breakdown products has, generally, involved measuring only one individual compound, such as hypoxanthine, or measuring a number of them and calculating ratios of the observed concentrations (Table 2.4).

2.2.1.3.2 Hypoxanthine Concentration

Partly because hypoxanthine is a result of both autolytic and microbial degradation (Table 2.3), its usefulness, as an index of freshness quality, has been thoroughly investigated.[100]

Hypoxanthine content is not affected by either thermal processing,[62] including the succeeding storage of the canned product, or by freezing and storage below −10°C.[63,82] Therefore, it has been suggested that the concentration of hypoxantine may be used to indicate the freshness quality (flavor and/or odor) of that particular product immediately before it was canned or frozen, even if freshness quality had been very high.[63,82] This is something that neither TMA nor TVB-N can accurately in-

Table 2.3. NUCLEOTIDE DEGRADATION THAT OCCURS IN FISH MUSCLE ONCE THE FISH DIES

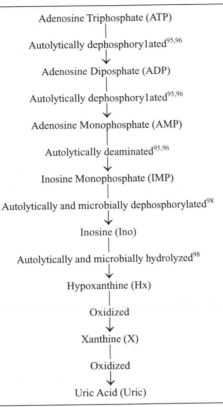

Adenosine Triphosphate (ATP)

Autolytically dephosphorylated[95,96]

↓

Adenosine Diposphate (ADP)

Autolytically dephosphorylated[95,96]

↓

Adenosine Monophosphate (AMP)

Autolytically deaminated[95,96]

↓

Inosine Monophosphate (IMP)

Autolytically and microbially dephosphorylated[98]

↓

Inosine (Ino)

Autolytically and microbially hydrolyzed[98]

↓

Hypoxanthine (Hx)

Oxidized

↓

Xanthine (X)

Oxidized

↓

Uric Acid (Uric)

Table 2.4. DIFFERENT RATIOS OF THE OBSERVED INDIVIDUAL CONCENTRATIONS OF NUCLEOTIDE DEGRADATION PRODUCTS

"Value"	Ratio of Concentrations
$K^a =$	$\dfrac{[\text{Inosine}] + [\text{Hypoxanthine}]}{[\text{ATP}] + [\text{ADP}] + [\text{AMP}] + [\text{IMP}] + [\text{Inosine}] + [\text{Hypoxanthine}]}$
$K_i^b =$	$\dfrac{[\text{Inosine}] + [\text{Hypoxanthine}]}{[\text{IMP}] + [\text{Inosine}] + [\text{Hypoxanthine}]}$
$H^c =$	$\dfrac{[\text{Hypoxanthine}]}{[\text{IMP}] + [\text{Inosine}] + [\text{Hypoxanthine}]}$
$G^d =$	$\dfrac{[\text{Inosine}] + [\text{Hypoxanthine}]}{[\text{AMP}] + [\text{IMP}] + [\text{Inosine}]}$

[a] K value.[112]
[b] K_i value.[109]
[c] H value, also called K' value[110]
[d] G value.[111]

dicate. TMA content is capable of measuring only medium to poor quality and is also unstable during thermal processing and during frozen storage, whereas TVB-N is capable of measuring only advanced spoilage.[73–75] Although these advantages are important, this chemical index of quality has several disadvantages. The rate of formation of hypoxanthine is greatly affected by the species being examined,[82,99] and therefore implementing single limits, regardless of species, to define different "grades" of freshness quality would lead to meaningless results.[99] The formation of hypoxanthine has been reported to vary considerably both within a given species[101] and within an individual fish, as its formation may be greater in red muscle than in white muscle.[102,103] In addition, using hypoxanthine content, without using any other index of freshness quality, may be misleading whenever a seafood has been processed during the latter stages of its chilled storage life. Hypoxanthine can be oxidized to xanthine, which in turn can be oxidized to uric acid (Table 2.3). Thus during chilled storage hypoxanthine content can reach a maximum and can then begin to decline.[100] Whenever a moderately high hypoxanthine content is observed, it is therefore unclear if this value reflects a relatively good freshness quality (of a fish processed prior to the maximum accumulation of hypoxanthine) or if it indicates a relatively poor freshness quality (of a fish processed after its maximum accumulation).[69] However, a decline in hypoxanthine content during latter stages of storages does not appear to always occur, as with chilled albacore, [104,105] iced hoki,[106] chilled orange roughy,[107] and iced shrimp[108] hypoxanthine concentration continued to increase long after the sensory quality became unacceptable. These exceptions emphasize the importance of clearly knowing the relationship between the chemical being analyzed and the freshness quality (determined by sensory evaluation), when a chemical is being used to indirectly measure freshness quality. These uncertainties in using only hypoxanthine content to indirectly determine freshness quality caused scientists to investigate the use of a ratio of the concentrations of numerous nucleotide degradation products to estimate freshness quality.[109–111]

2.2.1.3.3 Nucleotide Ratios of Content

Since the degradation of ATP to hypoxanthine involves numerous different nucleotides (Table 2.3), several different ratios (Table 2.4) that increase as freshness quality decreases have been suggested. The K value (Table 2.4) was the first ratio to be proposed,[112] but because ATP is normally completely degraded to IMP within 1 day it has been replaced by the K_i value,[109] which does not require the determination of ATP, ADP, or AMP concentrations (Table 2.4). Compared to using only hypoxanthine concentration, the K_i value does reduce variability, but its usefulness as an index of freshness quality clearly depends upon the species being examined. When used with some appropriate species the K_i value can be linearly related to the length of time (days) that the species was stored in ice.[99, 113] The clear establishment of such a relationship allows the K_i value to be used to predict the storage life of the fish being examined, which is an important advantage similar to that observed with the Tasmanian Food Research Unit fish quality grading system discussed in Chapter 4.

However, with some species the K_i value has been observed to increase very rapidly and then remain constant, even though the freshness quality continues to decrease greatly.[61,114,115] Such species have been observed to rapidly accumulate a large amount of inosine (Table 2.3) (relative to the accumulation of hypoxanthine), while the concentration of IMP (Table 2.3) rapidly decreases.[99,110] Although the K_i of these species does not accurately measure North American freshness quality,[61,115] it has been observed to accurately indicate Japanese freshness quality.[99] This may be a result of Japanese people eating a large amount of raw seafood,[99] rather than cooked seafood as in North America. Regardless of the reason, it clearly demonstrates that freshness quality is a concept and illustrates the desirability of the producer and buyer having a clearly written definition of freshness quality.[3,116] Therefore, when North American freshness quality of species such as Atlantic cod or Pacific cod (that rapidly accumulate inosine) is required, it is important not to determine the K_i value, but to consider determining a different ratio of nucleotide degradation products (Table 2.4). For example, the G value of iced Atlantic cod has been reported to be much superior to the K_i value, although it has been observed to decrease during the first 2 or 3 days of iced storage, prior to its subsequent steady increase.[111] Similarly the H value of iced Pacific cod has been observed to immediately begin to increase quite steadily and therefore also be much superior to the K_i value.[110] However, when used to evaluate the freshness quality of some species the K_i value has been observed to change very little during extended storage at 20°C.[62] This suggests that with some seafood no type of nucleotide ratio is appropriate.

In addition, nucleotide degradation has been stated to be dependent on the amount of dark muscle in a sample and may seriously depend upon the location of a fillet from which a sample was obtained.[38]

These significant variations, both between and within species, obviously limit the practical usefulness of measuring the concentration of a single nucleotide degradation product or a single nucleotide ratio to indirectly measure freshness quality.[117] It also clearly emphasizes the necessity of scientifically establishing the relationship between a nucleotide ratio and the freshness quality of species to be examined. Measuring the concentration of nucleotide degradation products can be a useful way of determining freshness quality, only once this is achieved.

2.2.1.3.4 Method of Analysis

Although using concentration of nucleotide degradation products to indirectly measure freshness quality has the important advantage of reflecting both autolytic and microbial degradation,[95,96,98] using wet chemistry to determine their concentration is extremely difficult and expensive.[63,94]

The development of HPLC to quantitatively measure the concentration of nucleotide degradation products[94,98,99,118,119] has greatly reduced some of these difficulties. A major advantage of HPLC analysis is that AMP, IMP, inosine, and hypoxanthine (Table 2.3) are simultaneously measured.[118] This allows the immediate determination of any of K_i, H, or G values (Table 2.4) and permits the analyses to be suitable for a wide range of species. In general, this type of analysis involves blending a finely chopped sample with perchloric acid for 2 min, filtering the mixture, neutralizing an aliquot of the filtrate, mixing, cooling, and filtering this solution, and injecting an aliquot of the final filtrate into an HPLC unit, which requires an additional 10–12 min to quantitatively determine each of AMP, IMP, hypoxanthine, and inosine.[118] Depending upon the HPLC method used, analysis of the prepared extracts is normally not rate limiting because HPLC units are often equipped with an autosampler (autoinjector) that is inside a refrigerated chamber. The cool temperature ensures that the extracts, within separate vials, do not deteriorate prior to being analyzed. Once a sample has been analyzed, the autosampler mechanically moves the next vial of extract to the intake port, which then automatically withdraws a predetermined amount of extract into the actual chromatographic system, which simultaneously separates and quantifies each of the different nucleotide degradation products present in an individual extract (Fig. 2.2). Such a system is capable of operating 24 hr per day, but depends upon vials of extracts being available to be analyzed. Consequently, lack of a sufficient number of skilled personnel (capable of preparing such extracts) is usually the rate-limiting factor, but this factor is often ignored by many laboratories.[120]

Major disadvantages of such HPLC analysis are the expensiveness of an HPLC unit, the lack of portability, and the necessary destructive sampling. Even if a chemical method of indirectly measuring freshness quality "hits the bull's-eye,"[70] it must be inexpensive, rapid, and nondestructive to the seafood being evaluated if it is to be used extensively for quality control purposes.[61,115] Thus HPLC analysis is believed to be primarily useful for research purposes, not for routine quality control analyses.[115]

Enzymes involved in the formation of nucleotide degradation products have been immobilized unto test strips.[121,122] Once reacted with an appropriate extract of fish muscle the test strip develops a color that is indicative of either the concentration of the degradation product or the value of the ratio being measured. Comparison of the developed color to that of standards allows the concentration or ratio value to be quantified. Although portable and rapid, these methods require destructive sampling, yield variable results, and are of limited practical use in the control of freshness quality.[61]

Other methods using enzymes, such as those involving enzyme sensors (Glossary),[123] to quantitatively measure nucleotide degradation products have also been investigated[109,115,124–130] and have resulted in the commercialization of meters designed to measure nucleotide ratio of seafood (Table 2.5). Although such enzyme methods may be very capable of accurately measuring these chemical products, when compared to HPLC analysis destructive sampling is still required, speed of analysis, including sample preparation, is similar, excluding initial capital cost, the cost per sample is similar, and the accuracy and precision are not superior.[61] These enzymatic methods are much more portable than HPLC analysis, but lack the capability of being readily used with a variety of species. This is because the concentrations of individual nucleotide degradation products are not simultaneously determined, instead the concentrations of different groups of compounds (e.g., inosine + hypoxanthine or IMP + inosine + hypoxanthine) are determined, which restricts the type of nucleotide ratio that can be calculated.

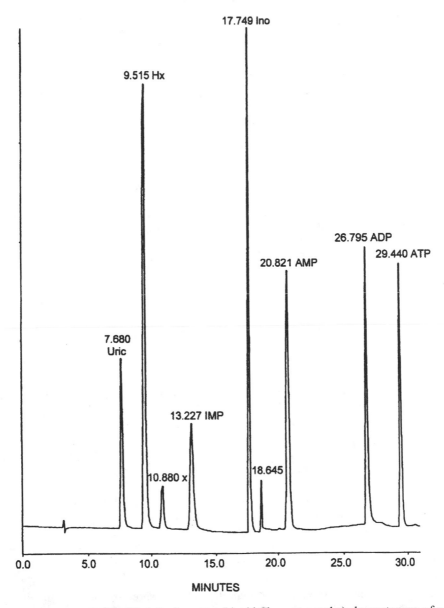

Figure 2.2.   An HPLC (High Performance Liquid Chromatography) chromatogram of nucleotide degradation products extracted from chilled stored Atlantic cod (*Gadus morhua*). The numbers associated with each peak are its retention time. See Table 2.3 for a definition of each abbreviation. Printed with permission from Canada Department of Fisheries and Oceans, Inspection Branch, St. John's, NF, Canada.

Table 2.5.   COMMERCIALLY AVAILABLE METERS FOR MEASURING THE
CONCENTRATION OF NUCLEOTIDE DEGRADATION PRODUCTS

Method	Description
KV-101 freshness meter[a]	Measures K_i value, by using a Clark oxygen electrode to monitor the oxygen consumption during the enzymatic degradation of IMP, inosine, and hypoxanthine.[109,199] Using different aliquots of a fish extract, the total concentration of inosine + hypoxanthine and the total concentration of IMP + inosine + hypoxanthine are determined, which are used to calculate K_i. A major drawback of this meter is the low sensitivity and rigid control of pH and oxygen tension.[127]
MICROFRESH meter[b]	Consists of a Clark electrode that contains an immobilized enzyme, capable of degrading hypoxanthine. One aliquot of a fish extract is reacted with enzymes that degrade inosine to hypoxanthine, which the electrode measures as immobilized enzyme degrades hypoxanthine to uric acid.[115,125–127] Analysis of this aliquot yields a quantitative determination of both inosine and hypoxanthine (the numerator of K_i value). A second aliquot of fish extract is reacted with enzymes that degrade IMP to hypoxanthine, which is degraded and measured by the electrode, thereby quantitatively measuring the concentration of IMP + inosine + hypoxanthine (the denominator of K_i value).

[a] Available from Orental Electric, 9–7 Nobidome 3–Chome, Niiza Saitama 352, Japan.
[b] Available from Pegsus Instruments, P.O. Box 319, Agincourt, Ontario, Canada M1S 3B9.

Nucleotide degradation products have also been measured using capillary electrophoresis.[110,131] This method is more expensive than enzymatic methods but less than HPLC analysis, involves destructive sampling, and requires approximately the same amount of time as HPLC analysis. In addition, this method simultaneously determines several of the degradation products,[110] may have higher resolution than HPLC analysis, but is not portable.

2.2.2 Other Chemical Methods

2.2.2.1 Ammonia Content

Since total volatile bases developed during storage consist primarily of ammonia and trimethylamine[78] the suitability of using ammonia content, itself, to evaluate the freshness quality of seafood has been investigated.[81,132–135] The practicality of this method is very dependent upon the species (see sections 2.4., 2.5., and 2.6.) being examined. In general, it has been reported to be a useful index of freshness quality of some cartilaginous fish,[135] some crustaceans,[132,135] squid,[134] but not of finfish.[81,135]

Ammonia concentration may be quantitatively measured by methods involving: diffusion;[133] accelerated micro diffusion;[136] enzymatic conversion of ammonia and keto-glutarate to glutamate[134] and a test kit in the form of a paper strip.[60] Enzymatic test kits are available from either Sigma Chemical Co. (St. Louis, Missouri, USA) or Boehringer Mannheim (Mannheim, Germany) whereas the paper strip test kit is available from Merck (Merckoquant, Darmstadt, Germany). Each of the different methods require destructive sampling as an extract (e.g, using perchloric acid) of the sample must be prepared.

2.2.2.2 Biogenic Amines

Depending on species being examined (see Sections 2.4, 2.5, and 2.6), the concentration of biogenic amines (Glossary) has been reported to be a reliable method of indirectly measuring seafood freshness quality.[100,134,137-140] Like both TVB-N and TMA, the formation of these chemicals is a result of microbial degradation and, therefore, is measurable, primarily during the later stages of chilled storage. These chemicals are normally determined using the same type of fish extract used to determine hypoxanthine concentration.[100] Therefore it has been suggested that the concentration of diamines (see definition of biogenic amines) be used to determine if a particular hypoxanthine value represents a premaximum or a postmaximum value (Section 2.1.3.2).[100] The presence of large quantities of diamines should clearly indicate that the hypoxanthine concentration represents a post-maximum value, but the presence of low quantities of diamines does not clearly indicate that hypoxanthine concentration is a premaximum value. Gill[60] stresses that the presence, not necessarily the absence, of biogenic amines is a useful indicator of freshness quality. Similarly Farn and Sims[137] emphasize that the presence of biogenic amines is important, but their absence must be regarded as inconclusive. This uncertainty concerning the relationship between the level of biogenic amines and freshness quality is a major disadvantage of this method. These chemicals are normally measured using HPLC analysis,[89,141,142] which is destructive as it requires TCA extraction of fish muscle, requires derivatization into fluorescent compounds using benzoyl chloride,[142] dansyl chloride,[89] orthopthalaldehyde,[141] or into strongly ultraviolet absorbing compounds using phenylisothiocyanate,[143] is expensive due to the high cost of an HPLC unit, and is slow, requiring at least 45 min per sample.

2.2.2.3 Ethanol

Microbial degradation of seafood may cause the concentration of ethanol to increase.[144-146] Investigations concerning its usefulness as a chemical index of freshness quality have revealed ethanol to be a useful index of the freshness quality of both chilled seafood[146,147] and canned seafood.[144,145,148,149] The capability of ethanol, itself, measuring the freshness quality of seafood when canned is somewhat unique, as other major chemical indices of freshness quality may not be suitable. For example, TMA is not stable during thermal processing[82] and low concentrations of hypoxanthine, by itself or in addition to low concentrations of biogenic amines, are not conclusive.[57,60]

Ethanol content in chilled seafood may be measured using commercially available enzyme kits,[60,146] which involves extracting the fish muscle with trichloroacetic acid (TCA) extraction (destructive sampling). Using headspace GC methods to measure ethanol content of canned seafood has been reported to be very useful.[144,148,149] Since the cans have to opened, this also involves destructive sampling. However, on adaption for chilled seafood, headspace analysis of the ethanol content of raw seafood may be a useful nondestructive method of measuring freshness quality.

2.2.2.4 Indole

An increased concentration of indole has been reported to be a useful chemical index of the freshness quality of shrimp during its nonfrozen storage, as microbial enzymes may cause the amino acid tryptophan to be degraded into this compound.[150-153] Since storage temperature rather than storage time has been observed to be the primary cause of indole formation in raw shrimp, it has been suggested that this test be used to determine if raw shrimp had undergone high temperature abuse.[150,153] However, it has also been reported that although high levels of indole definitely indicate decomposed (spoiled) shrimp, decomposed shrimp do not necessarily contain indole.[150,153] As with biogenic amines, this is a serious limitation of the test that causes great difficulty in interpreting the results. Thus indole should be used to determine freshness quality of shrimp only when it is used in conjunction with other methods.

The concentration of indole may be quantitatively determined using GC,[151] HPLC,[154,155] or spectrophotometry.[156] Each method requires destructive sampling as, depending on the method used, shrimp samples must be extracted with either carbonate buffer, ethyl acetate-*n*-hexane, methanol, or TCA.[154,156,157] Although the methods involving either GC or HPLC require both well-trained personnel and expensive equipment, the method involving spectrophotometric analysis of a TCA extract does not require either. In addition, this method may be completed within approximately 1 hr and is, therefore, potentially suitable for quality control purposes.[156]

2.2.2.5 Chemical Indices of Oxidative Rancidity

Oxidative rancidity can be a very serious problem with a wide variety of muscle foods, particularly those that have a high lipid ("fat") content, because when oxidative rancidity occurs it can cause toughened texture, undesirable flavor, and unsuitable odor.[45,158] Consequently the development and measurement of oxidative rancidity in both food oils and muscle foods have been thoroughly investigated.[158-165] The development of rancidity in seafoods, which usually contain highly unsaturated fatty acids, has been observed to be very complex.[45] This development is seriously affected by factors within the seafood such as the amount of unsaturated fatty acids and phospholipids, the physical distribution of the lipid, other chemicals that may either suppress or expediate rancidity, and external ("environmental") factors such as the temperature, the amount of oxygen (air), and the intensity of light to which the seafood is exposed.[158] In addition, anisidine value (AnV), peroxide value (PV), and thiobarbituric acid (TBA) value (Table 2.6), which are the major chemical indices of quantifying the extent of oxidative rancidity, are empirical methods.[45,157,159,161,163-165] Peroxide value measures hydroperoxides, which are primary products of lipid oxidation,[160,161] that break down to secondary products of oxidation or react with proteins.[161] Both AV and TBA value measure secondary products of lipid oxidation, which also break down to other chemical products.[57,161,163] This means that particularly during long-term storage of a muscle food, the magnitude of these different values may increase, reach a peak, and decline.[57,161] Alternatively, during storage of frozen fish substantial increases in TBA value have been reported

Table 2.6. MAJOR CHEMICAL METHODS USED TO QUANTITATIVELY MEASURE THE EXTENT OF OXIDATIVE RANCIDITY[a]

Method	Description
Anisidine value (AnV)	The An value of a sample is obtained by multiplying the absorbance, at 350 nm, of 1.0 g fat or oil that had been mixed with 100 ml of solvent and p-ansidine.[163] The intensity of the absorbance increases with the degree of oxidative rancidity. With all seafoods, except oils, the lipid must first be extracted from the sample. While determining AnV, extreme care must be taken to ensure that both the extracted lipid and all reagents that are used contain absolutely no water.[163]
Peroxide value (PV)	Lipid is quantitatively extracted from a preweighed seafood. This involves blending the sample with solvents, filtering the mixture, separating the different layers, and removing an aliquot, which is subsequently dried and weighed.[200] A weighed portion of this extracted lipid dissolved in solvents, reacted with potassium iodide solution, is allowed to stand (1 min).[201] The intensity of the resultant yellowish color is determined by adding starch, which causes the development, of a blue color, and carefully measuring the amount of added thiosulfate necessary to cause the color to disappear.[201]
Thiobarbituric acid (TBA) value	This frequently used test may be conducted using the water or acid extracts of the sample, a steam distillate of the sample, and lipid-extracted acid from the sample.[159] Regardless of the specific manner by which the TBA value is determined, the test is based on measuring the intensity of a pink color caused by the reaction of malonaldehyde (or other TBA-reactive substances) within the sample with 2-thiobarbituric acid.[159] The intensity of this color is determined by using a spectrophotometer to measure its absorbance. It is extremely difficult to compare results of tests conducted at different laboratories, because of the present existence of a large number of different types of tests used to determine TBA value.[157,159] Therefore, whenever the TBA test is used one must carefully estimate the effects of (1) presence of iron salts, which stimulate the test, (2) presence of antioxidants and metal chelators, which can inhibit the test, (3) the method of preparation, as different seafood products may require different acid conditions for the breakdown of the entire sample, (4) malonaldehyde and the acid-heating stage which may cause oxidation to occur, and (5) the chemicals being used, such as acetic acid (used to obtain an acid extract), which can contain high amounts of TBA-reactive substances.[157]
Malonaldehyde content	An alternative to using thiobarbituric acid to indirectly measure the concentration of malonaldehyde, within a sample is to directly measure it using HPLC.[141] Such a method involves blending with solvents, shaking, centrifuging (20 min), complete precipitation (60 min), additional centrifugation (15 min), millipore filtration, and column chromatography prior to an aliquot being injected into an HPLC for final separation (12 min) and quantification of malonaldehyde.[141]
Totox value	This total oxidation value, a combination of both the ansine value and peroxide value, is defined as the total of 2PV + AnV.[163]
Fluorescent products	1. A weighed quantity of lipid that has been quantitatively extracted from a preweighed seafood (see description, of peroxide value) is reacted with solvents, shaken for 1 min, aqueous and organic layers allowed to separate, and the fluorescence of the organic layer measured at specified excitation and emission wavelengths.[106] 2. An alternate, much less laborious method, is to place a weighed quantity of freeze-dried sample inside a solid sample holder (a disc with a quartz window) and to measure the fluorescence of the solid sample at specified excitation and emission wavelengths.[170]

(*Continued*)

Table 2.6.   (*Continued*)

Method	Description
Rapid headspace analysis	A preweighed small portion of minced tissue is placed inside a tightly sealed 5-ml vial and heated at 90°C for 15 min prior to using a gas-tight syringe to remove headspace volatiles, which are immediately injected into a GC column[171,185] (according to the procedures described by Young and Hovis[202]), which requires an additional 6 min to quantify the samples.

[a] The "description" of each method presented in this table is a general outline, not a detailed description. Whenever one of these methods is to be used to analyze a sample, it is extremely important that the exact procedures described in the original appropriate reference(s) be accurately followed.

to be caused by a breakdown (hydrolysis) of proteins rather than an increase in oxidative rancidity.[165]

Observed decreases in secondary products (e.g., malonaldehyde) of lipid oxidation are at least partially caused by the reaction of malonaldehyde with protein resulting in compounds that fluoresce.[161,166] Although fluorescent products have also been reported to be caused by the reaction of many other biological compounds,[164] quantitatively measuring the magnitude of these fluorescent products (Table 2.6) has been suggested as a method of measuring the extent of "advanced" rancidity.[161,166] Once lipid has been quantitatively extracted, this method is very rapid and, at least with some seafood products, has been reported to be a useful chemical method of measuring both the chemical aspects[106,167] and the sensory aspects of oxidative rancidity.[168,169] Whenever this method is to be used to measure freshness quality, data (obtained using both an identical product, under identical conditions, and an identical method of chemical analysis) clearly indicating that the results of the method were quantitatively related to the sensory quality (of the product being analyzed) must exist. If such background data do not exist, it is impossible to realistically interpret the results. Knowing that the chemicals (e.g., fluorescent products) being measured are definitely quantitatively related to the sensory quality of the product is much more important than knowing what chemicals cause the fluorescent products.

The magnitude of these fluorescence products may also be measured using solid sample fluorescence spectrophotometry.[170] Since this method does not involve lipid extraction (Table 2.6), it is a much less laborious procedure than other chemical methods of measuring rancidity and, therefore, may prove to be a very useful.[170]

Gas chromatographic analysis of volatiles present in headspace is another method that requires destructive sampling, but does not require the lipid to be extracted.[171,172] The concentration of total volatiles or individual volatiles (e.g., pentanal or hexanal), determined by either the "quick and dirty" method described by Erickson[171] (which can be completed within 24 min) or the more time consuming (approximately 75 min) purge and trap method described by Freeman and Hearnsberger[172] may be used as a chemical index of rancidity. The concentrations of both total volatiles and individual volatiles such as pentanal and hexanal have been reported to correlate well with sensory flavor scores.[172] The need for expensive equipment is a major disadvantage of these methods.

As previously mentioned, all of the various methods used to measure rancidity are generally classified as being empirical. Therefore, to correctly interpret the results of these chemical tests, it is advantageous to have some knowledge of the history of the seafood sample being analyzed, analyze the sample using more than one method (e.g., AnV, fluorescent products, headspace analysis, PV, or TBA), or have the chemical analysis accompanied by sensory analysis.

2.3 Effect of Species on Method Selected

The usefulness of any specific chemical method of evaluating seafood freshness quality depends on both the species being evaluated and the manner in which that species had been stored.[60,100] Thus the successful selection of a chemical method to evaluate freshness quality must involve careful consideration of these factors. During the sections discussing individual chemical methods some attention was given to the appropriateness of these methods for canned, chilled, or frozen seafood, but appropriateness of the different chemical methods for different species was seldom discussed. This will be considered now. A chemical method must be used only in circumstances in which both the type of "product" (including method of catching, handling, etc.) being analyzed and the chemical procedure being used are identical to what was used when a close relationship between the chemical method and freshness quality was clearly established (see Section 2.1). Thus, to determine if a particular method will, indeed, accurately evaluate freshness quality, the method must first be carefully investigated to determine if such a close relationship does indeed exist under the circumstances in which the test is to be used. The extremely large number of different species that are "processed" commercially means that it is beyond the scope of this book to provide a detailed discussion of specific methods of chemically measuring freshness quality of all of these different species. As a result, chemical methods that may generally be appropriate (worth investigating) for groundfish (Glossary), pelagic fish (Glossary), and shellfish (Glossary) will be discussed. The methods discussed are ones that may be appropriate, or, depending on the circumstances under which the test(s) are to be used, may possibly be found to be inappropriate. Alternatively, a method(s) other than those discussed may be found to be more appropriate.

2.3.1 Methods Appropriate for Groundfish

2.3.1.1 Measuring Early Stages of Deterioration

Whenever the test is to be conducted to determine either the early stages of deterioration or possibly both early and later stages, the appropriateness of measuring either DMA content (Section 2.2.1.2.2) whenever iced (chilled) haddock (*Melanogrammus aeglefinus*) and/or Atlantic cod (*Gadus morhua*) are to be analyzed,[81] or nucleotide degradation products (Section 2.2.1.3) should be seriously considered.

Hypoxathanine, not K_i value, has been observed to possibly be a suitable indicator of the freshness quality of chilled Pacific cod (*Gadus macrocephalus*)[114] and, to a lesser degree, of both Alaska pollock (*Theragra chalcogramma*)[114] and roughhead grenadier (*Macrourus berglax*),[173] as their hypoxanthine concentrations decreased during the latter stages of iced storage. Hypoxanthine (and possibly K_i value) has also been revealed to be a feasible indicator of the freshness quality of chilled rock sole (*Lepidopsetta bilneata*) and yellowfin sole (*Limanda aspera*).[117] Both hypoxanthine and K value have been reported to be very good chemical indicators of the freshness quality of hoki (*Macruronus novaezelandiae*),[174] whereas the IMP/hypoxanthine ratio (and possibly K_i value) was a very likely indicator of freshness quality of both chilled Dover sole (*Microstomus pacificus*) and flathead sole (*Hippoglossoides elassodon*), but for chilled rex sole (*Glyptocephalus zachirus*) only IMP or inosine concentrations were possible useful indicators.[117]

The H value has been suggested as a useful indicator of the freshness quality of chilled Atlantic cod (*Gadus morhua*)[110] and may also be useful with chilled (or iced) halibut (*Hippoglossus stenolepis* and *hippoglossus*), roundnose grenadier (*Coryphaenoides rupestris*), Pacific cod (*Gadus macrocephalus*), and Alaska pollock (*Theragra chalcogramma*), all of which accumulate substantial amounts of inosine during the degradation of ATP.[117,175–177]

The K value has been found to be useful for a number of different groundfish species, such as hoki (*Macruronus novaezelandiae*),[174] orange roughy (*Hoplostethus ananticus*),[178] bream (*Abramis brama*), and vimba (*Abrimis vimba*) during 12 days of iced storage,[179] but was observed to be appropriate for flounder (*Pleuronnectes flesus*) and white bream (*Abramis blicca*) only during the first 5 days of iced storage.[179]

2.3.1.2 Measuring Later Stages of Deterioration

Depending on the time of year, location of catching, type of processing and storage, and method of analysis, TMA content (Section 2.2.1.2) has been reported to be a useful method of determining the freshness quality of Atlantic cod (*Gadus morhua*), European hake (*Merluccius merluccius*), North American hake, haddock (*Meranogrammus aeglefinus*), and redfish (*Sebsates marinus*).[75,81,91,180]

Although it does not detect deteriorative changes as early as measuring TMA, TVB-N has been used to measure the freshness quality of a variety of groundfish such as Atlantic cod (*Gadus morhua*), European hake (*Merluccius merluccius*), haddock (*Melanogrammus aeglefinus*), and redfish (*Sebsates marinus*).[74,75,81] Whenever TVB-N is used to measure freshness quality, it is extremely important that the method recommended by WEFTA (Table 2.2) be strictly followed.

The freshness quality of Atlantic cod (*Gadus morhua*), Atlantic pollock (*Pollachius virrens*), redfish (*Sabastes marinus*), and winter flounder (*Pseudopleuonectes americanus*) may also be evaluated by determination of ethanol content,[146] which may be achieved without destroying the sample (Section 2.2.2.3).

2.3.2 Methods Appropriate for Pelagic Species

2.3.2.1 Measuring Early Stages of Deterioration

Whenever a chemical method is required to determine the early stages of deterioration in the freshness quality of pelagic species, measurement of nucleotide degradation must be seriously investigated.

The K_i value (or K value) has been observed to be a useful index of freshness quality of a variety of pelagic species such as chilled (iced) albacore (*Thunnus alalunga*),[104–105] Pacific herring (*Clupea harengus pallasii*),[115] mackerel (*Rastrelliger faughni Muatsui*),[181] (*Scomber japonicus*),[182] and sockeye salmon (*Oncorhynchus nerka*).[115]

Depending on the species to be evaluated, a serious investigation concerning chemically measuring early stages of deterioration in pelagic species should involve hypoxanthine concentration, as it has been reported to be a possible potential index of freshness quality of chilled (iced) albacore (*Thunnus alalunga*),[104,105] unfrozen yellowfin tuna (*Thunnus albacores*),[62] and anchovie (*Engraulis encrasicholus*) stored at both chilled and room temperatures.[183] Hypoxanthine by itself is generally not a reliable indicator of freshness quality as its concentration may decrease after reaching a maximum.[60] However, its concentration increased steadily, without declining, when albacore was chilled stored for 35–40 days.[104,105] Both the early and later stages of deterioration of albacore may also be measured by quantitatively measuring the decrease in IMP content,[105] whereas that of lake salmon and trout may be measured using the H value, rather than the K value.[110]

2.3.2.2 Measuring Oxidative Rancidity

Pelagic species (Glossary) are fast swimmers and thereby contain relatively large amounts of red (dark) muscle and lipid (fat).[184] Depending on how the pelagic species have been handled, stored, and processed, the development of rancidity is frequently a problem. Thus, it may be very desirable to investigate the usefulness of chemical methods of measuring rancidity, even though these methods are generally empirical (Section 2.2.2.5). Although peroxide value and TBA value are very common methods of chemically measuring the development of rancidity, their results often do not accurately indicate the level of freshness quality.[57,161] Quantitatively measuring the magnitude of fluorescent products (Table 2.6) has been reported to be a very useful method of measuring extensive oxidative rancidity in dried-salted mackerel (*Rastrelliger kanagurta*),[168] dried-salted sardines (*Sardinella longiceps* and *Sardinops neopilchardus*),[169] salted-dried marine catfish (*Arius thalassinus*),[106] and sun-dried fish.[167] These reported studies involving the measurement of fluorescent products all involve quantitative extraction of the lipid, which is time consuming. A much more rapid method of measuring oxidative rancidity is the method involving rapid headspace analysis, which is potentially useful for measuring oxidative rancidity of herring or mackerel as it has been reported to be very useful with bass and channel catfish.[172,185]

2.3.2.3 Measuring Later Stages of Deterioration

Measuring TVB-N concentration has been reported to be a useful method of determining freshness quality of canned albacore (*Thunnus alalunga*)[186] and unfrozen (5° and 22°C) anchovie (*Engraulis encrasicholus*),[183] but generally it has not been as widely used with pelagic species as it has been with groundfish (Section 2.3.1.2). This difference between groundfish and pelagic species is also observed with TMA, which has been observed to be a useful chemical indicator for only a few pelagic species, such as anchovie (*Engraulis encrasicholus*).[183]

Determination of ethanol concentration has been revealed to be a useful chemical index of freshness quality of canned albacore, chum salmon (*Oncorhynchus keta*), coho salmon (*Oncorhynchus kisutch*), pink salmon (*Oncorhynchus gorbuscha*), and sockeye salmon (*Oncorhynchus nerka*).[144,148,149] In addition, ethanol may also be appropriate to measure freshness quality of chilled albacore, horse mackerel, mackerel, and sardine.[145,147]

Measurement of specific biogenic amines, which are seldom used to determine freshness quality of groundfish, has been suggested as a method of determining freshness quality of pelagic species such as canned skipjack (*Kstsuwanus pelamus*) and canned yellowtail (*Neothunnus macropterus*),[137] unfrozen (4–6 and 18–22°C) anchovie (*Engraulis encrasicholus*),[183] and chum salmon (*Oncorhynchus keta*).[134] However, Farn and Sims[137] state that the absence of biogenic amines in a seafood sample must be regarded as inconclusive, and Gill[60] states that the absence of biogenic amines does not necessarily indicate a wholesome product. This serious limitation must be critically compared to the written reasons for measuring freshness quality, before the concentrations of specific biogenic amines are used to determine freshness quality.

2.3.3 Methods Appropriate for Shellfish

In general, the use of chemical methods to measure freshness quality of shellfish has not been investigated to the same extent as they have been for either groundfish or pelagic species. However, depending on the species of shellfish, some chemical methods have been observed to be useful indices of freshness quality.

The freshness quality of chilled shellfish such as brackish-water prawns,[187] tiger prawns (*Penaeus japonicus*),[182] spiny lobster (*Panulirus argus* and *Panulirus laevicauda*) tails,[188] and common squid (*Todarodes pacificus*)[189] has been reported to have been reliably measured by determining the *K* value (see Section 2.2.1.3.3). However, with common squid, a ratio of the individual concentrations of hypoxanthine and AMP (Table 2.3) was observed to be a superior index of freshness quality.[189] Ammonia content and TVB-N value have, individually, been reported to be very useful indicators of the freshness quality of chilled squid, although the TVB-N value was most useful during the latter stages of storage.[134,190]

Both TMA and TVB-N have also been revealed to be useful chemical methods of measuring the freshness quality of both lobster (*Panulirus polyhagus*)[191] and shrimp (*Penaeus merguiensis*).[153] In addition, measurement of hypoxanthine concentration, itself, has been observed to be a useful chemical index of the freshness quality of iced shrimp (*Penaeus merguensis*).[108] Although the concentration of either biogenic amines or indole may be used to measure the freshness quality of shrimp, it must be remembered that although the presence of biogenic amines or indole clearly indicates the presence of decomposition,[134,150,153] their absence does not necessarily indicate the absence of decomposition.[60,137,150,153]

2.4 Analysis and Interpretation of Results

Whenever chemical methods are being used to ensure that the expectations of the buyers, users, or regulatory agencies are being met, it is very common to analyze the results by determining the highest, lowest, and mean values. These values are then compared to an upper limit, lower limit, or both upper and lower limits that had been previously established. Alternatively, the frequency distribution of the observed results may be calculated and tables and/or graphs (e.g., quality control charts with identified upper and lower control limits; see Section 4.3.1 of Chapter 4) prepared. This procedure allows the results to be readily analyzed by management.

When (such as during product development) analyses are conducted to determine if the freshness quality between two or more products is different, analysis of variance is frequently used to analyze the results. Generally, the use of analysis of variance is more appropriate for results of chemical analyses than it is for the results of sensory evaluations since chemical analyses do not produce categorical data. However, once the results of the chemical analyses have been used to estimate the level of a specified sensory attribute, analysis of variance should not be used, as categorical data have now been produced.

During the interpretation (explanation) of the analyzed results, it is extremely important to answer a number of critical questions. Has the method of chemical analysis been altered so as to possibly make the results meaningless (i.e., once the alterations occurred, has subsequent monitoring revealed the method was correctly predicting the sensory quality of that specific product)? Have the samples been randomly collected and has a sufficient number of samples been analyzed? Once the samples were collected, have they been stored (prior to being analyzed) in a manner that possibly affected the meaning of the results. Unless scientifically sound procedures of sample collection, storage and preparation, and analysis are actually carried out, the results will not ensure that the expectations of the buyers, users, and regulatory agencies are being met.

3

Physical Methods of Evaluating Freshness Quality

3.1 Introduction

Physical methods consist of measuring the magnitude of a physical parameter (e.g., color, distance, force). This magnitude is normally measured either by using instruments or by comparing the observed magnitude to a physical standard (e.g., comparing an unquantified distance to that of a ruler). Regardless of the procedure used to quantify the magnitude, physical methods indirectly measure seafood freshness quality by using their results to estimate the "level" of a specific sensory attribute and then comparing this estimated "level" to those specified in the appropriate grade standard.

Since the determination of these magnitudes is often very precise (exact), physical methods (along with chemical methods) have been called "objective" methods.[203] However, unless a close relationship between the results of the physical method being used and the sensory attribute being estimated has been clearly established, the results of these methods may be precise without being accurate[70] and of little use for measuring freshness quality. Therefore before any physical method is used, scientifically sound investigations concerning the results of this physical method and the results of an "objective" sensory evaluation method (i.e., a descriptive, discriminative, or grading method) must have definitely revealed that a close relationship between the results of these specific physical and sensory evaluation methods does indeed exist. The results proving such a close relationship apply only to the conditions (method of catching and handling, time of season during which the seafood was harvested, species being examined, specified physical method, and specified sensory evaluation method, etc.) under which the investigation was conducted. Altering only one of these conditions may alter the relationship to such a degree that the close relationship may no longer apply, causing the estimated "level" of the sensory attribute to be of questionable value. Also during these investigations, the sensory evaluations must have been conducted using scientifically sound procedures. Whenever a physical method has met these requirements, it can be an extremely useful,[70,72] and, depending upon its cost effectiveness,[204] should be used.

The major types of physical methods used to determine freshness quality are those used to determine texture of seafood, appearance of seafood, and specific electrical methods (designed to measure overall quality). Each of these types will be described and discussed, focusing on factors that affect the relevance of using these different methods.

Unless there are clearly defined written reasons for measuring freshness quality,[3] the numerous known factors that affect the results of the physical method under consideration cannot be promptly and reliably compared to these reasons. Such a comparison is essential to maximize the benefits and minimize the limitations of any physical method that is to be selected.

3.2 Physical Methods Used to Measure Texture

The terms adhesiveness, chewiness, cohesiveness, fibrous, gaping, hardness, and springiness describe different food textural attributes and are defined in the Glossary. Additional terms, each of which refers to a specific level of one of the aforementioned attributes, are summarized in Table 3.1.

Table 3.1. INTERRELATIONSHIP OF TERMS FREQUENTLY USED TO DESCRIBE TEXTURE OF SEAFOOD[a]

| Sensory Attribute | Level of Attribute to Which the Descriptive Term Refers | | |
	Low	Moderate	High
Adhesiveness	Sticky	Tacky	Gooey/gluey
Chewiness[b]	Tender	Chewy	Tough
Fracturability[b]	Crumbly	Crunchy	Brittle, crispy, and/or crusty
Gumminess[b]	Short	Mealy, pasty, and/or powdery	Gummy
Hardness	Soft	Firm	Hard
Springiness	Plastic	Malleable	Elastic, springy, and/or rubbery
Viscosity	Fluid	Thin	Viscous

[a] Defined by International Standards Organization Vocabulary.[272]
[b] Related to cohesiveness (mechanical textural attribute relating to the degree to which a substance can be deformed before it breaks).

3.2.1 Measuring Texture of Cooked Seafood

Punching and shearing have been major physical methods used to measure texture of cooked seafood.

When compared to the results of a texture profile panel (Chapter 5), the puncture test (Table 3.2) has been revealed to be capable of measuring the level of chewiness, hardness, and, to a lesser degree, fibrousness of fillets from a wide variety of unfrozen groundfish and pelagic species,[205] as well as a variety of snapper and rockfish species.[206] Kramer shear force (Table 3.2) determined using either a 4 blade modified shear cell,[207–211] as shown in Figure 3.1, or a 10 blade shear cell[212–215] attached to a force measuring system (e.g., Ottawa Texture Measuring System or Instron Universal Testing Machine) has also been observed to be a useful mechanical method of measuring hardness of canned as well as frozen and subsequently cooked seafood.

Both the puncture test and Kramer shear force method are effective mechanical techniques of measuring hardness and cohesivenness of seafood.[216] The muscle of a finfish is made up of myotomes (flakes), which are connected to each other by myocommata (connective tissue).[57,101] During handling and storage of finfish this connective tissue may readily break down causing the flakes to separate ("gap") from each other seriously affecting the appearance of a fillet or split fish,[57,101] as the fillet is no longer, visually, a "continuous" muscle (Fig. 3.2). Gaping also affects the physical continuity of a fillet, which is at least one reason why both the puncture test and the shear test methods involve flaking (destructive sampling) the cooked fillets (Table 3.2). Since both methods also require expensive equipment and the combined speed of preparing and measuring samples is slow, they are used primarily for research (including product development) rather than for routine testing.

Table 3.2 MAJOR PHYSICAL METHODS USED TO MEASURE TEXTURE OF COOKED SEAFOOD

Method	Description
Puncture test	The force required to force ("punch") a cylindrical plug a predetermined distance, which is usually held constant, into the seafood is measured.[206,273] The method requires a force measuring instrument such as an Instron Universal Testing Machine, an Ottawa Texture Measuring System,[273] or a TA-TX2 Texture Analyzer (Fig. 3.3), which are expensive. Once cooked, fillets are separated into individual flakes or, when appropriate, into 1-cm-thick strips, and flakes with minimum curvature and greater cross-sectional area than the plug are selected for testing.[206]
Kramer Shear Cell	The force required for the blades of a Kramer shear cell (Fig. 3.1), moving at a specified speed, to be pushed through a predetermined amount of seafood placed within the Kramer Shear Cell.[211,273] Although originally designed as a separate instrument, a Kramer Shear Cell is often attached to an Ottawa Texture Measuring System (Fig. 3.1) or an Instron Universal Testing Machine. Prior to the shear force being measured, pieces of seafood are steamed, cooled, flaked, and mixed.[209]

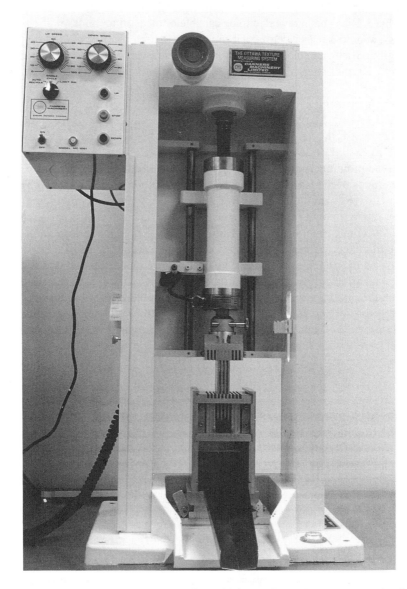

Figure 3.1. A modified Kramer Shear Cell attached to an Ottawa Texture Measuring System and a view of the bottom part of a Kramer Shear Cell, showing the guide ridges and the bottom guide bars. Printed with permission from Canada Department of Fisheries and Oceans, Inspection Branch, St. John's, NF, Canada.

Figure 3.1. (*continued*)

3.2.2 Measuring Texture of Raw Seafood

3.2.2.1 Raw Finfish

3.2.2.1.1 Hardness and Springiness

Whenever the texture of cooked seafood is mechanically measured, chewiness, fibrousness, and hardness are important attributes that need to be quantified, whereas when the texture of raw fish is mechanically measured, hardness and springiness are often the major variables that need to be measured.[217]

A modified (4 blade) Kramer Shear Cell (Fig. 3.1) attached to an Instron Universal Testing Machine has been revealed to give reproducible measurements of hardness of raw haddock and red hake fillets[208] and of raw Atlantic cod fillets that had been frozen, commercially, and subsequently stored at −12, −15, −22, and −30°C or under a set of simulated industrial fluctuating temperature conditions.[210] Similarly, a 10 blade Kramer shear cell attached to an Instron Texturometer provided reproducible results concerning the texture of raw fillets from several different groundfish and pelagic

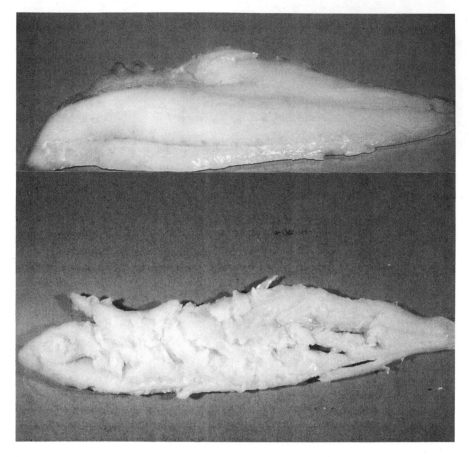

Figure 3.2.   Raw groundfish fillets exhibiting no gaping (top fillet) and considerable gaping (bottom fillet). Printed with permission from Canada Department of Fisheries and Oceans, Inspection Branch, St. John's, NF, Canada.

species.[218] However, a statistical relationship between these values and the texture, determined using sensory evaluation methods, of either raw or cooked samples was not[207,210] or could not[218] be confirmed. Even if such a relationship was established, the practicality of using this procedure for routine testing would be limited by both the expense and the necessity of destroying the sample to determine its hardness.

Azam et al.[219] used a 15-mm-diameter hemispheric end probe attached to a force measuring system to measure the springiness of raw rainbow trout fillets. The probe was descended past the point of contact with the flesh, automatically reversed, retracted to its initial contact point, driven forward to the same depth, and again retracted.[219] The distance between the first and second contact points was taken as a measure of the springiness of the fillet, although reproducible results were obtained, a close relationship between them and storage time was not observed.[219] The overall deformation of intact cod and salted herring has been determined by using a simple mechanical electromagnetic device to measure the depth of penetration of a plunger, into the fish, under the action of a constant load for a specified period of time.[220] The freshness of raw fish has also been measured using a hand-held probe.[221] Although these devices could nondestructively measure the hardness of raw fish flesh, slow speed and/or difficulty of obtaining repeatable results,[220,221] which depends on the person using the instrument, limited their practical usefulness. Alternatively (to reduce dependence on the individual operator), the use of a puncture probe attached to a more stationary force measuring system, such as a TA-TX2 texture analyzer (Fig. 3.3), may be investigated.

Botta[217] developed a transportable electronic instrument capable of measuring texture attributes of raw Atlantic cod fillets. As described (Figs. 3.4, 3.5, and 3.6; Table 3.3), once a fillet is placed under the probe, thickness, firmness (d_i), resilience (d_r), and

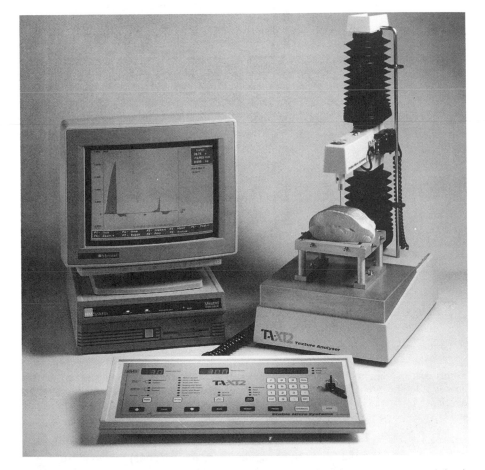

Figure 3.3. A TA-XT2 Texture Analyzer being used to conduct the puncture test on Atlantic Salmon. Printed with permission from Mono Research Laboratories Ltd., Brampton, ON, Canada.

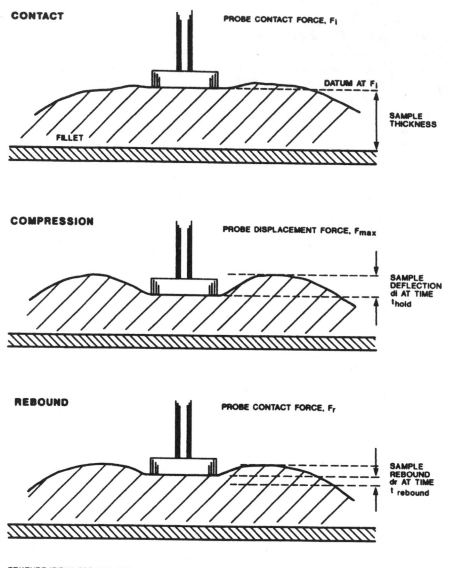

TEXTURE (FIRMNESS AND RESILIENCE) INDEX IS CALCULATED USING BOTH d_i AND d_r.

Figure 3.4. Diagram of nondestructive mechanical determination of hardness (d_i), springiness (d_r), and texture index (d_r/d_i) of a raw Atlantic cod fillet, as measured by the instrument developed by Botta (1991).[217] Printed with permission from Canada Department of Fisheries and Oceans, Inspection Branch, St. John's, NF, Canada.

texture index (d_r/d_i) of a fillet can be rapidly (very few seconds) but nondestructively measured, without the measurements being affected by the operator of the instrument.

When the texture of a large number of Atlantic cod was assessed using both a research prototype to determine the texture index and the overall results of three differ-

Table 3.3. RAPID NONDESTRUCTIVE MEASUREMENT OF THE TEXTURE OF RAW FILLETS[a]

Attribute Measured	Method of Measurement
Fillet thickness	This is automatically measured and recorded by an especially developed electronic instrument when a 2.5-cm-diameter flat probe, with a force of 10.0 g and speed of 20 mm/sec, contacts the surface of a fillet (Fig. 3.4).
Firmness (hardness)	Once the thickness has been determined, the force is, immediately, automatically increased to 500 g for a period of 1.0 sec, at which time the distance the probe depresses the fillet (deformation distance, represented as d_i in Fig. 3.4) is electronically measured and recorded.[b]
Resilience (springiness)	Immediately after the deformation distance has been measured the probe's force automatically decreases to 1.0 g for 1.0 sec, to allow the fillet to rebound (Fig. 3.4), with the probe "just touching" the surface of the fillet. Once this rebound time has lapsed, the distance the fillet rebounded (i.e., d_r in Fig. 3.4) is measured and recorded.
Texture index	Using both the deformation distance (d_i) and the rebound distance (d_r) a texture (firmness and resilience) index (d_r/d_i) is automatically calculated.

[a] Printed with permission from Canada Department of Fisheries and Oceans, Inspection Branch, St. John's, NF, Canada.
[b] This deformation force, revealed to be appropriate for raw Atlantic cod fillets, may be different when used with other species.

ent experienced expert assessors (Glossary), this instrument was observed to be quite capable of determining whether raw Atlantic cod fillets were suitable for high value premium packs.[217]

Using a second less complicated and more durable prototype (Fig: 3.5) to evaluate another large number of raw unfrozen cod fillets, the texture index was observed to correctly identify 90% of raw fillets suitable for and 84.5% of the raw fillets not suitable for premium packs.[217] Also, preliminary unpublished results suggest that by reducing both the deformation force and the size of the probe it could be a reliable method of measuring the texture of raw silver hake (*Merluccius bilinearis*).

Regardless of the species being evaluated, once a fillet is placed under the probe, the measurements are obtained within a few seconds. However, if measurements at several locations are required, the time necessary to physically move the fillet to these locations greatly increased the time to assess a single fillet. The time required for this instrument ("an electronic finger") to conduct the "finger test" at various locations of a fillet was slow compared to time required for an expert assessor to determine the firmness and resilience at numerous locations and determine the texture of an "entire" fillet. During the development of the instrument, a location just posterior to the belly cavity (Fig. 3.6) was observed to be the best single location to nondestructively determine the texture of raw Atlantic cod fillets. Although very satisfactory results were observed when this one location was utilized,[217] the necessity of using only one specified location on the fillet is a drawback.

During its testing this second prototype was shown to be durable under commercial situations, nondestructive, rapid, reliable, and readily portable.

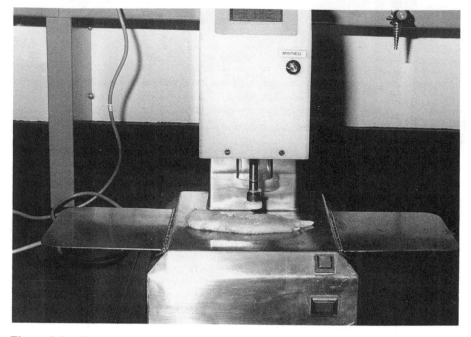

Figure 3.5. Transportable electronic/mechanical instrument capable of rapidly and nondestructively measuring texture attributes (firmness and resilience) of raw Atlantic cod fillets. Printed with permission from Canada Department of Fisheries and Oceans, Inspection Branch, St. John's, NF, Canada.

Although the cost (approximately, $15,000, Canadian funds) of the commercialized version (Oceans Ltd., St. John's, NF) is less than the cost of either an Ottawa Texture Measuring System or an Instron Universal Testing Machine, it is still substantial.

3.2.2.1.2 Gaping

Gaping (Fig. 3.2) may be indirectly determined using the aforementioned "electronic finger," because fillets that are firm and resilient usually do not gap.[217] An alternate method is to place a sample of a fish fillet between two parallel metal plates, which are each equipped with numerous 2-cm-long spikes. Once attached to a force measuring system (e.g., an Instron Universal Testing Machine) the force required to tear the fillet apart is measured to determine the softness (potential gaping) of the fillet.[101] Whenever either of these indirect procedures is used it is important to first confirm that a close relationship between the respective measurement and gaping does indeed exist, particularly under the situation in which it is then being used.

Since gaping (in addition to being considered an aspect of texture) is a very serious aspect of appearance, computer vision has been reported to be a reliable method of measuring this aspect of appearance (see Section 3.3).

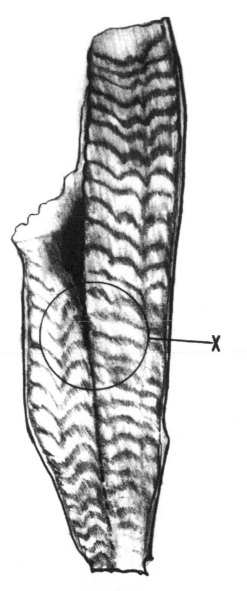

Figure 3.6   Diagram of an Atlantic cod fillet, indicating the best single location (X) to assess the texture attributes (firmness and resilience), using the instrument shown in Figure 3.5. Printed with permission from Canada Department of Fisheries and Oceans, Inspection Branch, St. John's, NF, Canada.

3.2.2.2 Raw Shellfish

Depending on both the species and the buyer's product standards, it may be desirable to determine whether the raw intact shellfish is soft shelled (i.e., recently molted), thereby having a higher mortality when landed and low meat yield. This determination has, traditionally, been achieved by using the "thumb test," to determine if the claw shell can be easily bent with thumb pressure and by observing if the shell is both brightly colored and the outer edge of the claw is iridescent.[222] However, Foyle et al.[223] reported that the hardness of a snow crab's shell could be physically measured using a hand-held durometer (Fig. 3.7), which had a maximum force of 31.14 N (7.0 lb). It was equipped with an indentor, which did not penetrate the shell, an extension rod to separate the indentor from the body of the instrument, and a secondary pointer ("lazy hand") in the dial, which held the highest durometer reading until it was reset with a thumb screw (Fig. 3.7). The indentor of the portable durometer is placed on a crab's claw (Fig. 3.8) and adequate force applied to the durometer so that the indentor is no longer visible.[223] Even if the gauge has been removed from the shell the "lazy hand" promptly indicates the reading.[223] The results of using this durometer on one claw of each of over 1,100 snow crab have been compared to re-

Figure 3.7. Hand-held durometer used to determine shell hardness of snow crab.[224] Indentor diameter, maximum force of indentor, and length of extension rod are 3.175 mm (1/8 in.), 31.14 N (7.0 lb), and 2.5 cm (1.0 in.), respectively. Printed with permission from Canada Department of Fisheries and Oceans, Inspection Branch, St. John's, NF, Canada.

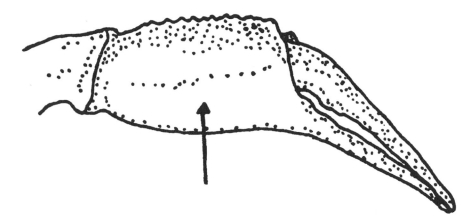

Figure 3.8. Diagram of a snow crab claw, indicating (arrow) suggested location of placement of durometer (or thumb) when determining hardness of the shell. Printed with permission from Canada Department of Fisheries and Oceans, Inspection Branch, St. John's, NF, Canada.

sults of the "thumb test" (conducted by Canada Department of Fishery officers experienced at conducting this test) on the other claw of the same crab.[224] Depending on whether the results were evaluated on a batch basis or on an individual basis, they were observed to be either practically indistinguishable or to have an overall difference of less than 10%, respectively.[224] Thus this instrument has been observed to be

Table 3.4. MEASURING TEXTURE OF SURIMI USING PUNCH TEST[a]

Sample Preparation
Raw chopped surimi, having the moisture content adjusted to 78%, is stuffed into a 25-mm-diameter sausage casing prior to being subjected to cold (either 4°C, refrigeration temperature, or 22°C, room temperature) setting, partial heat (40–50°C) setting, or heat (80–95°C) setting.[229,274,275]
Whenever surimi is cold set or partially heat set, it must be cooked prior to being tested. Whether heat set or cooked, the surimi gel must attain room temperature and (prior to being tested) be cut into samples 25 mm long.[276]

Sample Testing
Individual pre-cut samples are subjected to the punch test by measuring the force required for a 5-mm-diameter probe, having either a flat or a spherical end, to penetrate 90% of the sample length.[275] During testing the probe is attached to a force and distance measuring system (such as an Instron Universal Testing Machine or an Ottawa Texture Measuring System attached to chart recorder, or a digital system such as an electronic rheometer or an Okada gelometer) with a crosshead speed of 50–60 mm/min[229,276] and, when outfitted with a chart recorder, a chart speed of 100 mm/min.[276]
The force required for the probe to penetrate the surimi gel and the distance that the probe penetrated the surimi gel (at the point when it ruptured) measure the degree of hardness and degree of cohesiveness, respectively.[229]

[a] This "description" of the punch test is a general outline, not a detailed description. Whenever the punch test is to be used to analyze a sample, it is extremely important that the exact procedure described in the appropriate reference(s) be accurately followed.

an inexpensive, nondestructive, portable, rapid, and reliable method of determining if crab are soft-shelled.

3.2.3 Measuring Texture of Surimi

A major advantage of using surimi (Glossary) to make fabricated seafoods[225-227] is its excellent textural forming (gelling) properties, such as cohesiveness, chewiness, elasticity, hardness, and water-binding capacity.[57,225,226,228]

The measurement of both a surimi's cohesiveness and its hardness is extremely important, as these two results are often used, together, to determine if the surimi being evaluated is brittle (low cohesiveness and high hardness), mushy (low cohesiveness and low hardness), rubbery (high cohesiveness and low hardness), or tough (high cohesiveness and high hardness).[229] The punch test (Table 3.4), compression test (Table 3.5), and torsion test (Table 3.6) are the three major physical tests used to mechanically measure the texture of surimi. Results of the punch (penetration) test are used to indicate the extent of hardness and the magnitude of cohesiveness of surimi gels (Table 3.4), results of compression tests are used to determine the level of cohesive-

Table 3.5. USING COMPRESSION AND TENSILE TESTING TO MEASURE TEXTURAL ATTRIBUTES OF SURIMI GELS[a]

Sample Preparation
Samples of surimi gels to be tested using the compression test should be prepared using procedures that are identical to those used to prepare samples for testing using the punch test (Table 3.4).

Sample Testing
A force measuring system, operating at a crosshead speed of 50 mm/min and a recorder chart speed of 100 mm/min, is required for both compression testing and tensile testing.[276] During compression testing, a steel plate, whose surface area is a at least six times that of the surface of the surimi gel being tested, is used to compress the sample, whereas during tensile testing, clamps are required to attach the sample of surimi to the texture measuring system. Depending on the specific test being conducted, a variety of different texture attributes can be measured.

Texture Attributes That May be Measured
Chewiness of the gel is determined by measuring the energy (area of second and third peaks) used during three repeated compressions of cylindrical specimens at 90% deformation.[225]
Cohesiveness of the gel is the compression force required to rupture a cylindrical specimen, when it is compressed 90% of its height (e.g., compressed from 25 to 2.5 mm).[225] Cohesiveness cannot be measured unless the gel ruptures, even if the extent of deformation has to be increased to greater than 95%.[225,275]
Elasticity of the surimi gel is equivalent to the tensile force required to break (pull apart) a 2-mm-thick sheet of extrudate (25 mm wide × 70 mm long) partially heat set at 50°C for 15 min.[225]

[a] These "descriptions" of compression and tensile testing are general outlines, not detailed descriptions. Whenever either of these tests are to be used to analyze a sample, it is extremely important that the exact procedures described in the appropriate reference(s) be accurately followed.

ness, chewiness, and elasticity (Table 3.5), and results of torsion tests reveal the degree of cohesiveness and hardness (Table 3.6).

The traditional procedures used to prepare surimi gels for punch testing or for compression testing are basically identical (Tables 3.4 and 3.5). These procedures involve stuffing raw chopped surimi inside sausage casings prior to the setting and cooking of the gel, which is then removed from the casing prior to its being tested. However, the successful development of the torsion test to measure surimi quality resulted in the development of improved preparation methods (Table 3.6), which reduce the variability of the surimi gel's cohesiveness and hardness.[229] Two major changes were the use of a vacuum cutter-mixer to ensure that no pockets of air remained in the surimi gel and the use of sealed rigid tubes (rather than flexible sausage casing) for the formation and cooking of the surimi gel.[229] The presence of these procedures does not mean that torsion testing must be conducted using only these specific procedures

Table 3.6. MEASURING TEXTURAL ATTRIBUTES OF SURIMI USING THE TORSION TEST[a]

Sample Preparation[b]

Using a sausage stuffer, rigid tubes[c] are stuffed, completely, with raw surimi, immediately prior to being tightly sealed and the surimi gel's allowed to set using either low temperature and long time (0–4°C for 12–18 hr), medium temperature and medium time (25°C for 2 hr), or high temperature and short time (40°C for 30 min).

Each set surimi gel is immediately cooked (15 min at 90°C), cooled to 0°C, and removed from the rigid tubes.

Prior to being tested each sample must be allowed to attain room temperature, cut into specified lengths (28.7 mm), mounted (glued) unto styrene mounting discs, and milled into dumbbell-shaped samples with a minimum diameter of 1.0 cm (Fig. 3.9).

Sample Testing

The dumbbell-shaped samples are mounted unto a torsion device (Fig. 3.10) that is attached to a strip chart recorder operating at 20 cm/min. The sample is twisted until it breaks. Both the maximum digital viscometer reading and the distance the chart traveled during the testing are recorded.

Using these results both hardness (also referred to as shear stress) and cohesiveness (also referred to as true shear strain) are calculated, as described below.

Hardness = T = 1581 × maximum digital viscomter units, that were recorded during test.

Strain = Y = 0.150 × [distance (mm) chart traveled during testing/chart velocity) – 0.00847 × (maximum digital viscometer units, recorded during testing).]

Cohesiveness = $\ln[1+(Y^2/2) + Y(1+Y^2/4)^{0.5}]$

[a] This "description" of the torsion test is a general outline, not a detailed description. Whenever the torsion test is to be used to analyze a sample, it is extremely important that the exact procedures described by Lanier et al.[229] be accurately followed.

[b] While preparing surimi gels (from frozen surimi blocks) to be subjected to torsion testing, either a regular or a vacuum cutter-mixer is used. The vacuum cutter-mixer is preferred, as its use eliminates the presence of air pockets inside the surimi gel.

[c] Although rigid tubes are recommended, torsion testing may also be conducted using gels that have been packed inside sausage casings.

nor does it mean that these new procedures cannot be used to prepare surimi gel for either the punch test or the compression test. Thus it is extremely important that whenever the compression test, punch test, or torsion test is to be used, the type (ambient or vacuum) of cutter, the length of chopping, the type (rigid or flexible) of casing, the crosshead (or probe) speed, and (in the case of the probe test) the probe size each be clearly defined.[229]

The preparation of the necessary surimi dumbbells (Figs. 3.9 and 3.10; Table 3.6) requires additional time, but determination of surimi hardnesss by torsion testing has been reported to be less variable than when determined using the punch test.[216] This is at least partially caused by the change of shape that the gel undergoes during the punch test.[216] Since the extent of this change depends on the cohesiveness and hardness of the surimi gel being tested,[216] so does the observed variability of a particular surimi gel. However, if a buyer is primarily interested in hardness, this variability can be reduced by decreasing the size of the plunger that is being used or if the buyer is primarily interested in cohesiveness, it can be reduced by increasing the size of the plunger.[229] There are situations, such as the development of a product using different blends of raw surimi, in which both hardness and cohesiveness are very important and thus necessitate using the torsion test. The choice of testing method is extremely dependent on the written reasons for measuring the seafood freshness quality.

Figure 3.9. Photograph of a dumbbell, necessary to conduct the torsion test, being prepared from surimi. Printed with permission from Canadian Institute of Fisheries Technology, Halifax, NS, Canada.

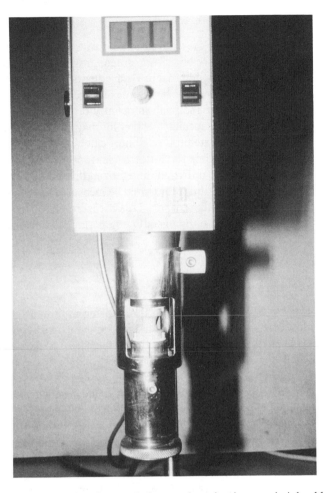

Figure 3.10. Photograph of torsion test being conducted, using a surimi dumbbell, to measure both cohesiveness and hardness of a surimi gel. Printed with permission from Canadian Institute of Fisheries Technology, Halifax, NS, Canada.

3.3 Physical Methods of Measuring Appearance

The term appearance (Glossary) of food refers, primarily, to color (as well as being opaque, translucent, or transparent), size, shape, and uniformity of the food[230] and is an extremely important sensory characteristic.[233] In addition to greatly influencing a buyer's or consumer's decision to purchase a seafood product a second time,[53] appearance greatly affects the purchasing of a product for the first time. A variety of different physical methods have been developed to measure different aspects of seafood appearance.

3.3.1 Measuring Color of Seafood

The characteristic external color of fish frequently varies among species. Although it often involves colors such as dark blue, dark green, gray, and silver, it also involves colors such brown and red.[234] The internal or flesh color of groundfish, species is predominantly white to off-white or pinkish, whereas that of pelagic species is pink, orange, red, or white, and that of shellfish is usually brown, ivory, pink, white, or yellow.[3,234] Within an individual species, flesh color may be seriously affected by location of catching, method of catching, season of catching, and how the seafood is handled and stored.[207,235-238] Thus the color of seafood being produced (such as canned Pacific salmon, canned, unfrozen, and frozen/thawed tuna, raw and cooked Atlantic salmon, shrimp, and surimi) often must be measured to ensure that the product standards are being achieved.[229,239-245] This measurement may be achieved by using instrumental methods and/or by visually comparing the color of the product to that of physical standards.

3.3.1.1 Instrumental Methods

Instruments capable of rapidly measuring three different dimensions (lightness to darkness, yellowness to blueness, and redness to greeness) of color are very frequently utilized to rapidly measure (define) the surface color of the seafood being examined.[229,233] Such devices (tristimulus colorimeters) frequently use either the Hunter L, a, b system and/or the CEILAB L*, a*, b* system, as described in Figure 3.11.[230,241] Which of these two scales is most appropriate depends on the nature of the color of the seafood being examined. A major problem associated with the Hunter L, a, b scale is its lack of uniformity in the blue region, whereas the CEILAB L*, a*, b* scale, although more uniform in the blue region, is overexpanded in the yellow region.[246] In general, tristimulus colorimetry is a very versatile procedure that has been used, successfully, to measure the color of cooked crawfish meat,[247] cooked Atlantic salmon,[244,245] cooked surimi,[229] raw minces,[248] flesh of raw Atlantic salmon,[243-245] flesh of raw rainbow trout,[249] minced cooked crab meat by-products,[250] tuna meat,[242] and skin color of raw rockfish.[251]

Whenever the results of such instruments are to be used to compare the color of either different seafoods or to compare the color of very similar seafoods (which had been produced and/or evaluated on different dates), the preparation and measuring procedures must be carefully standardized.[243,252] Unless this was accomplished, it is very possible that observed differences are actually the result of variations in such preparation and/or measuring procedures.

Whenever the surface color of an intact seafood is to be measured without destroying the sample (e.g., placing the instrument directly on the seafood), it is very important to ensure that the sample's surface is always at least twice the diameter of that of the instrument's sampling port.[229] The accuracy of such nondestructive color measurements is normally increased by using a larger measuring port and/or a standard tile (that approximates both the color and the texture of the seafood being evaluated) to calibrate the instrument.[229] For example, a calibration tile that approximates

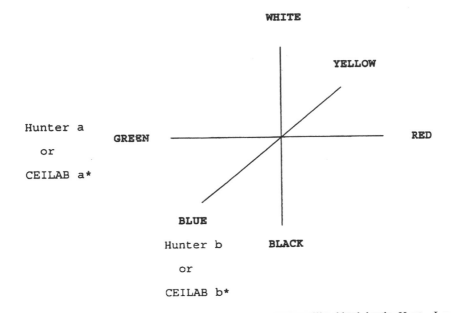

Figure 3.11. Diagram of the three-dimensional color space utilized both by the Hunter L, a, b and CIELAB L*, a*, b* systems. L (or L*) values range from 0, for white, to 100, for black. a (or a*) values: greenness increases with the size of the number associated with the − sign, whereas redness increases with the size of the number associated with the + sign. b (or b*) values: blueness increases as the size of the number associated with the − sign increases and yellowness increases as the number associated with the + sign increases. Printed courtesy of Francis and Clydesdale.[241]

both the color and surface texture of high quality pollock surimi is indirectly available through the National Fisheries Institute, Arlington, VA.

Whenever such a calibration tile is not available and particularly when the surface (color and texture) of the seafood appears to be inconsistent, it may be desirable to measure the color using a thoroughly ground (homogenized) sample. This homogenized sample may consist of the entire seafood product or, alternatively, only a homogenized "plug" (subsample) that has been removed using a cork borer. When using this procedure it is important to place the homogenized sample inside a commercially available measuring cell prior to its being measured two, three, or four times, ensuring that the sample is rotated 180°, 120°, or 90°, respectively, between the different measurements.[244,245,253] In addition, whenever a food has been ground prior to the color being measured, the results may have to be interpreted very cautiously, particularly if the grinding has drastically altered the light-scattering properties of the sample.[253] Thus, depending upon the nature of the original sample, the visual characteristics of the ground sample may not be representative of those of the original sample. Therefore, the nature of the seafood being assessed greatly affects the speed, the nondestructive sampling aspects, and the relevancy of results of using tristimulus colorimetry to physically measure color of seafood.

Although tristimulus colorimetry can be an extremely useful method of measuring color of seafood, factors such as cost of the necessary instruments, time required (i.e., cost) to measure large numbers of samples, and unacceptable variability and incapability of accurately measuring the color of specific seafoods can easily limit the usefulness of this procedure. A major alternative to using only tristimulus colorimetry is the use of physical standards that are visually or instrumentally compared to the seafood being analyzed.

3.3.1.2 Physical Standards

3.3.1.2.1 Manual Comparisons

Whenever this method is used, it is also extremely important that the preparation and measuring procedures be carefully standardized.[239,254] Unless this is achieved any differences in results from different products may also easily be due, entirely, to differences in these procedures and not related to differences in the actual color of the products themselves.

Physical standards made of ceramic tiles fired on steel plates have been developed to measure the very strict color tolerances of five species (chinook, *Oncorhynchus tshawytscha*; chum, *O. keta*; coho, *O. kisutch*; pink, *O. gorbuscha*; and sockeye, *O. nerka*) of canned Pacific salmon.[239] Three different specifically colored tiles (Nos. 2, 4, and 6) were developed for each of the five different species. The color of a canned product of a particular species is compared to the color of the three different tiles representative of that individual species and, by interpolation or by extrapolation, the product may readily be assigned one of seven different color grades distinctive for that species.[239] During the comparison of the color of the product to the closest matching colored tile the examination area is strongly illuminated by standardized light (e.g., Standard Source C), the physical standards are placed on a rack over an inspection table, at an angle of nearly 45° to the vertical, the canned product is placed on the inspection table, and the samples to be compared are removed from the can, broken in the examiner's hands, and held close to the physical standards.[239] Since variations among examiners have been observed to be very rare, this method has been observed to be a very rapid and accurate method of determining the color of canned Pacific salmon.[239] Despite problems in manufacturing the reference tiles, this method has been regularly used throughout the British Columbia canned salmon industry during the more than 25 years since it was developed. Thus, whenever rigid color standards exist for any particular seafood the use of physical standards (adapted to the specific product) may be a very appropriate method of ensuring that the product conforms to these rigid standards.

Rather than using colored steel plates, a physical standard system using colored cards has been successfully used to measure color of both raw Atlantic salmon (*Salmo salar*) flesh[254] and raw Pacific salmon (*Oncorhynchus tshawytscha*) flesh.[255] However, to achieve accurate and reproducible measurements it has been recommended that the color cards used as reference standards allow for a range in color intensity, allow for variations in levels of blackness, and ensure that all colors, within the range of that represented by the cards being used, are evenly spaced.[243] Also during the comparison of the flesh color to that of the color cards fish samples should be cut out of the flesh to prevent misleading influence from the skin, fat, and bone, fish samples should be evaluated at a defined distance from each color card, and each sample should be evaluated against a gray background under standardized light (see Chapters 4 and 5) conditions.[243]

In addition to the flesh color of raw and cooked seafood being very important,[234,239,243,254,255] the skin color of some fish may also be very important. For example, throughout each particular commercial catching season the external features of individual Pacific salmon gradually change as a fish approaches its spawning stream so that eventually, within an individual fish, very dramatic changes occur. This has led the Alaska Seafood Marketing Institute to develop different color evaluation guides for each chum, coho, pink, and sockeye salmon.[237,238] Proper use of these physical standards allows a fish's external features to be accurately sorted into one of six to eight different categories, which potentially allows some of the fish to enter the higher value fresh and frozen market rather than the traditional, but lower value, canned salmon market.[237,238]

3.3.1.2.2 Instrumental Comparisons

Utilizing a colored physical background that is the same color as acceptable shrimp, an automated physical machine capable of rapidly, but nondestructively, sorting colored shrimp has been developed commercially.[240] Rubber belts gently move wet shrimp between the colored background, at a particular wavelength of light and a photoelectric cell. Whenever the color of an acceptable shrimp is compared to the acceptable shrimp color of the background (which is the same as that of an acceptable shrimp), the acceptable shrimp appears invisible. In contrast, whenever the color of an off-colored shrimp is compared to the acceptable shrimp color of the background, the off-colored shrimp is observed, by the photoelectric cell to be visible. This visible presence of a shrimp automatically causes a high-speed jet of air to immediately blow the off-colored shrimp into a reject container.[240] Thus, at the end of the belt, all of the acceptable colored shrimp have been rapidly, but nondestructively, sorted from all off-colored shrimp, such as those with shell remnants. Since the capacity of the machine has been observed to be approximately 300 kg of shrimp (250–300 count per pound) per hour, it has been reported to be cost effective.[240] Depending on the development of an appropriately colored background, this machine also has potential use with other seafood.

3.3.2 Measuring Shape, Size, and Sex of Seafood

Depending on both the buyer and the type of seafood being processed, shape (e.g., preformation, presence, or resolution of rigor mortis), size, and/or sex can be vital product specifications and thus should, when appropriate, be completely satisfied by the producer.

Rapid physical techniques, often involving computer vision, are being developed to sort seafood species, sort according to specific sex, sort according to preset sizes, and determine if a fillet is from the left side or the right side of the fish.[256-261] Some equipment is available commercially.

3.3.2.1 Finfish

3.3.2.1.1 Determining (Sorting) Sex

Utilizing the different degree to which infrared light (at a specified frequency) penetrates milt and roe, equipment capable of rapidly, but nondestructively, grading and immediately sorting herring into roe-bearing female herring or milt-bearing male herring has been developed.[204] Since becoming available commercially, this instrument has been successfully utilized within the herring industry (of several different countries) for a number of years.[204] Once the herring have been manually aligned on a conveyor belt, such instruments are capable of sorting up to 200 herring per minute. Once automatically sorted, additional equipment may be utilized to, immediately, automatically remove the roe.[204] Interested readers should contact either the Fisheries Technological Research Institute in Norway or Neptune Dynamics Ltd., Richmond, B.C., Canada.

3.3.2.1.2 Measuring Size

Some commercially available grading systems are now capable of accurately, nondestructively, and rapidly size grading (sorting) fish. For example, Marel Ltd., employing computer vision, produces a system that can very accurately (± 0.5 cm) sort the length of 120 to 150 fish per minute even if fish on the conveyor belt are bent, not especially aligned, or placed side by side.[204]

3.3.2.2 Shellfish

3.3.2.2.1 Measuring Shape

In addition to being used to sort them into species, the shape of raw shellfish is an important attribute that may be measured to indirectly determine the shellfish's level of freshness (Table 3.7). The shape of shellfish, such as crabs (Fig. 3.12) lobsters, and mussels, is often used to determine if these shellfish are definitely alive immediately prior to their being processed. The processing of only live shellfish often occurs because it is common commercial practice, but some countries (e.g., Canada and Norway) enforce regulations that forbid the cooking or processing of shellfish that are not alive.

Traditional methods of using the observed shape of shellfish to measure its liveliness (freshness quality) have serious limitations (Table 3.8). However, researchers have developed an electrical instrument (Fig. 3.13; Table 3.9) that has been reported to be readily capable of reliably determining liveliness of a variety of shellfish.[262,263] The in-

Table 3.7. USING OBSERVED SHAPE OF SHELLFISH TO INDICATE ITS
FRESHNESS QUALITY[a]

Species	Shape	Importance
Raw crab	Extreme drooping of legs and claws with no visible sign of movement	Indicates that the crab *may* not be alive and, therefore, should not be processed (consumed)
Raw lobster	Extreme drooping of legs, body, and tail	Indicates lobster *may* not be alive and should not be cooked (consumed)
Cooked lobster	Tail of cooked lobster, once straightened, will not recurl	Indicates lobster was dead when it was cooked and thus should not be consumed
Raw mussels	Opened (gaped) shell	Indicates mussel *may* not be alive

[a] Printed with permission from Canada Department of Fisheries and Oceans, Inspection Branch, St. John's, NF, Canada.

strument is based on the well-known scientific observation that when electrically stimulated, the muscle of any living animal will contract. At least when used with snow crab,[262,263] American lobster,[264] and blue mussels[263] this instrument has been revealed to be an inexpensive ($800, Canadian funds), nondestructive, objective, portable, rapid (very few seconds), and reliable method of determining if any of these shellfish, suspected of being dead, are indeed alive, and, therefore, capable of being processed. When utilized commercially, it could reduce wastage of valuable resources by allowing seafood that would otherwise be discarded to be processed without affecting the freshness quality of the seafood. For example, the sensory quality of cooked meat from snow crab that had been chilled (raw) for 26–45 hr (after the heart stopped beating), but then visually responded (very weakly) to electrical stimulation, did not differ from the sensory quality of meat from comparable snow crab that were extremely active prior to being cooked.[263,264] However, when utilized with lobster (unlike with snow crab) care must be taken to ensure that a very strong response is observed.

Preliminary unpublished results have revealed that clams, sea scallops, and pre-rigor Atlantic cod also respond to the crab life detector (electrical stimulation), but the existence of a close relationship between such responses and freshness quality of these species has not been investigated.

3.3.2.2.2 Measuring Size

Equipment, based on utilizing computer vision and the calculation of weights from three-dimensional (3-D) images, has also been made commercially available, for the rapid nondestructive size grading (sorting) of shrimp.[265] The system, which is capable of size grading shrimp at a speed of 450 shrimp per minute with an accuracy of ± 1 g, consists of a feeder, a grading section, and a discharge unit for as many different groups of output as required. The system has been regularly utilized during some commercial processing of black tiger prawns where it has been observed to allow processors of such high value premium products to accurately ensure weight stan-

Figure 3.12. Photograph of (a) a typical snow crab showing only some signs of physical movement and, therefore, defined as a weak (but alive) crab and (b) a typical snow crab showing no signs of physical movement and, therefore, defined as a critically weak crab that can be determined to be alive only if it visibly responds to electrical stimulation or if (after removing the carapace) visible heart action is observed. Printed with permission from Canada Department of Fisheries and Oceans, Inspection Branch, St. John's, NF, Canada.

Table 3.8. LIMITATIONS OF TRADITIONAL METHODS USED TO DETERMINE
LIVELINESS OF SHELLFISH[a]

Traditional Method	Limitations
Observing physical movment of body, and/or legs of raw shellfish	The appearance of physical movement may often not be closely related to sensory attributes of the cooked shellfish meat
Observing resiliency of the tail of cooked lobster	Can be applied only after the lobster is cooked "processed"
Observing if opened shell closes, once it is given a sharp tap.	These results are very reassuring whenever an opened shell closes, but are very uncertain whenever the shell does not close

[a] Printed with permission from Canada Department of Fisheries and Oceans, Inspection Branch, St. John's, NF, Canada.

dards are strictly achieved without having to include excess valuable overpack (for which no payment is received).

3.3.3 Measuring Uniformity of Appearance

Various physical devices potentially capable of rapidly and automatically detecting the presence of defects such as blood, bones, parasites, skin, and gaping (each of which may seriously detract from the uniformity of seafood's appearance), are being developed.

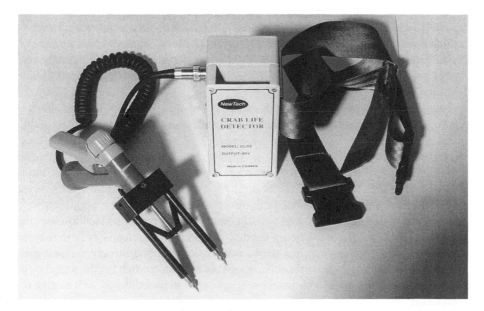

Figure 3.13. Photograph of "Crab Life Detector" developed by Botta and Kiceniuk.[263] Printed with permission from Canada Department of Fisheries and Oceans, Inspection Branch, St. John's, NF, Canada.

Table 3.9.   ELECTRICAL INSTRUMENTS READILY CAPABLE OF DETERMINING LIVELINESS OF SHELLFISH[a,b]

	General description of Crab Life Detector
Power source	Ten 9-V dry-cell batteries, inside a noncorrosive splash proof housing, that may be comfortably attached to the operator using a belt.
Stimulator ("gun-shaped")	Two probes, a lever (at the back of the "gun") capable of adjusting the distance between the tips of the probes, a trigger to allow a direct current of 60 V and 160 mA to flow between the two probes for 1 sec, and a buzzer that rings whenever the current is actually flowing between the two probes. A holster, to store the "gun," is attached to the power source.
Operation	The probes are placed on two different joints that connect the legs to body of a crab, the underside of an attached lobster tail, the mantle of an open mussel (or clam), or the abductor muscle of an open scallop. Once the buzzer rings, indicating current is flowing between the probes, any movement of the crab's leg, lobster's tail, or bivalves's shell reveals that the animal is alive, whereas no movement indicates the animal is dead.

[a] Printed with permission from Canada Department of Fisheries and Oceans, Inspection Branch, St., John's, NF, Canada.
[b] Available from Newtech Instruments Ltd., St. John's, NF, Canada.

Using visible light, color filters, video camera, and simple image analysis, Emsholm et al.[266] were able to accurately, but automatically, rapidly, and nondestructively measure both the extent of blood stains and the extent of gaping present in cod fillets. Using this method it is possible to develop a mechanical device to in-line sort fillets according to the presence of blood stains and/or gaping.[266] Nevertheless, the usefulness of such a system may depend on it being actually able to sort an adequately large number of fillets during a sufficiently short period of time (e.g., one fillet per second).

However, these strict time limitations do not apply to all types of seafood. For example, saltfish is normally both produced and graded on a batch basis and Marel Ltd. of Iceland has developed a physical device capable of automatically and nondestructively grading salt fish.[204,267,268] Utilizing vision technology similar to that reported by Emsholm et al.[266] the system is able to accurately measure the extent of blood stains and gaping in salted fish.[267,268] This accuracy is possible, at least partially, because the system is situated inside an enclosed cabinet allowing strict control of lighting that is necessary to ensure that the grading will not be affected by either the location (or time of day) at which the device is being used.[267,268] Since the enclosed system may be placed on top of a conveyor belt it allows automatic, but nondestructive assessment and sorting (according to preset specifications) of each salted fish for the presence of surface defects (e.g., discolorations, bones, gaping, and parasites) as well as size requirements.[267,268]

Utilizing X-rays to scan individual fish fillets, instruments have been reported to be capable of nondestructively, but reliably detecting bones (as small as 0.5 mm in diameter) present in such fillets.[204]

3.4 Measuring Dielectric Properties of Seafood

Electric properties (e.g., conductance and capacitance) within fish skin and fish muscle have been observed to change in an orderly manner as a fish undergoes postmortem spoilage.[269] Therefore measuring the magnitude of these properties has been repeatedly reported to be a useful. nondestructive physical method of indirectly measuring the extent of postmortem odor and appearance changes that have occurred.[38,81,203,204,269–271]

Measuring the magnitude of these electric properties may involve placing a hand-held device (e.g., Torrymeter) on the external side of the fish and manually obtaining individual readings.[203] Alternatively, these electrical properties may be very rapidly measured as the electrodes of the RT Freshness Grader spontaneously contact individual fish (on a moving conveyor belt) and automatically, within 1 sec, take approximately 200 independent measurements, which are immediately averaged and presented as one value ranging between 0 and 15.[38,204,270] Thus the RT Freshness Grader is capable of nondestructively assessing up to 60 fish per minute.[270] Following the successful development of the processing line model, a hand-held RT-Freshmeter (Fig. 3.14) was produced. While evaluating a fish, this freshmeter is held in a horizontal position, on the skin of a whole fish, gutted fish, or skin-on fillet and pulled across the middle of the "fish" (Fig. 3.14) for 1 or 2 sec, after which the fish may be turned to its other side and scanned again. However the RT-Freshness meter must be used only with unfrozen samples, as thawed fish give unreliable results.[270]

Regardless of which specific instrument is used to quantify these electric properties, this method has been observed to be a potentially reliable nondestructive method

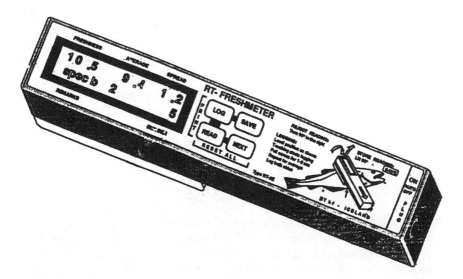

Figure 3.14. Diagram of hand-held RT-Freshmeter Type TR-2E. Printed with permission from Rafagnataekni Electronics, Reykjavik, Iceland.

of determining the freshness quality of Atlantic cod (*Gadus morhua*), butterfish (*Peprilus tricanthus*), haddock (*Melanogrammus aelefinus*), plaice (*Pleuronectes platessa*), redfish (*Sebastes marinus*), scup (*Stenotomus chrysops*), whiting (*Merlangius merlangus*), and yellowtail flounder (*Limanda ferruginea*).[81,203,270] This method is particularly useful to rapidly determine if chilled seafood has been subjected to temperature abuse, thereby substantially reducing the seafoods' freshness quality.[38] However, the value of the results can be seriously affected by the season during which the seafood was harvested.[38,269] This method has also been reported to be less useful with fatty fish rather than lean fish.[203] In addition, such procedures may produce reliable results, but may not be cost effective.[204] For example, the processing line model of the RT Freshness Grader, which is capable of automatically and accurately evaluating the freshness quality, was not widely used within the Icelandic fishing industry, because of its high cost. The Icelandic seafood industry repeatedly observed that the freshness quality could be obtained much less expensively by knowing the length (and manner) of chilled storage to which the seafood (that was to be processed) had been subjected.[204]

3.5 Effect of Species on Method Selected

As observed with the usefulness of specific chemical methods of measuring freshness quality (see Section 2.3), it is strongly believed that the species being evaluated may greatly affect the usefulness of a specific physical method of measuring freshness quality. However, often such information may not actually be available. This is primarily because a large number of these physical methods have been investigated with only a small number of different species, since they have been developed quite recently.

Whenever considering a physical method to indirectly measure the freshness quality of a certain seafood "product" it is extremely important that information concerning the usefulness of that physical method for that product (species, method of handling, processing, storage, etc.) be obtained. If such information is not available, investigations must be conducted. Only then will it be known if the physical method is indeed capable of indirectly measuring the specific aspect of appearance, flavor, odor, and/or texture (of that product) needed to be measured.

3.6 Analysis and Interpretation of Results

Whenever the physical methods used involve instruments producing noncategorical data, the results should be analyzed in a manner identical to that used to analyze results of chemical methods (see Section 2.4). However, when the physical methods involve manual comparisons with a physical standard (e.g., colored ceramic tiles), thereby producing categorical data, the results must be analyzed in a manner similar to that used to analyze the results of freshness quality grading (see Section 4.3.1).

Once the results of physical methods have been analyzed, numerous critical questions (outlined in Section 2.4) must be asked. These questions are extremely important as their answers can critically affect the usefulness of the results obtained, possibly making that physical method capable of ensuring that the buyer's and user's expectations will be satisfied.

4

Sensory Evaluation: Freshness Quality Grading

4.1 Introduction

Freshness quality grading to determine seafood freshness quality is becoming widely used within the seafood industry[3,277] It may be used by commercial seafood companies to ensure that the product being produced will meet the expectations of both buyers and regulatory agencies, seafood buyers to ensure that the product being purchased is meeting their expectations, and seafood regulatory agencies to confirm that the seafood being produced is meeting their regulations (expectations).

Freshness quality grading involves the use of a structured category scale (Section 5.4.3.1.1) by either highly trained expert assessors (Glossary) or highly trained specialized expert assessors (Glossary), rather than panelists, to determine freshness quality.[278,279] These assessors (graders) individually use their appropriate senses (sight, smell, taste, and/or touch) to determine the "level" of each sensory characteristic in the defined grade standard (i.e., a structured category scale) appropriate for the seafood being examined. Once the "level" of each assessed sensory characteristic is compared to that described in the defined grade standard being used, the freshness quality is directly determined (i.e., it has been sorted into defined categories or grades).[52]

Although this type of sensory evaluation is used in a variety of different food industries, these assessors are usually trained to evaluate only one class of product, such as coffees, dairy products, seafoods, teas, or wines.[278] In addition, these assessors are often not part of an evaluation panel, but operate as individual assessors.[3,36,101] Both Connell[36] and Huss[101] state that when a panel of assessors is utilized, a maximum of six assessors is required. In addition, Huss[101] states such panels should primarily be used during experimental investigation or with large companies that produce branded products.

Since seafood quality grading (when conducted using technologically sound procedures) involves the use of both a structured category scale and highly trained graders who have been taught to function as analytical instruments, the procedure is objective (Glossary) not subjective (Glossary).[67] This is because, in addition to the graders functioning as analytical instruments, the words (employed to define the respective points of the particular defined grade standard being utilized) describe specific sensory properties.[52,63,66] Therefore the criticism that freshness quality grading (since it is based on sensory evaluation) is subjective, causing the results to be extremely variable and of limited use,[62] is not valid.[67–69] Although both freshness quality grading (Chapter 4) and attribute assessment (Chapter 5) involve sensory evaluation, there are considerable differences between them. Regardless of the seafood being evaluated, technologically sound freshness quality grading directly measures freshness quality by quantifying the characteristics of appropriate sensory attributes. This is achieved by using a single type of sensory test (i.e., a structured category scale, which is commonly called a grade standard) and a small number of highly specialized graders (evaluators), who have been trained to function as analytical instruments.[278,279] In contrast, when attribute assessment procedures are used, the subsequent results may be used either to directly or indirectly measure the freshness quality of seafood (see Section 5.4.2.3 of Chapter 5). This is because attribute assessment is a general term that refers to any one of a large number of different specific sensory tests. Also unlike freshness quality grading, attribute assessment tests usually require a relatively large number of panelists (evaluators) who, depending on the sensory test being utilized, either may or may not be well trained.[64,280] The selection of a specific attribute assessment test primarily involves determining if the assessment is being conducted to determine the preference and/or acceptance of a sample, determine the perceived difference of certain sensory characteristics between two or more samples, precisely describe the characteristics of particular sensory attributes, or quantify the characteristics of particular sensory attributes.[47,64,66,280] In addition, the structured category scale is one of several (e.g., magnitude estimation, structured category scale, unstructured interval scale) sensory tests that may be utilized to quantify the characteristics of a particular attribute when attribute assessment is conducted,[64,280] but it is (by definition) the only type of sensory test used when freshness quality of seafood is graded (sorted into defined categories).[52]

This chapter discusses the technologically sound procedures required to ensure that graders conduct objective and accurate evaluations; it also discusses the analysis and interpretation of those evaluations.

4.2 Ensuring Graders Conduct Accurate Assessments

It is extremely difficult to ensure the accuracy of the graders sensory assessments without first clearly defining, in writing, all of the reasons why the freshness quality of a particular product is being graded.[67] The importance of each factor that affects the objectivity of the assessments can then be readily established by comparing it with these written reasons.

4.2.1 Factors Affecting Graders

Ensuring that all graders do indeed always function as analytical devices eliminates (or at least minimizes) the number of incorrect grades that are assigned.[36,101] Consequently, effects within the surroundings such as distraction by noise, other people, foreign odors, appearance of surroundings or samples, and being uncomfortable (all of which are discussed in Chapter 5) should never be overlooked. Similarly, the negative effect of psychological factors such as capriciousness, contrast effect, convergence effect, error of central tendency, error of habituation, expectation error, halo effect, leniency error, logical error, motivation, mutual suggestion, pattern effect, position effect, and stimulus error (Table 5.2) must not be ignored, but must always be seriously considered. The negative effect of these factors can be greatly reduced (if not actually eliminated) using the corrective procedures outlined in Table 5.21.

Some of the corrective procedures utilized during sensory assessment (see Chapter 5) have been considered restrictive[101,281,282] and primarily suitable for quality grading of experimental samples,[101] large companies,[101] and any situation in which a wide range of products is assessed using a wide range of sensory evaluation methods, thereby making sensory evaluation a major activity.[282]

This does not mean that the effect of the surroundings or psychological factors should be overlooked. Instead, alternate corrective procedures that are more appropriate for small and/or medium sized commercial companies, that produce only seafood and assess the samples using only one type of sensory evaluation such as attribute rating using a structured category scale (commonly referred to as grading), must be used.[282]

4.2.1.1 Minimizing Effects of Immediate Surroundings

A large number of "effects of the surroundings" may be eliminated by having all samples assessed inside a room that is well ventilated, illuminated to give an intensity of approximately 1,000 lux/m^2 and a color temperature of 5,000–5,500 K, and used only for sensory assessment.[36,282] Whenever the entire "grading room" is not properly illuminated, either a properly illuminated semipermanent grading cabinet (Fig. 4.1) or a properly illuminated portable grading cabinate (Fig. 4.2) must be used, whenever the color of the product is to be assessed. In addition, samples to be evaluated must not be prepared, but only evaluated, inside this room.[67]

Since it is not an expensive corrective measure, all of the surfaces of the entire assessment area (booths, cabinets, ceilings, countertops, doors, floors, and walls) should be of a neutral color(s) (Glossary). Similarly, within this assessment area, distraction by noise (including talking) should be minimized. However, depending on the specific situation, some of the more expensive (restrictive) corrective procedures may not be essential. Thus the assessment area does not necessarily have to be

Figure 4.1. Photograph of a semiportable, but properly illuminated, grading cabinet. Printed with permission from Canada Department of Fisheries and Oceans, Inspection Branch, St. John's, NF, Canada.

equipped with pass-through(s), which makes it essential for the assessment area to be adjacent to where the samples are prepared, outfitted with positive pressure, purified air, constant temperature, and constant relative humidity, and equipped with separate evaluation booths; instead it may have open benches,[282] which often depends on the number of graders assessing the samples at any one time.

Grading freshness quality within facilities that do not have these desirable features is extremely important if the failure to implement these corrective procedures prevents the accurate determination of freshness quality. The function of these features is to provide constant conditions enabling the sensory evaluations conducted at any specific time of year to be realistically compared to those conducted at any other specific time of year. Using expert graders (rather than nonexperts) reduces the effect of the surroundings.[36,282]

However, in some situations, it is extremely important that very detailed guidelines be rigidly followed. For example, whenever visual evaluation is required to detect parasites within fish muscle (Fig. 4.3), the detailed recommendations presented in Table

Figure 4.2. Photograph of a readily portable, but properly illuminated, grading cabinet. Printed with permission from Canada Department of Fisheries and Oceans, Inspection Branch, St. John's, NF, Canada.

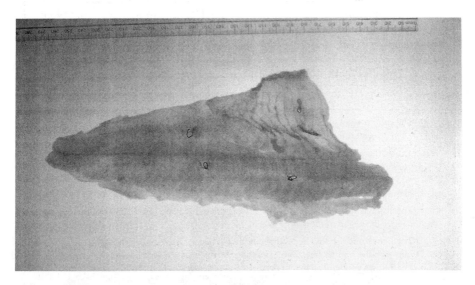

Figure 4.3. Photograph of an Atlantic cod fillet placed on a candling table, demonstrating the presence of parasites. Printed with permission from Canada Department of Fisheries and Oceans, Science Branch, St. John's, NF, Canada.

4.1 must be followed closely. To do otherwise seriously decreases both the validity and the usefulness of the results.

Regardless of the type of facilities being used, if graders do not perform as analytical devices, thereby accurately assessing the freshness quality, the grading should not be conducted.

4.2.1.2 Minimizing Effect of Psychological Factors

Whenever possible, the grader(s) who assess the seafood must not have been involved with placing the order and/or actually obtaining the seafood.[3] This is because the knowledge acquired concerning where the seafood was caught, how the seafood was caught, how the seafood was handled, and length of time the seafood was stored can cause the assessor to have specific expectations concerning the results[64,132] and he or she will no longer be acting as an analytical device.[283,284] Similarly, the grader(s) should not be involved with the preparation of the seafood. Labeling each sample with a three-digit random number (see Chapter 5) will also reduce the occurrence of expectation error.

Almost all of the remaining psychological factors can be minimized by presenting the samples in a random order, ensuring that the order by which the samples are graded by the grader is balanced so that each different product appears in a given position an equal number of times, and using experienced graders (Table 5.20). Although grading different products in a balanced manner sounds very simple, it can be extremely difficult to achieve whenever a large number of different products are to be assessed. This is because under such circumstances, a small increase in the number of different products to be evaluated at any one time greatly increases the number of different combinations that must be evaluated, to ensure that each combination is

Table 4.1. SPECIFICATIONS NECESSARY TO OPTIMIZE VISUAL DETECTION OF PARASITES IN FISH MUSCLE[a]

Item	Specification
1	"The color of the light source should be **cool white** with a color temperature of **4200°K**. At least two 20-watt fluorescent tubes are recommended in a candling table."
2	"The working surface on top of a candling table should be an acrylic sheet or other suitable material 5–6 mm thick with 45–60% translucency. The length and width of this sheet depend on on the size of the fillets being examined and the size of the light source. A 30 × 60 cm sheet is suggested for most applications."
3	"The average light intensity above a candling table should be 1500–1800 lux as measured 30 cm above the center of the acrylic sheet."
4	"The light source should be arranged to give a distribution of illumination in a ratio of 3:1:0.1 through the acrylic sheet. In other words, the brightness directly above the light source should be 3 times greater than that of the outer field and the brightness of the outer limit of the visual field should not be more than one-tenth that of the inner field."
5	"The overhead illumination (incident light) should be at least 500 lux."

[a] Reprinted with permission from Valdimarrsson et al.[300]

evaluated an equal number of times. For example, the required number of different combinations increases from 1 to 2 to 6 to 24 to 120 when the number of different products being evaluated (at any one time) is increased from 1 to 2 to 3 to 4 to 5, respectively (Table 4.2). Thus only one, two, or three different products should be evaluated at the same time, as then only one, two, or six different combinations would be required (Table 4.2).

4.2.1.3 Screening, Selecting, and Training Graders

Screening primarily involves testing the potential grader's basic ability to assess each type of attribute (appearance, odor, flavor, and/or texture) that he or she will likely be required to evaluate.[285] These abilities are often determined by subjecting the person to a broad range of triangle tests, which vary in only appearance, aroma, flavor, or texture.[285] However, screening also involves assessing an individual's health, general attitudes, availability, and ability to communicate (e.g., work habits and willingness to evaluate the type of samples needed to be evaluated).[279,285] Potential candidates may be people who have not been screened or trained, but are currently grading freshness quality of samples, people who are designated, because of their current duties, to begin grading freshness quality, or people who have been chosen, because of their individual interest, attitude, knowledge, and health.[272,282]

Table 4.2. DIFFERENT ORDER IN WHICH MULTIPRODUCTS MUST BE PRESENTED TO ENSURE THE PRODUCTS ARE PRESENTED IN A BALANCED MANNER

Products to Be Evaluated	Different Combinations in Which the Different Products Must Be Presented If a Balanced Presentation Is to Be Achieved
A, B	AB and BA
A, B, C	ABC, ACB, BAC, BCA, CAB, CBA
A, B, C, D	ABCD, ABDC, ACBD, ACDB, ADBC, ADCB, BACD, BADC, BCAD, BCDA, BDAC, BDCA, CABD, CADB, CBAD, CBDA, CDAB, CDBA, DABC, DACB, DBAC, DBCA, DCAB, DCBA
A, B, C, D, E	ABCDE, ABCED, ABDCE, ABDEC, ABECD, ABEDC, ACBDE, ACBED, ACDBE, ACDEB, ACEBD, ACEDB, ADBCE, ADBEC, ADCBE, ADCEB, ADEBC, ADECB, AEBCD, AEBDC, AECBD, AECDB, AEDBC, AEDCB, BACDE, BACED, BADCE, BADEC, BAECD, BAEDC, BCADE, BCAED, BCDAE, BCDEA, BCEAD, BCEDA, BDACE, BDAEC, BDCAE, BDCEA, BDEAC, BDECA, BEACD, BEADC, BECAD, BECDA, BEDAC, BEDCA, CABDE, CABED, CADBE, CADEB, CAEBD, CAEDB, CBADE, CBAED, CBDAE, CBDEA, CBEAD, CBEDA, CDABE, CDAEB, CDBAE, CDBEA, CDEAB, CDEBA, CEABD, CEADB, CEBAD, CEBDA, CEDAB, CEDBA, DABCE, DABEC, DACBE, DACEB, DAEBC, DAECB, DBACE, DBAEC, DBCAE, DBCEA, DBEAC, DBECA, DCABE, DCAEB, DCBAE, DCBEA, DCEAB, DCEBA, DEABC, DEACB, DEBAC, DEBCA, DECAB, DECBA, EABCD, EABDC, EACBD, EACDB, EADBC, EADCB, EBACD, EBADC, EBCAD, EBCDA, EBDAC, EBDCA, ECABD, ECADB, ECBAD, ECBDA, ECDAB, ECDBA, EDABC, EDACB, EDBAC, EDBCA, EDCAB, EDCBA

Training involves teaching the people (1) the general principles and practices of sensory evaluation; (2) to readily identify and accurately assess each sensory characteristic defined in each of the different product standards that he or she will be expected to use, (3) to have a long-term memory so that standards that have not been recently used can be readily and accurately implemented, (4) to grade a large number of samples at a single session, and (5) to evaluate his or her own performance.[272,282]

The grader's learning of general principles and practices usually involves formal lectures and demonstrations concerning topics such as the operation of each of the different senses (sight, smell, taste, and touch), how the perception of color (and other types of appearances), flavor, odor, and texture is affected by a wide range of variables, the different types (affective, discriminative, descriptive) of sensory assessment, and technologically sound testing procedures.[278,282]

The importance of a sound knowledge of the principles and practices of sensory evaluation must not be underestimated. This is because many of the skills learned by a potential grader are often learned during formal practice sessions and by apprenticing with a grader(s) who consistently demonstrates these skills, These skills are obviously best learned and utilized when the potential grader understands why such skills are necessary.

Although all graders must be properly screened (so their basic sensory skills will not inhibit any future training that may be required), the necessary minimum extent of training depends on the specific duties of the grader. Some graders are required to assess a very wide range of products, using very specific and detailed (e.g., a 10-point structured category scale) product standards. Such graders may be required to assess a wide variety of seafood such as single ingredient fillets, shellfish, and numerous types of value added seafood products that may also contain poultry, red meat, sauces, and vegetables. In these circumstances, appropriate training methods would need to be more extensive,[282] possibly similar to those mentioned in Chapter 5 and described by other references.[64,65,220,285,286]

Extensive training is also necessary whenever graders are required to assess specific off-odors and off-flavors, commonly referred to as taints.[282]

Other graders may be required to assess a narrow range of seafood products (e.g., fresh groundfish and/or single ingredient fresh groundfish fillets that are not value added) using a specific, but not detailed, product standard that consists of two categories (accept or reject). In such circumstances, appropriate training would not need to be as extensive.

Since it depends on the specific situation, the extent of training that is actually necessary is best established by critically examining the written reasons for determining freshness quality. This is very important because if the extent of training is not closely related to the duties expected, a person may receive costly training for a specific grading duty he or she may never perform or, conversely, a person may be requested to conduct a specific grading duty for which he or she has not been adequately trained.

Regardless of the extent to which a grader (who has been properly screened) has been trained, the practicing grader must accurately implement the grade standards. Monitoring the accuracy of assigned grades may be achieved by having the grader check his or her consistency, comparing the grader's assessments with those of other graders, and conducting formal examinations.[279] A grader's performance may also be monitored by having the grader, without his or her knowledge, assess samples with sensory characteristics of a known "level." The necessity of monitoring the assessments of graders who have been screened and trained (to operate as analytical instruments) is similar to the necessity of periodically checking the accuracy of a pH meter, even though it had previously been calibrated.

4.2.2 Defined Grade Standards

4.2.2.1 Importance

Since grading the freshness quality of seafood consists of having graders use their relevant senses [(sight, smell, taste, and/or touch) to sort that seafood into specified categories (Tables 4.3 to 4.16)], the defined grade standards, which describe each category, are extremely important. Even if the effects of both immediate surroundings and psychological factors are minimized and the graders are well screened and well trained, the assigned grades will probably not be valid unless the grade standards clearly allow the grader to objectively assess the samples. Consequently, the individual terms that are used to describe an individual grade of a single criterion must be precise rather than vague, technically correct, objective rather than subjective, independent (not redundant of any other terms used to describe other grades within the grade standard), and a primary term rather than a cluster of terms.[67,72,287,288] Descriptive terms of any sensory attribute that are vague, subjective, or part of a cluster of terms describing a particular grade can easily cause the grader to be confused and less objective, thereby increasing the chances of assigning an incorrect grade.[288]

4.2.2.2 Traditional Freshness Quality Grading Systems

During the past few decades, seafood freshness quality grades have often been determined using intact (i.e., not filleted, split, or steaked) gutted fish using a grading standard such as that presented in Table 4.3. This type of a quality grading standard has frequently consisted of specified sensory characteristics of three to six different criteria (e.g., visual characteristics of eyes, gills, outer slime, peritoneum, skin, and odorous characteristics of the gills) associated with the fish (Table 4.3). Depending on the specific grade standard, each criterion of the sample being assessed is categorized as being one of two grades (accept or reject), three grades (grade A, grade B, or grade C), or four grades (grade A, grade B, grade C, or grade D), etc., whichever is specified in the grading standard being used. Once each criterion has been graded, a final grade (based on the grades assigned each of the different criteria) of the sample being evaluated is determined. Prior to being categorized into grades, each of the three to six different criteria are evaluated according to the specifications of the grade standard being used, which often consist of three to six subdescriptions for each of the different grades (Table 4.3). These numerous subdescriptions often increase the time required to assess an intact fish, whenever the sensory characteristics of the criterion being assessed do not agree with all of the three to six subdescriptions of any specific

Table 4.3. EUROPEAN COMMUNITY (EC) FISH FRESHNESS GRADES FOR WHOLE WHITE FISH, DOGFISH, HERRING, AND MACKEREL[a]

	Grade E	Grade A	Grade B	Grade C (Unfit)
	"White Fish": cod, haddock, whiting, plaice, redfish, ling, hake			
Skin	Bright; shining; iridescent (not redfish) or opalescent	Waxy; slight loss of bloom; very slight bleaching	Dull, some bleaching	Dull; gritty; marked bleaching and shrinkage
Outer slime	Transparent, water white	Milky	Yellowish-gray; some clotting	Yellow-brown; very clotted and thick
Eyes	Convex; black pupil; translucent cornea	Plane; slightly opaque pupil; slight opalescent	Slightly concave; gray pupil; opaque cornea	Completely sunken; gray pupil opaque discolored cornea
Gills	Dark red or bright red; mucus translucent	Red or pink; mucus slightly opaque	Brown/gray and bleached; mucus opaque and thick	Brown or bleached; mucus yellowish gray and clotted
Peritoneum	Glossy; brilliant; difficult to tear from flesh	Slightly dull; difficult to tear from flesh	Gritty; fairly easy to tear from flesh	Gritty; easily torn from flesh
Gill and internal odors all except plaice	Fresh; seaweedy; shellfishy	No odor; neutral odor; trace musty, mousy, milky, capryllic, garlic, or peppery	Definite musty, mousy, milky, capryllic, garlic, or peppery; bready; malty; beery; lactic; slightly sour	Acetic; butyric; fruity; turnipy; amines, sulfide; fecal
plaice	Fresh oil; metallic, fresh-cut grass; earthy; peppery	Oily; seaweedy; aromatic; trace musty, mousy, or citric	Oily; definite musty, mousy or citric; bready; malty; beery; slightly rancid; painty	Muddy; grassy; fruity; acetic; butyric; rancid; amines; sulfide; fecal
	Dogfish			
Eyes	Convex; very bright and iridescent; narrow pupils	Convex to flat; green; clear but some loss of brightness and iridescence; oval pupils	Flat to sunken; some yellowing; slightly cloudy	Sunken; yellow; cloudy

Table 4.3. *Continued*

	Grade E	Grade A	Grade B	Grade C (Unfit)
Appearance	In or partly in rigor; small amount of clear slime on skin	Loss of rigor; no slime on skin and particularly no slime in mouth or at gill opening	Sticky slime in mouth and at gill openings; some flattening of snout	Copious slime in mouth and gill openings; obvious flattening of snout
Odor	Fresh marine	Odorless or slightly musty; not ammoniacal	Ammoniacal; sour	Very ammoniacal; very sour
		Herring		
Skin	Full bloom; bright; shining; iridescent; clean	Slight dullness and loss of bloom	Definite dullness and loss of bloom	Dull; no bloom
Outer slime	Transparent or water white	Milky; slight browning	Brownish	Brown
Gill covers	Silvery	Silvery; slight browning; slight bright red blood	Some browning and blood staining	Very brown and blood stained
Eyes	Convex	Plane	Slightly concave	Concave; sunken
Firmness	Very stiff and firm	Fairly stiff and firm	Stiffness nearly absent, fairly soft	Soft or very soft
Gill odors	Fresh seaweedy	Less fresh seaweedy, slight oily	Slight stale seaweedy; definite oily; trace or slight H_2S (sulfide), "salt cured" or rancid oil	Definite H_2S (sulfide); rancid oil; amines; fecal; sour
		Mackerel		
Skin	Strong blue and turquoise colors; iridescence over all body; well-defined lateral line; reticulations on upper surface; clear distinction between upper and lower surface	Loss of bright colors with fading of reticulations; pale golden tinge on lower surface	Golden tinge over all body; skin wrinkles on flexing; washed-out appearance of colors; patchy iridescence	Yellow slime; little distinction between upper and lower surfaces

(Continued)

Table 4.3. *Continued*

	Grade E	Grade A	Grade B	Grade C (Unfit)
Texture of body	Stiff	Firm	Some softening	Limp and floppy
Eyes	Bulging with protruding lens; shiny jet black/blue pupil with metallic brown iris; transparent eye cap	Convex; slight clouding of lens and wrinkling of iris; clouding of eye cap	Plane; cloudy lens with black specs in iris; pale golden eye cap	Sunken eye covered with yellow slime
Gill appearance	Uniformly dark red/purple with free blood and water clear slime	Loss of color with red/brown slime; pale margins to gills	Further loss of color with patchy bleaching; increase red/brown slime	Bleached; thick yellow slime
Gill odor	Fresh seaweed; sharp; halogens; pepper; fresh-cut grass; metallic; blood; fresh, sweet oil	Dull; muddy; musty mousy; cardboard; fish oil	Yeast; sour rotten fruit; "wet dogs"; old grass cuttings; strong oily	Compost heap; rotten turnips; sour cheese; ammonia; sulfides; rancid oil

[a] Reprinted with permission from Howgate et al.[301]

Table 4.4.   AN ATLANTIC COD WHOSE SENSORY CHARACTERISTICS DO NOT ENTIRELY AGREE WITH EITHER THOSE SPECIFIED FOR GRADE B OR GRADE C OF THE EUROPEAN COMMUNITY FISH FRESHNESS GRADES (TABLE 4.3)

	Specified Sensory Characteristics of a Cod to Be Classified as Grade B	Sensory Characteristics of the Cod Being Assessed	Specified Sensory Characteristics of a Cod to Be Classified as Grade C (Unfit)
Skin	Dull, some bleaching	Dull; gritty; some bleaching; slight shrinkage	Dull; gritty; marked bleaching and shrinkage
Outer slime	Yellowish-gray; some clotting	Yellowish-gray; some clotting	Yellow-brown; very clotted and thick
Eyes	Slightly concave; gray pupil; opaque cornea	Slightly concave; gray pupil; opaque discolored cornea	Completely sunken; gray pupil opaque discolored cornea
Gills	Brown/gray and bleached; mucus opaque and thick	Bleached; mucus opaque and thick	Brown or bleached; mucus yellowish gray and clotted
Peritoneum	Gritty; fairly easy to tear from flesh	Gritty; easily torn from flesh	Gritty; easily torn from flesh
Gill and internal odors	Definite musty, mousy, milky, capryllic, garlic, or peppery; bready; malty; lactic; slightly sour	Bready; malty; slightly sour; fruity; turnipy	Acetic; butyric; fruity; turnipy; amines; sulfide; fecal

grade (Table 4.4). This is because the lack of agreement (Table 4.4) often causes the grader to be confused, which increases the time to decide which grade to assign and decreases the objectivity of these types of seafood freshness quality grading systems. Therefore, scientists have attempted to develop seafood freshness quality grading systems that are both rapid and objective.

4.2.2.3 Modifying Traditional Freshness Quality Grading Systems

One method of increasing both speed and objectivity of a quality grading system is to increase both the number of grades within a criterion and the number of criteria to be assessed. For example, the traditional grading system for hake (Table 4.3) consists of four grades for each of six criteria, whereas the grading system for hake presented in Table 4.5 includes six grades for each of 11 different criteria. These changes produce a reduced number of subdescriptions for each grade of each criterion (Tables 4.3 and 4.5). This increases the chances that a sample's sensory characteristics agree with all of the subdescriptions within an individual grade of a specific criteria, thereby decreasing confusion and increasing objectivity. However, depending on the system and the sample being evaluated, the increased number of grades may increase the probability of an individual sample's sensory characteristics, of one or more specific criteria, agreeing with the subdescriptions of more than one specific grade. This would also cause the grader to be confused, resulting in both decreased speed and reduced objectivity.

An alternative method of increasing both the speed and objectivity of a grading system is to increase the number of criteria but decrease the number of grades within each criteria (Table 4.6).

4.2.2.4 Tasmanian Food Research Unit (TFRU) Freshness Quality Grading System for Intact Fish

This freshness quality grading system (Table 4.6) has several unique characteristics. Unlike traditional methods of freshness quality grading, the number of different grades (different demerit points) within each criteria depends on the criterion being evaluated. Second, it involves specifying the sensory characteristics of a very large number (e.g., 18) of clearly defined criteria associated with the seafood. In addition, the freshness quality of the fish being evaluated is not based on an average of different grades, but on the total number of demerit points it was assigned (Table 4.6).

Once the sensory characteristic of a criterion is determined it is immediately assigned a demerit point ranging from 0 to 3 (Table 4.6). Every description of each demerit point of each criteria is very brief, usually involving only one or two words, and, if possible, is very precise (Table 4.6). Thus, while assessing each criterion, a grader is exposed to minimum confusion. Individuals using the TFRU system have been reported to be able to both rapidly and objectively assess the freshness quality of intact fish.[113,289,290]

Whenever this system is used to determine a seafood's freshness quality, it is extremely important to ensure that every one of the specified questions concerning sen-

Table 4.5. ORGANOLEPTIC SCORE: UNGUTTED HAKE[a]

	Organoleptic Score					
	0	1	2	3	4	5
Skin						
Outer slime	Transparent, not colored	Transparent, not colored	Milky	Opaque	Clotted	Yellowish
Pigmentation	Bright, iridescent	Natural	Less natural, not bright, not iridescent	Faded	Discolored	Gray
Eyes						
Color	Black pupil translucent cornea (bright)	Black pupil translucent cornea (less bright)	Translucent cornea, (not bright)	Opalescent cornea	Gray pupil, milky cornea	Opaque, discolored
Sinking	Completely convex	Completely convex	Less convex	Plane	Slightly concave	Completely concave, sunken
Gills						
Color	Bloody red	Bloody red	Dull red	Pale red	Dirty yellow	White–grayish
Odor	Fresh (algae, sea)	Neutral sweet	Neutral sweet	Slightly rancid	Slightly disagreeable	Off odors, nauseous
Flesh quality						
Meat	Firm (rigid)	Firm (slightly elastic)	Elastic	Flexible	Soft	Very soft
Belly	Intact (firm–rigid)	Intact (not rigid)	Distended (firm)	Soft (not firm)	Fragile	Perforated
Peritoneum	Difficult to tear from flesh (bright black)	Difficult to tear from flesh (black)	Easy to tear from flesh	Teared	Damaged (incomplete)	Burst
Backbone						
Color of meat next to bone	Bright white	White, not bright	Slightly pale red	Pale red	Red	Grizzly
Meat adherence to bone	Very adherent	Very adherent	Adherent	Slightly adherent	Not adherent	Meat separated from bone

[a] Reprinted with permission from Lupin et al.[302]

Table 4.6. FRESHNESS QUALITY ASSESSMENT SYSTEM FOR ROUND FISH[a]

Factor Being Assessed	Observed Characteristic	Demerit Points
Appearance of surface	Very bright	0
	Bright	1
	Slightly dull	2
	Dull	3
Skin	Firm	0
	Soft	1
Scales	Firm	0
	Slightly loose	1
	Loose	2
Slime	Absent	0
	Slightly slimy	1
	Slimy	2
	Very slimy	3
Stiffness	Prerigor	0
	Rigor	1
	Postrigor	2
Eyes		
Clarity	Clear	0
	Slightly cloudy	1
	Cloudy	2
Shape	Normal	0
	Slightly sunken	1
	Sunken	2
Iris	Visible	0
	Not visible	1
Blood	No blood	0
	Slightly bloody	1
	Very bloody	2
Gills		
Color	Characteristic	0
	Slightly dark/slightly faded	1
	Very dark/very faded	2
Mucus	Absent	0
	Moderate	1
	Excessive	2
Smell	(Fresh oily)/(metallic seaweed)	0
	Fishy	1
	Stale	2
	Spoiled	3
Belly		
Discoloration	Absent	0
	Detectable	1
	Moderate	2
	Excessive	3
Firmness	Firm	0
	Soft	1
	Burst	2

Table 4.6. *Continued*

Factor Being Assessed	Observed Characteristic	Demerit Points
Vent		
Condition	Normal	0
	(Slight break)/(exudes)	1
	(Excessive)/(opening)	2
Smell	Fresh	0
	Neutral	1
	Fishy	2
	Spoiled	3
Belly cavity		
Stains	Opalescent	0
	Grayish	1
	Yellow-brown	2
Blood	Red	0
	Dark red	1
	Brown	2
Total demerit points (0–39)		

[a] Reprinted with permission from Branch and Vail.[90]

sory characteristics be answered.[113] Although graders can readily use a pencil and paper to record their assessments of each "part," programming this grading system into a hand-held computer or into a hand-held device developed specifically for the TFRU helps ensure that all appropriate questions have been answered and decreases the time required to assess a fish.[291] Other important aspects of the TFRU system are (1) no undue emphasis is placed on a single feature and the sample cannot be rejected on the basis of a single criterion, (2) minor differences in judgments in any one criterion being assessed do not unduly influence the total score, and (3) the combination of the number of the different criteria and different demerit scores gives a total possible score of a reasonable magnitude.[291]

Even though the TFRU grading system is both objective and nondestructive, it is extremely rapid, requiring only 5 min to grade 10 fish.[289] It has been shown to be a very applicable means of evaluating the freshness quality of a variety of different temperate and tropical species (e.g., anchovy, Atlantic cod, herring, hoki, plaice, redfish, saithe, sardine, whiting, *A. spinifer*, *L. vittus*, *N. peronii*, and *P. pictus*) stored in ice.[113,270,289,290,292] The developers of the TFRU system appropriate for iced anchovy (Table 4.7), Atlantic cod (Table 4.8), Atlantic herring (Table 4.9), plaice (Table 4.10), redfish (Table 4.11), saithe (Table 4.12), and sardine (Table 4.13) observed that it was necessary to modify the general TFRU system (Table 4.6). Thus, whenever one intends to use the TFRU system for a "new" species, preliminary studies must be conducted to ensure that all the criteria and their corresponding defined characteristics incorporated in the grade standards are appropriate and will actually be used.

When the TFRU (or modified TFRU) system was used to assess the freshness quality of the previously mentioned temperate and tropical species, the total de-

Table 4.7. FRESHNESS QUALITY GRADING SYSTEM FOR ANCHOVY (*ENGRAULIS ENCRASICOLUS*)[a]

Parameter Being Assessed	Defined Characteristic	Demerit Points
General appearance		
Surface	Bright	0
	Less bright	1
	Dull	2
Firmness	Tense, firm, hard (rigor)	0
	Less tense, firm	1
	Flaccid, soft (postrigor)	2
Eyes		
Clarity	Clear, transparent	0
(cornea)	Central opacity	1
	Opaque	2
Pupil	Black and circular	0
	Gray	1
	Gray and distorted	2
Shape	Slightly convex, normal	0
	Plane, flat	1
	Concave, sunken	2
Gills		
Cover	None	0
(bloodiness)	Slight <10%	1
	Some <50%	2
	Bloody >50%	3
Color	Red	0
	Brownish-red	1
Slime	None	0
	Slight	1
	Slats stick together	2
Smell	Slight seaweedy, peppery	0
	Metallic, oily	1
	Metallic, acid, rancid	2
	Sour, stale blood	3
Abdomen		
Postgill	Intact, firm	0
(belly-burst)	Stretch-marks	1
	Torn	2
Spinal column		
Rupture	Breaks with force (knife)	0
strength	Breaks (hands)	1
	Comes apart (hands)	2
Flesh		
(-head and viscera)		
Appearance and	Fresh bloom, translucent	0
color	Some opacity	1
	Dense, bloody	2
Total demerit points (0–25)		

[a] Reprinted with permission from Nielsen et al.[290]

Table 4.8. FRESHNESS QUALITY ASSESSMENT SYSTEM FOR GUTTED ATLANTIC COD[a]

Parameter Being Assessed	Defined Characteristic	Demerit Points
Appearance of surface	Very bright	0
	Bright	1
	Slightly dull	2
	Dull	3
Skin	Firm	0
	Soft	1
Stiffness	Rigor	0
	Postrigor	1
Slime	Clear	0
	Unclear	1
	Slightly cloudy	2
	Very cloudy	3
Eyes		
Clarity	Clear	0
	Slightly cloudy	1
	Cloudy	2
Shape	Normal	0
	Slightly sunken	1
	Sunken	2
Gills		
Color	Characteristic, red	0
	Slightly faded	1
	Faded, discolored	2
Smell	Fresh, seaweed/metallic	0
	Fishy	1
	Stale	2
	Spoiled	3
Mucus	Absent	0
	Moderate	1
	Excessive	2
Flesh color (in open surfaces)	Translucent	0
	Gray	1
	Yellow-brown	2
Blood (in throat, cut)	Red	0
	Dark red	1
	Brown	2
Total demerit points (0–23)		

[a] Reprinted with permission from Larsen et al.[289]

merit points (either by themselves or as a percentage of maximum demerit score) was always observed to be linearly related to the length of time (days) the individual species were stored in ice.[113,270,289–292] Once such a statistical relationship between these two variables has been established (for each species of interest), the total demerit scores of the fish being assessed may be used to readily predict the storage life of those fish. This prediction of "future" freshness quality of fish that

Table 4.9. FRESHNESS QUALITY GRADING SYSTEM FOR HERRING[a]

Parameter Being Assessed	Description	Demerit Points
Appearance consistency and odor		
Skin	Very shiny	0
	Shiny	1
	Mat	2
Blood on gill covers	None	0
	Very little (10–30%)	1
	Some (30–50 %)	2
	Much (50–100 %)	3
Consistency	Hard	0
	Firm	1
	Yielding	2
	Soft	3
Belly	Firm	0
	Soft	1
	Burst	2
Odor	Fresh sea odor	0
	Neutral	1
	Slight secondary odor	2
	Strong secondary odor	3
Eyes		
Brightness	Bright	0
	Somewhat lusterless	1
Shape	Convex	0
	Flat	1
	Sunken	2
Gills		
Color (can be omitted in tank herring)	Characteristic red	0
	Somewhat pale/nonglossy/ opaque	1
Odor	Fresh, seaweedy, metallic	0
	Neutral	1
	Some secondary odor	2
	Strong secondary odor	3
Total demerit points (0–20)		

[a] Reprinted with permission from Jonsdottir.[292]

have been sorted into both species and batches (with the same "catching history") allows them to be processed at an iced storage time that best suits the product specifications[290] to which both the processor and the buyer had previously agreed. However, at times, the assessment of intact (round or gutted) fish may not reveal whether the product specifications have been satisfied, as the buyer may be very concerned about sensory characteristics that can be determined only by examining actual fillets.

Table 4.10. FRESHNESS QUALITY GRADING SYSTEM FOR RAW INTACT PLAICE[a]

Parameter Being Assessed	Defined Characteristic	Demerit Points
Skin		
Surface appearance	Bright shining	0
	Not lustrous	1
	Discolored	2
Slime	Aqueous transparent	0
	Slightly mucus	1
	Milky mucus	2
	Opaque mucus	3
Eyes		
Clarity	Translucent cornea	0
	Slightly opalescent	1
	Opalescent cornea	2
Shape	Bulging	0
	Convex sunken	1
	Flat	2
Gills		
Color	Bright color	0
	Less colored	1
	Discolored	2
	Yellowish	3
Odor	Fresh oil, peppery	0
	Oily, aromatic	1
	Musty, slightly rancid	2
	Rancid, fecal	3
Mucus	No mucus	0
	Trace of mucus	1
	Excessive mucus	2
Flesh		
Stiffness	Rigor	0
	Postrigor	1
Cut from abdomen	Bluish translucent	0
	Less colored	1
	Waxy	2
Total demerit points (0–20)		

[a] Reprinted with permission from Nielsen et al.[290]

4.2.2.5 Freshness Quality Grading of Fillets

Unlike grading of intact fish, grading of fillets allows additional sensory characteristics such as gaping (Glossary, Fig. 4.4, Tables 4.14 and 4.15), color of the flesh (Figs. 4.5, 4.6, and 4.7; Tables 4.14 and 4.15), and presence of parasites (Fig. 4.3; Tables 4.14 and 4.15) to be determined. The actual system of grading the freshness quality of fillets that is to be employed usually depends on a variety of factors such as the species being evaluated, the fillets being skinned or unskinned, whether the fish being filleted had been gutted, and if the fillets (or fish) had been frozen and

Table 4.11. FRESHNESS QUALITY GRADING SYSTEM FOR REDFISH[a]

Parameter Being Assessed	Description	Demerit Points
Appearance, consistency		
Skin	Very shiny	0
	Shiny, some discoloration	1
	Mat, discoloration	2
Consistency	Rigid	0
	Hard	1
	Firm	2
	Yielding	3
Eyes		
Brightness	Bright	0
	Somewhat lusterless	1
	Lusterless	2
Shape	Convex	0
	Flat	1
	Sunken	2
Color	Black eyeball	0
	Grayish ring	1
	Gray ring	2
Gills		
Color	Characteristic red color	0
	Somewhat pale/nonglossy	1
	Faded, discolored, brown spots	2
	Brown spots, brown	3
Odor	Fresh, seaweedy, metallic, sea-like	0
	Neutral, grassy, slightly musty	1
	Malt, yeast, beer, lactic acid, sour milk	2
	Acetic acid, sulfur, decay	3
Slime	Clear	0
	Milky	1
	Discolored, cloudy	2
Fillets		
Color of flesh	Mother-of-pearlish, bluish	0
	Milky	1
	Discolored, cloudy	2
Entrails		
Decomposition	Normal	0
	Beginning decomposition	1
	Strong decomposition	2
Total demerit points (0–23)		

[a] Reprinted with permission from Martinsdottir and Arnason.[270]

Table 4.12. FRESHNESS QUALITY GRADING SYSTEM FOR ICED SAITHE[a]

Parameter Being Assessed	Defined Characteristic	Demerit Points
General appearance		
Elasticity	Elastic	0
	A press leaves a minor mark	1
	A press leaves a clear mark	2
Slime, skin	Slippery, supple	0
	Pigment colored slime	1
	Skin appears leathery	2
Flesh color	Translucent	0
in open	Characteristic meat color	1
surface	Yellowish	2
Stiffness	Rigor	0
	Postrigor	1
Eyes		
Clarity	Clear	0
	Slightly cloudy	1
	Cloudy and milky	2
Shape	Convex, normal	0
	Flat, slightly convex	1
	Slightly sunken, lens appears	2
	Hole in eye is sunken, concave	3
Gills		
Color	Characteristic red-like aorta blood	0
	Red-brown	1
	Brownish color with red shade	2
	Excessive rust brown	3
Slime	Normal slime formation, gill slats apart	0
	Gill slats starting to stick together	1
	Yellowish slime	2
	Excessive slime, red-brown color	3
Smell	Sweat, seaweed	0
	Neutral/slight sweet	1
	Slight sourness, trace of "off" odor	2
	Sour and cabbage-like smell	3
Total demerit points (0–21)		

[a] Reprinted with permission from Nielsen et al.[290]

Table 4.13. FRESHNESS QUALITY GRADING SYSTEM FOR SARDINE
(*SARDINA PILCHARDUS*)[a]

Parameter Being Assessed	Defined Characteristic	Demerit Points
General appearance		
Surface appearance	Very bright, iridescent	0
	Bright	1
	Less bright	2
	Slightly dull	3
Stiffness	Flexible (prerigor)	0
	Tense (rigor)	1
	Less tense	2
	Soft	3
Flesh firmness	Firm, springy	0
	Firm, hard	1
	Springless	2
	Soft	3
Eyes		
Clarity (cornea)	Clear, transparent	0
	Central opacity	1
	Opaque	2
Pupil	Black and circular	0
	Black and distorted	1
	Gray and distorted	2
Shape	Slightly convex, normal	0
	Plane, flat	1
	Concave, sunken	2
Gills		
Cover (bloodiness)	None	0
	Slight <10%	1
	Some <50%	2
	Bloody	3
Color	Bluish-red	0
	Brownish-red	1
	Faded	2
Smell	Fresh, oily, marine	0
	Oily, musty, slightly rancid	1
	Rancid, sour	2
	Rancid, acrid	3
Abdomen		
Postgill (belly-burst)	Intact, firm	0
	Stretch-marks	1
	Torn	2
Spinal column		
Rupture strength	Breaks with force	0
	Breaks	1
	Comes apart	2
Flesh		
Appearance and color	Fresh bloom, translucent	0
	Opaque	1
	Dense, bloody	2
Total demerit points (0–29)		

[a] Reprinted with permission from Nielsen et al.[290]

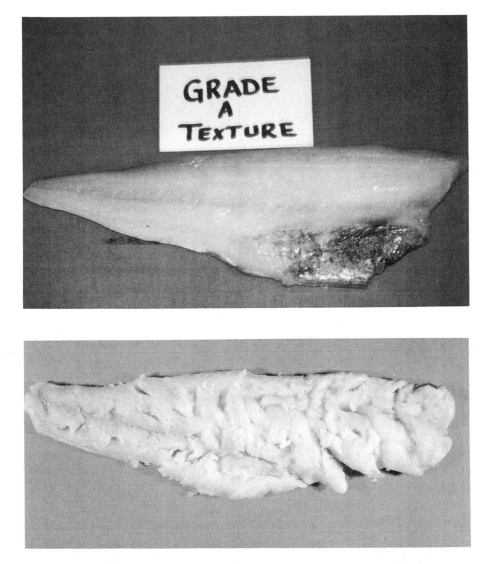

Figure 4.4. Photographs of Atlantic cod fillets that (a) exhibit no gaping and (b) exhibit extensive gaping. Printed with permission from Canada Department of Fisheries and Oceans, Inspection Branch, St., John's, NF, Canada.

thawed prior to being assessed. Thus whenever a grading system for fillets is being utilized, it is also important to ensure that the system contains all of the appropriate criteria and their corresponding defined characteristics. The results of the TFRU system for grading fillets (Table 4.15), like those of the TFRU system for assessing intact fish, have been reported to be linearly related to the length of chilled storage.[113,291,293]

Figure 4.5. Photograph of bruised flounder fillets. Printed with permission from Canada Department of Fisheries and Oceans, St. John's, NF, Canada.

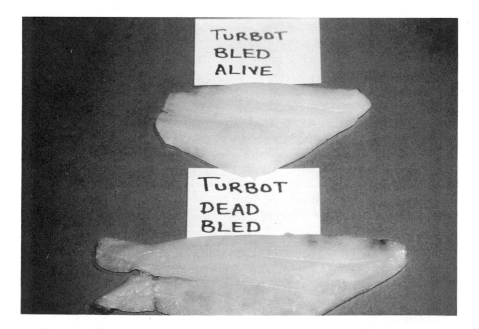

Figure 4.6. Photograph of white (fish had been alive, when bled) and discolored (fish had been dead, when bled) turbot fillets. Printed with permission from Canada Department of Fisheries and Oceans, Inspection Branch, St. John's, NF, Canada.

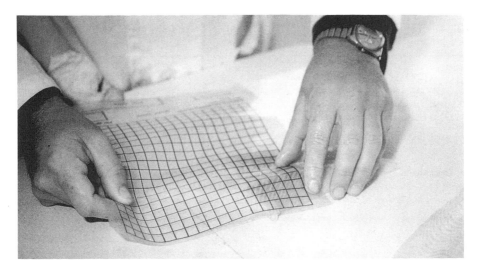

Figure 4.7. Rapidly, but objectively, measuring the extent of discoloration present on a fillet. Printed with permission from Canada Department of Fisheries and Oceans, Inspection Branch, St. John's, NF, Canada.

Table 4.14. FRESHNESS QUALITY GRADING SCHEME FOR ATLANTIC COD FILLETS AND SPLIT FISH[a]

Sensory Variable	Description of Variable	Assigned Grade
Smell	Fish has a normal smell	1
	Faint normal smell, no abnormal smell	2
	Normal smell absent, abnormal smell may be noticed	3
	Sour or putrid smell	4
Gaping	Fish muscle firm, with no gaping	1
	Fish muscle firm, slight gaping	2
	Gaping quite noticeable	3
	Torn muscle and excessive gaping	4
Blood veins in belly flaps	No visible blood veins	1
	Blood veins slightly noticeable	2
	Blood veins noticeable, but neither continuous nor forming blood patches	3
	Blood veins continuous or forming blood patches	4
Color of muscle	Color normal and characteristic for the species	1
	Different color hues just noticeable	2
	Normal color absent	3

Number of blood patches that are each > 3 cm^2
Number of areas (each > 3 cm^2) damaged by guts
Number of gaff stabs
Number of visible codworms

[a] Reprinted with permission from Martinsdottir and Stefansson.[284]

Table 4.15.   FRESHNESS QUALITY ASSESSMENT SYSTEM TO EVALUATE
              RAW FILLETS[a]

Factor Being Assessed	Observed Characteristics	Demerit Points
Appearance		
Color of fish	Translucent	0
	Slightly discolored	1
	Slightly opaque	2
	Opaque	3
Blood stains	Absent	0
	Detectable	1
	Moderate	2
	Excessive	3
Clotting	Unclotted	0
	Slightly clotted	1
	Moderately clotted	2
	Excessively clotted	3
Skin color	Very bright	0
	Bright	1
	Slightly dull	2
	Dull	3
Texture	Firm	0
	Slightly soft	1
	Soft	2
Condition		
Gaping	Absent	0
	Detectable	1
	Moderate	2
	Excessive	3
Bruising	Absent	0
	Slight	1
	Severe	2
Autolysis		
Discoloration	Absent	0
	Moderate	1
	Severe	2
Parasites		
Infestations	Absent	0
	Moderate	1
	Severe	2
Other discolorations or contaminations (bones, membranes, tissues, etc.)	Absent	0
	Present	1
Ease of filleting[b]	Easy	0
	Slightly difficult	1
	Difficult	2
Ease of skinning[b]	Easy	0
	Slightly difficult	1
	Difficult	2
Wetness[c]	Normal	0
	Slightly dry or	

| | slight drip | 1 |

Table 4.15. *Continued*

Factor Being Assessed	Observed Characteristics	Demerit Points
	Moderately dry or moderate drip	2
	Excessive dryness or freezer burn or excessive drip	3
Total demerit points (0–31)		

[a] Reprinted with permission from Brenner.[113]
[b] Applicable only if intact fish has to be filleted prior to fillet being assessed.
[c] Applicable only if intact fish or fillet was frozen and thawed prior to being assessed.

4.2.2.6 Grading Elasticity of Surimi

Elasticity, an extremely important sensory attribute of surimi, has been traditionally graded using the folding test (Table 4.16). Surimi paste is stuffed into a 30-mm-diameter casing, linked into 25-cm lengths, heated in water at 90°C for 40 min, cooled in cold water, and left at room temperature for 18–48 hr[225] prior to being cut into 3-mm slices[294] and tested by folding, individual slices, between the thumb and the index finger.[225] The degree of elasticity is determined by comparing the observed extent of cracking to a very specific grading system (Table 4.16). Once the grader is

Table 4.16. TRADITIONAL SURIMI FRESHNESS GRADING SYSTEM (FOLDING TEST) TO DETERMINE ELASTICITY OF THE SURIMI GEL[a,b]

Sensory Characteristic	Grade	Degree of Elasticity
No cracks observed when a surimi slice is folded into quarters[c]	AA	Extremely elastic
Cracking observed when folded into quarters, but not when folded in half[d]	A	Moderately elastic
Some cracking observed when it is folded in half[d]	B	Slightly elastic
Breaks into pieces when it is folded in half[d]	C	Not elastic
Breaks into fragments when pressure (using one's finger) is applied to sliced surimi	D	Poor

[a] Reprinted courtesy of Kudo et al.[294]
[b] Preparation of the surimi to be assessed is described in the text.
[c] Folded between the thumb and the index finger twice.
[d] Folded once.

trained to successfully fold the surimi, this procedure (which utilizes a five-point cat-egory scale) yields objective (Glossary) measurements.[67]

4.3 Analysis and Interpretation of Results

4.3.1 Analyzing Seafood Freshness Quality Grades

How the results of freshness quality grading are analyzed depends on both the writ-ten reasons why the freshness quality had been graded and the type of defined grade standards that were used.

Whenever freshness quality grading is conducted as part of a quality control (QC) program, analysis of the data often consists of comparing the results to a lower limit, an upper limit, or to both lower and upper limits, which had previously been estab-lished by management and the buyer.[3,72,287] When using the more traditional grading systems, such limits may be based on one, some, or all of the sensory variables that were evaluated. However, whenever the TFRU grading system is used these limits refer to the total demerit points that were assigned. Depending on the grading system that is used, these limits the may also refer to either mean value or the frequency of observed values. One method of analyzing QC results is to prepare a control chart.[72] Once a QC sample(s) has been evaluated, the results are plotted (Fig. 4.8), with the mean line, upper control limit, and lower control limit clearly identified,[72] allowing the data to be readily analyzed, which in turn allows rapid implementation of appro-priate action. When control charts are used to monitor seafood freshness quality of a specific seafood over time, they permit immediate detection of trends and out-of-con-trol conditions allowing appropriate handling and processing procedures to be cor-rected and the variability of the freshness quality to be reduced.[295] The preparation of bar graphs (histograms) of the observed freshness quality grades of a particular group of samples such as a specific batch of samples or the samples from an entire produc-tion lot (Fig. 4.9) readily reveals both the variability and central tendency of the grades.[295]

Alternatively, measurements of central tendency, such as mean, median, and mode, as well as measurements of variability such as minimum and maximum values, range (an absolute number), and standard deviation of the freshness quality grades may be tabulated.[287,296]

The previously mentioned methods of data analysis may also be utilized when the freshness quality grading is conducted as part of a new product development pro-gram. However, since the purpose of new product development is to develop a "dif-ferent" product, the results of such freshness quality grading is often analyzed using statistical methods designed to determine if a difference does indeed exist. Thus, such results are often subjected to analysis of variance, but it is extremely important to re-member that traditional seafood quality grading systems (Section 5.2.2.2) are a type of structured category scale, which means the results may often not meet the under-lying assumptions necessary to conduct analysis of variance.[297–299] Therefore one must be cautious when using analysis of variance to analyze the results of traditional

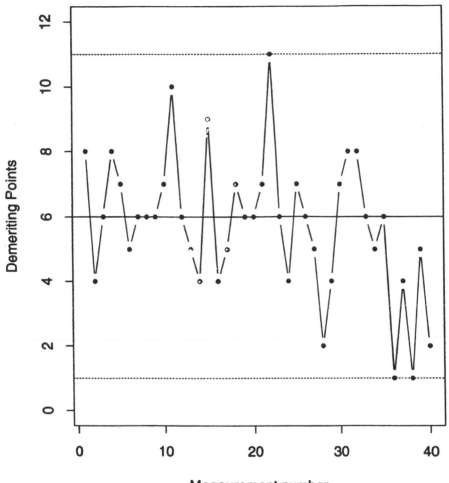

Figure 4.8. A graph of "total demerit points" that may be observed during the examination of representative samples from a day's production.

types of freshness quality grading systems. Although the TFRU freshness quality grading system is also a type of structured category scale, analysis of its results is based on total demerit points that were assigned, not on individual assigned grades. This causes the range of such total demerit points to be 0–39, 0–24, 0–23, 0–20, 0–20, 0–23, 0–21, 0–29, and 0–31 for each of the TFRU or modified TFRU systems described in Tables 4.6, 4.7, 4.8, 4.9, 4.10, 4.11, 4.12, 4.13, and 4.15, respectively. Since these ranges are much larger than the range (two to four different grades) normally observed with traditional freshness quality grading systems, some assumptions that do not apply when statistically analyzing the results of traditional freshness quality grading systems may indeed apply to the results of the TFRU system. However, the

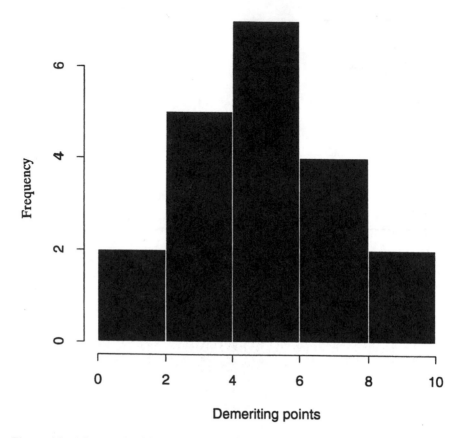

Figure 4.9. A bar graph of the distribution of the "total demerits points" that may be observed during examination of samples from a day's production.

applicability of these assumptions, to the data being analyzed, must be checked before such statistical analyses are conducted.[297-299]

4.3.2 Interpreting Seafood Freshness Quality Grades

Although measurements concerning central tendency and variability are necessary to summarize the data concerning the assigned freshness quality grades, these summarized data need to be explained. Accurate interpretation of freshness quality grades involves critically reviewing all actions that were carried out to obtain the data. The following important questions must be answered: Were the samples collected randomly and were the number of samples collected sufficient to ensure this number was indeed representative of the seafood product whose freshness quality was being evaluated? Were the collected samples handled, stored, and prepared (to be evaluated) in a manner that did not unduly affect the sensory criteria of the sample? Had the samples been evaluated in both a random order and a balanced manner? Were the graders unaware of the history of the samples they evaluated? Did the facilities allow necessary reduction of effects of immediate surroundings? Had recent monitoring proven that the grader(s) were indeed conducting both objective and reliable evaluations.

The validity of the grades is extremely important as the use of invalid results will not ensure that the expectations of the buyers, users, and regulatory agencies are being met. Since such validity easily decreases as the number of negative answers (to the above mentioned questions) increases, whenever a negative answer occurs the situation must be critically reviewed and (if necessary) the problem corrected immediately. By comparing the summarized data, as affected by these answers, to the expectations of the buyers or users (i.e., written product specifications), a realistic and accurate determination of the product's freshness quality can be confirmed.

Although it may initially be somewhat more expensive to ensure that scientifically sensible procedures are always used, such methods easily reduce long-term expenses, as they will most likely yield valid results that allow the processor to regularly meet the expectations of the buyers and users, thereby encouraging them to purchase or use the product again.

CHAPTER

5

Sensory Evaluation: Attribute Assessment

5.1 Introduction

Freshness quality (Glossary) of seafood cannot be determined unless the "level" of sensory attributes, such as appearance, flavor, odor, and/or texture (Glossary), are first directly or indirectly determined.

The previously discussed chemical methods (Chapter 2) and physical methods (Chapter 3) are both indirect procedures of determining the "level" of a specific sensory attribute (i.e., the results of any specific chemical or physical method are used to estimate the "level" of a specific sensory attribute). In contrast, the freshness quality grading method (Chapter 4) is a technique that directly determines the "level" of a specific sensory attribute(s). This is achieved by having a small number of graders (who have been highly trained) use their appropriate senses (sight, smell, taste, and/or touch) and a written grade standard (consisting of words that clearly describe specific sensory properties) to "sort" the seafood into clearly defined categories (grades).[3,52,63,278]

Attribute assessment also involves having people (panelists) use their senses to evaluate sensory attributes such as appearance, flavor, odor, and/or texture. However, such attribute assessment may be achieved using one of a very large number of different sensory tests that have been developed to assess sensory attribute(s).[47,64,66,280] Both the number of panelists required and the extent of training required by the respective panelists vary greatly among the different sensory tests used to conduct attribute assessment. Some of these numerous sensory tests may be used to measure the "level" of sensory attributes directly, whereas other sensory tests may be used to measure such "levels" only indirectly.[47,64,66,280] These

99

many different sensory tests are usually categorized into one of three major groups: (1) affective, (2) discriminative, and (3) descriptive.[64,66,280] In general, the criticism that sensory evaluation of freshness quality is subjective (Glossary), making the results highly variable and of limited use,[60,61] does not apply to either discriminative or descriptive sensory tests.[67] This is because during these tests the sensory evaluation panel must function as an analytical instrument utilizing the sensory systems (sight, taste, smell, and/or touch) of each panelist without any one of them involving his or her own personal reaction.[64,67,280,303] However, like all other methods of evaluating freshness quality, it is extremely important that the sensory assessment of a seafood's sensory attributes be conducted using technologically sound procedures. To do otherwise would make the results highly variable and of little value, just as not following recognized chemical or microbiological procedures greatly reduces the reliability of the subsequent chemical or microbiological results.

Providing a detailed description of the different sensory tests that have, in the past, been used to assess sensory attribute(s) of food is beyond the scope of this chapter. Readers who are interested in becoming informed about a wider variety of sensory tests are referred to other publications.[47,64,65,66,280]

This chapter will discuss the numerous physiological and psychological factors that must always be considered when conducting sensory assessment, the selection of appropriate facilities, selection of appropriate sensory tests, screening, selecting, training, and monitoring panelists, preparation and presentation of samples, and analysis and interpretation of results. Serious application of this information should readily allow readers to conduct sensory assessment of sensory attributes, and obtain data that are not highly variable and not of limited use.

However, readers will have great difficulty applying this information unless they have first clearly defined (in writing) all of the reasons why the freshness quality (of the specific seafood to be assessed) needs to be determined.[3] The presence of such written reasons allows comparison to both the advantages and disadvantages of any methodology that is being considered. This comparison thus allows methods to be selected that will most likely permit the achievement of those written reasons.

5.2 Important Physiological and Psychological Factors

5.2.1 Physiological Factors

Each of the several different factors described in Table 5.1 has been observed to affect the physiology of panelists and hence the results of attribute assessment.[64] Thus it is very important for anyone conducting sensory assessment to be aware of each of these factors so that, when appropriate, necessary corrective action may be taken or the effect of the factor(s) on the panelists may be considered very seriously during the subsequent interpretation of the results.

Table 5.1. PHYSIOLOGICAL FACTORS THAT INFLUENCE THE RESULTS OF SENSORY EVALUATION

Factor	Definition
Adaptation[64]	When panelists are continually exposed to a particular type of sample/product, a decrease (or change) in the panelists' sensitivity to that particular type of sample/product occurs.
Enhancement[64]	When panelists are presented with a mixture of substances, one substance increases the perceived intensity of the other substance.
Synergy[64]	When panelists are presented with a mixture of substances, one substance causes an increase in the perceived intensity of both substances yielding a mixture that has a perceived intensity greater than that of the sum of the individual substances that make up the mixture.
Suppression[64]	When panelists are presented with a mixture of substances, one substance decreases the perceived intensity of the mixture.

5.2.2 Psychological Factors

All of the different psychological factors described in Table 5.2 have been reported to affect sensory panelists and the subsequent results of attribute assessment.[64,280,303] This means that whoever conducts sensory evaluation panels to assess sensory attribute(s) must be aware of each of these psychological factors. Otherwise, appropriate corrective and/or interpretive action may not occur, possibly causing the results to be extremely variable and of little use. Important, and suitable, corrective methods that may be readily applied (particularly during the presentation of the samples) are presented in Table 5.20.

5.3 Selection of Appropriate Facilities

5.3.1 Evaluation Area

The sensory evaluation area must be readily accessible to all panelists and adjacent, but completely separate, from the sample preparation/serving area.[303,304] This latter requirement is often achieved by separating the evaluation area and the preparation/serving area by only a single wall, but without a door between the two areas (Fig. 5.1). Thus to go from the preparation/serving area to the evaluation area requires the use of two different doors. This is extremely important as the panelists must not be able to go through the preparation/serving area to enter or leave the evaluation area because this would enhance expectation error (Table 5.2).

During assessment of the seafood's appropriate attributes, sensory evaluation panels must often function as analytical instruments.[67] During every evaluation, each panelist must not be distracted by noise, other panelists, foreign odors, appearance of anything within the evaluation area itself, and anything that makes them physically uncomfortable.[64,65] If this is not achieved, the panelist may not be evaluating only the specific attribute (of the sample being assessed) requested, but may be evaluating a

Table 5.2. PSYCHOLOGICAL FACTORS THAT INFLUENCE THE RESULTS OF
            SENSORY EVALUATION

Factor	Description
Capriciousness	This is when panelists tend to use the extremes of the sensory evaluation scale, thus having an abnormal amount of influence on the results of the sensory evaluation being conducted.[64] This factor is the opposite of the factor "timidity."[64]
Contrast effect	When the difference between two samples (presented after each other) is very large, this factor causes the difference to be overrated.[280]
Convergence effect	This effect occurs when the distinctive differences between two (or more) samples disguises smaller differences that occur between other samples, during the same sensory evaluation session.[280,303] This factor is also called group effect.[64]
Error of central tendency	Some panelists, particularly if they are not familiar with the type of samples being presented or with the test method being used, will score the samples using the center part of the scale or will prefer samples placed at the center part of the set of samples being evaluated.[64] This factor has also been defined as the tendency of panelists to use the mid range of a scale and to avoid extremes[280,303] (i.e., timidity).[64]
Error of habituation	This factor occurs when the stimulus of the samples being presented to the panelists panelists either slowly increases or slowly decreases, which may result in the panelists' ratings being at least partially based on habit and not entirely on the sensory attribute itself.[64,303] This factor is also called error of anticipation.[303]
Expectation error	Since most people, including panelists, "find what they expect to find" this factor is the result of panelists obtaining information about the samples being evaluated or the study being conducted, causing them to have expectations concerning the results.[280,303]
Halo effect	When, during any one panel session, more than one sensory attribute is evaluated, this factor causes one or more of the attributes to affect the actual ratings of one or more of the other attributes being evaluated.[64,280,303]
Leniency error	This factor is caused by the ratings of the panelists being influenced by the panelists' feelings about the person conducting the evaluations, and not by the sensory attribute itself.[280,303]
Logical error	Even if only one sensory attribute (e.g., flavor) is evaluated during each panel session, the actual rating of the flavor (of the sample being evaluated) may be influenced because, in the minds of panelists, it is logically related to another sensory attribute (e.g., appearance) that is not being evaluated, resulting in a combination of flavor and appearance (not flavor itself) being rated.[64,280,303]
Motivation	The performance of panelists, like that of most people, is seriously affected by the degree of interest each panelist has in conducting the assessments of the samples, which ultimately affects the precision and accuracy of the ratings.[64,280,303]
Mutual suggestion	This factor is a result of the ratings of panelist(s) being modified by the response of other panelist(s).[64,280,303]
Pattern effect	If there is any pattern in the order that the samples are presented panelists' ratings may be partially based on this pattern of presentation and not entirely on the sensory attribute of the sample being evaluated.[64]
Position effect	Although only one sample may be individually evaluated, the position of the sample (relative to the other samples being evaluated during that evaluation session) may affect the panelists' ratings.[64,280] This effect is also referred to as order effect and/or time effect.[64]

Table 5.2. *Continued*

Factor	Description
Stimulus error	Irrelevant characteristics of the sample being presented may "stimulate the panelist," which will yield ratings that are not entirely based on the sensory attribute being evaluated.[64,280,303]
Timidity	This is when panelists tend to use the center part of the sensory evaluation scale, thereby minimizing differences between samples.[64] This factor may also be referred to as "error of central tendency."[64]

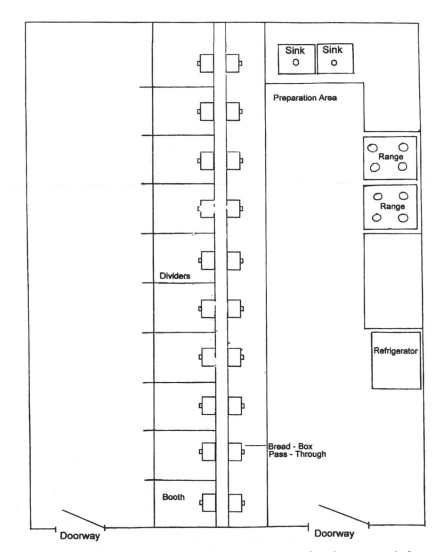

Figure 5.1. Diagram of a sensory assessment area that is separated from the preparation/serving area by a solid wall equipped with breadbox pass-throughs.

combination of the distraction(s) and the sensory attribute. Similarly, the facilities must provide constant conditions, so that the sensory assessments do not depend on the actual day and time when the evaluations were conducted.[64,65,304]

5.3.1.1 Elimination of Distraction by Noise and by Other People

The sensory evaluation area must not be adjacent to any area in which noise is normally produced.[304] Although not related to selection of facilities, strictly prohibiting any talking (or other practices that generate noise) by the panelists while inside the sensory evaluation area is also necessary to eliminate distraction by noise. Other types of distractions by people are often eliminated by two common procedures. First, extra care is taken to ensure that every panelist uses an individual booth (Fig. 5.2) while he or she assesses the attributes of the sample. Second, the experimenter always uses a pass-through (Fig. 5.2) (from each booth to the preparation area) to present individual samples to individual panelists, thereby allowing the presentation of a sample to a particular panelist, without disturbing any other panelists. Suggested specifications concerning such booths and pass-throughs are presented in Table 5.3.

5.3.1.2 Elimination of Distraction by Foreign Odors

Odors foreign to those of the particular sample being assessed may be generated by samples that were previously assessed inside the evaluation area, materials inside the evaluation area, the preparation of samples in the preparation area, and/or materials/areas outside either the preparation area or the evaluation area. In addition, foreign odors, which are not directly related to selection of facilities, may be generated by cosmetics worn by panelists. Regardless of their source, odors foreign to that of the sample being assessed must be eliminated. This is often achieved by having an air exhaust system within the evaluation area that is capable of quickly exchanging the air near the booths and thereby removing odors from previous assessments, a slight positive air pressure inside the evaluation area to prevent foreign odors from entering the evaluation area, all booths, cabinets, ceilings, countertops, floors, walls, etc. made of nonodorous materials that are also nonporous and therefore can be readily cleaned, and all air entering the evaluation area filtered using activated charcoal. Although not related to selection of facilities, it is important to instruct panelists not to use perfumed products (cosmetics, aftershave, etc.) and to clean the facilities using only non-odor-generating cleaners.

5.3.1.3 Elimination of Distraction by Appearance

The major method of eliminating this type of distraction is to have all booths, cabinets, ceilings, countertops, floors, walls, etc. colored white, cream, or gray (Fig. 5.2), thereby being a neutral (Glossary) stimulus to the panelists.[304] Similarly, the lighting used must not alter the appearance of the sample being assessed, not produce any shadows, and provide sufficient intensity.[304] Usually the evaluation area is equipped with either incandescent lighting or fluorescent (cool white, warm white, and simulated north light) lighting.[64,304] However, Stone and Sidel[303] recommend that within

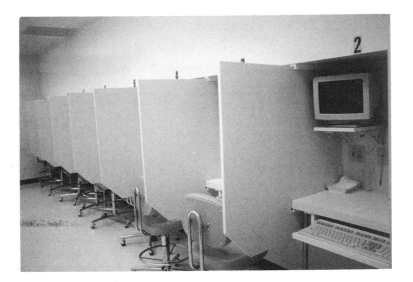

Figure 5.2. Photograph of sensory evaluation booths equipped with (a) dividers extending over the edge of the counter, (b) breadbox pass-throughs, and (c) computer terminals. Printed with permission, Canada Department of Fisheries and Oceans, Inspection Branch, St. John's, NF, Canada.

Table 5.3.   SUGGESTED SPECIFICATIONS CONCERNING THE BOOTHS OF A
SENSORY ATTRIBUTE ASSESSMENT AREA[a]

A medium sized evaluation area often contains 6 to 10 booths.

The countertop within each booth is usually 45.7–55.9 cm (18–22 in.) deep.

Booths are often 68.6–81.3 cm (27–32 in.) wide.

The most common height of a booth countertop is 91.4 cm (36 in.), particularly if there is a pass-through between each booth and the preparation/serving area.

For the samples to be effectively served, every booth should be separated from the sample preparation/serving area by only a single solid wall that extends from the solid floor to the ceiling.

Each booth should have a pass-through in this single wall so that individual samples may (with minimum distraction) be directly presented to individual panelists.

These pass-throughs should be flush with both the countertop in the assessment area and the countertop in the preparation/serving area.

A very effective type of pass-through is the breadbox type (Figs. 5.1 and 5.2), which prevents the panelist(s) from observing activities in the sample preparation area. The breadboxes are usually 30.5–40.6 cm (12–16 in.) wide and 25.4–30.5 cm (10–12 in.) high.

Booth dividers must extend from the ceiling to the countertop (or below). When the amount of space is limited, it may be desirable to have removable dividers, which would be removed during training sessions.

Booth dividers must extend out past the edge of the booth countertop (Fig. 5.2) to give each panelist sufficient privacy.

It is also desirable to have each booth equipped with a switch (which turns on a light in the preparation area) that the panelist uses to indicate that he or she is ready to be served the next sample.

[a] Printed courtesy of Eggert and Zook.[304]

the booth itself, only incandescent light be used. Whenever incandescent lighting is used, the production of shadows is reduced by having the lights tilted toward the panelist and spotlighting is eliminated by placing opalite diffusion glass beneath the bulbs.[303] Regardless of the type of lighting used, dimmer switches are often used so that, when necessary, the intensity may be increased from the normal 753–861 lux (70–80 footcandles) to 1184 lux (110 footcandles).[304]

Colored lights have, in the past, been used to eliminate distraction by appearance (of the samples themselves) when flavor, odor, and/or texture were being evaluated. However, it is now recommended that this procedure not be used, because the colored lights do not eliminate, but only alter, differences in the color density of the samples being evaluated[64,280,303] and it increases the variability in the panelist's ratings as the panelists are now exposed to an entirely different environment.[303] Whenever the difference in appearance (between two or more samples being presented simultaneously) is distracting to the panelist(s), it is now recommended that samples not be presently simultaneously, but sequentially and scored with reference to a common standard.[64]

5.3.1.4 Elimination of Distraction by Being Uncomfortable

This type of distraction is normally minimized by ensuring that the chairs or stools in the booths are both comfortable and stable and that the temperature and humidity of the evaluation area do not make the panelist(s) uncomfortable.[304] The American

Society for Testing and Materials (ASTM) recommends that swivel chairs or stools, with a 5-prong base, be used and that the evaluation area be kept at a constant temperature of approximately 22°C (72°F) and a relative humidity of 45–50%.[304] The necessity of having constant environmental conditions within the evaluation area cannot be over emphasized.

5.3.2 Preparation and Serving Areas

Unlike large facilities that prepare and serve a large number of samples, with medium or small sized facilities these two areas are often combined (Fig. 5.1 and Fig. 5.3).[64,304] Since the actual design of the preparation/serving area depends on both the type of samples and the volume of samples being assessed, it is difficult to present a detailed description of such an area. However, some suggested specifications for a medium sized preparation/serving area are listed in Table 5.4.

Figure 5.3. Photograph of a sensory evaluation preparation and serving area. Printed with permission, Canada Department of Fisheries and Oceans, Inspection Branch, St. John's, NF, Canada.

Table 5.4.   SUGGESTED SPECIFICATIONS CONCERNING A MEDIUM-SIZED
PREPARATION/SERVING AREA

The preparation/serving area (Fig. 5.1) is usually in a rectangular (or square) room, with the counters, sink(s), stove(s), and refrigerator(s) being positioned in an L-shape or a U-shape.[304]

The importance of both adequate counter space and adequate cabinet space cannot be overemphasized.[280,303]

The panelists must not be able to see inside the preparation and serving area.[304]

There must be an air exhaust system that is capable of quickly removing odors that are generated while the samples are being prepared and/or served.[280]

Unless breadbox pass-throughs are used, the cabinets, ceilings, countertops, floors, walls, etc. of the preparation area must also provide a neutral appearance.[303]

It is important that the preparation/serving area also be constructed using materials that are not odorous or porous, so they can be easily cleaned.[280,303]

A system of keeping the samples warm after they are prepared but before they are served is often desirable.[280] This is particularly true for seafood samples, since they are often served "hot." One way of achieving this is to place the samples on warming trays (that do not have a hot spot) that have been previously set at the appropriate temperature.

It is desirable to have special lighting (e.g., cool white, warm white, simulated North light, etc.) available in the preparation/serving area so that the experimenter is able to examine each type of product using appropriate lighting.[303]

5.3.3 Training Area

When a large number of samples are regularly evaluated (involving a substantial number of experimenters) it is desirable to have a separate training area. However, with medium or small sized facilities the training area may be part of the evaluation area (e.g., a table inside the room in which the booths are located).[280] Regardless of its location, a number of important points must always be considered, during the selection of an appropriate training area. While being trained, the "panelists" must not be located in separate booths, since the booth dividers do not allow free discussion among the people being trained. Thus, during training, 6 to 12 "panelists" are often seated around a table.[304] Alternatively, the booth dividers may be removed (Fig. 5.4) whenever the evaluation area is utilized as a training room. The training area should be adjacent to the sample preparation/serving area, but the "panelists" must not have to enter the preparation/serving area before entering the training area.[304] While being trained, as during evaluation sessions, the "panelists" must not be distracted by noise, other than the discussion related to the training, foreign odors, such as that given off by some markers, appearance, and being uncomfortable.[280,304] Methods of eliminating these types of distraction have been discussed.

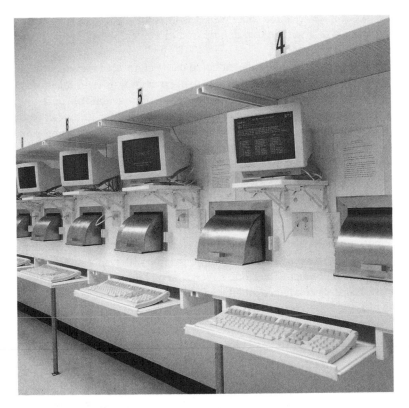

Figure 5.4. Photograph of sensory assessment area, with individual booth dividers removed, so the assessment area may be used as a training area. Printed with permission, Canada Department of Fisheries and Oceans, Inspection Branch, St. John's, NF, Canada.

5.4 Selection of Appropriate Sensory Tests

Regardless of the degree of excellence of the facilities used, if the appropriate sensory test is not used during the assessment of the samples, the results of these assessments may be of little use to those who requested that the sensory attribute(s) be assessed. Thus, before any sensory attributes are assessed, the reason for conducting the assessments must be clearly defined.[67] Only when such reasons are compared to clearly understood capabilities of the different sensory evaluation techniques can the appropriate sensory test be accurately chosen.

5.4.1 Affective Sensory Tests

Affective sensory tests (unlike either descriptive or discriminative sensory tests) are subjective and measure the original and spontaneous impressions of the panelists.[67] Thus whenever the reason for conducting the sensory assessments is to determine the panelists' acceptance/rejection (how well it is liked/disliked) of a sample or the panelists' preference of a sample (e.g., compared to a reference sample), affective sensory tests should be used.[64,280,305]

Affective sensory tests may be conducted using controlled facilities, such as those suggested in the first part of this chapter, using a central or field location, such as a booth at a shopping mall, and in the home of actual or potential consumers.[64,280,303,305] The conduction of affective sensory tests using controlled facilities will be discussed in this chapter, whereas the conduction of affective sensory tests using central/field locations or within the home will not be discussed in this book. Readers seeking information concerning this method of conducting affective sensory tests are referred to other publications.[47,64,303,305]

Although the use of controlled facilities provides "constant conditions," so that the results will not depend on the time and day the assessments were conducted, they do not provide realistic conditions as "the realism of a test kitchen is never that of the real eating environment."[305] This must not be overlooked during the interpretation of such results. Also the response to a small sample may be different than the response to a full portion of the product. Therefore, depending on both the reason(s) for having the sensory assessments conducted and the actual results obtained, it may be desirable to have the results of affective tests (conducted using controlled facilities) verified using field or home tests.

5.4.1.1 Assessing the Acceptance of Seafood

The hedonic scale test is very often used to assess the degree to which a sample is liked or disliked (accepted or rejected).[64,66,280] The hedonic scale (Table 5.5) is a series of statements that allows the panelist(s) to express how much he or she likes or dislikes the sample being assessed. Partly because the hedonic scale is simple to use and has no numbers on the evaluation form, this scale has, historically, proven to be a very practical sensory method of assessing the level of acceptance or rejection of the sample being evaluated.[303] Although numbers are not on the evaluation form, the ratings from an hedonic scale can be readily changed to numbers that, depending on the hedonic scale used, range from 1 for dislike extremely to 9 for like extremely.[66,303]

The example given in Table 5.5 is a 9-point hedonic scale, but hedonic scales with fewer, or more, points may be used.[64] However, regardless of the number of points within a given scale, it is extremely important that it be a balanced sensory scale (Glossary).[64] In practice, the 9-point hedonic scale has, historically, been proven to give reliable and valid results.[303]

Although the example given in Table 5.5 does not specify the attributes that the panelist(s) should assess, the hedonic scale may be used to assess the acceptance of any (one at a time) specified sensory attribute.[64] Thus, to assess the acceptance of each of four different sensory attributes (e.g., appearance, flavor, odor, and texture) would require four different sessions of the sensory panel.

Whenever the acceptance of a seafood sample is being assessed, the sensory test must measure only acceptance, nothing else.[303] For example, the experimenter using

Table 5.5. SUGGESTED QUESTIONNAIRE (9-POINT HEDONIC SCALE) USED FOR ASSESSING THE LEVEL OF ACCEPTANCE OF A SEAFOOD SAMPLE

PANELIST _____   DATE _____

Evaluate the coded samples in the order (left to right) presented on the evaluation form. While assessing each sample, check the statement that best describes your feelings about the sample being assessed. Once a sample is assessed, please rinse your mouth with water before assessing the next sample.

CODE _____	CODE _____	CODE _____
___ Like extremely	___ Like extremely	___ Like extremely
___ Like very much	___ Like very much	___ Like very much
___ Like moderately	___ Like moderately	___ Like moderately
___ Like slightly	___ Like slightly	___ Like slightly
___ Neither like	___ Neither like	___ Neither like
nor dislike	nor dislike	nor dislike
___ Dislike slightly	___ Dislike slightly	___ Dislike slightly
___ Dislike moderately	___ Dislike moderately	___ Dislike moderately
___ Dislike very much	___ Dislike very much	___ Dislike very much
___ Dislike extremely	___ Dislike extremely	___ Dislike extremely

the hedonic scale must not ask the panelists what they did or did not like about the sample as this procedure will cause the panelist to be confounded (Glossary).[303]

5.4.1.2 Assessing the Preference of Seafood

In addition to determining the level of acceptance and rejection of a sample, it is often desirable to determine if that sample is preferred (Glossary) when it is compared to another sample or compared to a standard.

The preference of a sample may be indirectly determined by having each sample/standard assessed using an hedonic scale (which by itself measures only acceptance) and comparing the results,[303,305] to determine which sample is liked the most (i.e., preferred). However, the preference of a sample may also be determined by directly comparing the samples/standards of interest.[64,280,305]

One such direct procedure is the paired comparison preference test (Table 5.6), during which the panelist(s) are "forced" to decide which of two samples (presented simultaneously) he or she prefers.[64,280,303] This test may be modified to allow the panelist to indicate there is no preference without indicating if the samples were liked equally or were disliked equally.[280,303] Alternatively, this test may also be modified to allow the panelist to indicate the samples were liked equally or the samples were disliked equally.[280,303] The use of either of these modifications is not recommended if fewer than 50 panelists are used to assess a specific pair of samples, as both of these modifications reduce the likelihood of finding a statistical difference.[303] In fact, it has been stated that "only the forced choice method is amenable to formal statistical analysis,"[64] which limits the practical applicability of these modifications.

Table 5.6. SUGGESTED QUESTIONNAIRE (PAIRED COMPARISON PREFERENCE TEST) FOR DIRECTLY ASSESSING WHICH SAMPLE IS PREFERRED BY THE PANELISTS

PANELIST _____ DATE _____

Assess the coded samples in the order (left to right) presented on the evaluation form. Once the first sample has been assessed, please rinse your mouth with water before assessing the second sample. When both samples have been assessed, indicate which sample was preferred, by writing the code of the preferred sample underneath the term "preferred sample." **You must make a choice, even if it is guess.**

CODE _____   CODE _____

PREFERRED SAMPLE

_____

The paired comparison preference test, just like the hedonic scale, may be modified so that different specified sensory attributes may be individually assessed, one at a time.[64] The example, given in Table 5.6, involves the comparison of only two samples. However, this direct preference test may be modified to be a multiple comparison test, during which three to six samples are presented to the panelist(s), who are "forced" to indicate the sample that they preferred.[64] Whenever the preference (of more than two samples) is to be assessed, it is often desirable to use the rank preference test (Table 5.7). During such a test three to six samples are simultaneously presented to the pan-

Table 5.7. SUGGESTED QUESTIONNAIRE (RANK PREFERENCE TEST) TO ASSESS THE RELATIVE PREFERENCE OF MULTIPLE SAMPLES

PANELIST _____ DATE _____

Assess the coded samples in the 'order (left to right) presented on the evaluation form. Once a sample is a assessed, please rinse your mouth with water before assessing the next sample. When all samples are evaluated, rank all samples in order of which each sample is preferred by writing the code of each sample in the space opposite the appropriate rank. **Do not give any two samples the same rank.**

CODE	CODE	CODE	CODE	CODE	CODE
_____	_____	_____	_____	_____	_____

RANK IN ORDER OF PREFERENCE

First _____
Second _____
Third _____
Fourth _____
Fifth _____
Sixth _____

elist(s) and ranked according to the panelist's preference. Consequently, when this test is used, the relative preference of all "six" samples is readily obtained. However, the actual degree of difference (only the relative difference) in preference is not measured.

Regardless of the sensory test used to directly assess preference, the method must measure preference, nothing else.[303] It is extremely important not to combine methods of directly assessing preference with other methods of sensory evaluation such as methods of assessing acceptance, difference/discriminative testing, or methods of descriptive testing.[303] Sometimes, during direct preference testing, questions concerning acceptance and difference/discriminative or description of the sensory attributes need to be answered. Whenever this occurs, each type of question (acceptance, difference, or description) must be answered separately, using different tests that are appropriate only for the type of question being asked.[64,303]

5.4.2 Discriminative Sensory Tests

Whenever it is desirable to know if there is a perceived difference in the sensory characteristics of different samples, discriminative tests (Glossary) should be used.[66,303]

Discriminative sensory tests are extremely useful in both product development and quality control.[66,280] Actually, compared to other sensory procedures, discriminative tests have been reported to be the most useful.[306,307] Frijters[308] stated that the great usefulness of discriminative sensory tests was due to the simplicity of the experimentative procedure of such tests and that discriminative tests had specific purposes.

The importance of determining if there is a perceived sensory difference between two different samples is widely recognized. However, the complexity of determining if there is indeed a perceived sensory difference is often not appreciated.[308] This complexity is largely caused by two important principles of sensory response behavior: (1) "two physically different stimuli can evoke two identical sensory responses and (2) the same stimulus can evoke a variety of sensory responses on different occasions."[308] These two principles have the practical results of clearly necessitating that determination of a difference in sensory attributes between two samples be determined only by sensory examination, not by chemical/physical analyses and during the determination of sensory differences, a number of different trials be conducted.[308]

In general, the exact discriminative test used to determine if there is a perceived sensory difference between two different samples depends on whether the specific characteristic (of an individual sensory attribute) of interest (e.g., yellowness characteristic of appearance, bitterness characteristic of flavor, ammoniacal characteristic of odor, and resilience characteristic of texture) can be identified.

5.4.2.1 Tests Using Specified Sensory Characteristics

5.4.2.1.1 Paired Comparison Difference Test

Whenever the specific sensory characteristic of interest can be identified, the paired comparison difference test (Table 5.8) is recommended, as this test is more efficient than either the duo-trio test (Table 5.9) or the triangle test (Table 5.10).[309] During the

Table 5.8.   PAIRED COMPARISON DIFFERENCE TEST FOR DETERMINING IF
             THERE IS A DIFFERENCE IN A SPECIFIED SENSORY CHARACTERISTIC
             (SUCH AS BITTERNESS) BETWEEN TWO DIFFERENT SAMPLES

PANELIST _____   DATE _____

Assess the coded samples in the order (left to right) presented on the evaluation form. Once the first sample has been assessed, please rinse your mouth with water before assessing the second sample. When both
samples have been assessed, indicate which coded sample was most bitter by placing an X underneath the
coded sample that was most bitter. **You must make a choice, even if it is a guess.**

CODE _____   CODE _____

_____ _____   _____

paired comparison difference test the two samples are simultaneously presented to a
panelist.[280] Once each panelist has evaluated both samples, he or she is "forced" to
indicate which sample has more (i.e., a difference) of the specific sensory characteristic being assessed.[303] A panelist must not be allowed to indicate that neither sample
has the most intense characteristic.[303]

The results of the paired comparison difference test reveals whether there is a perceivable difference (in the sensory characteristic being assessed) between the two
samples being evaluated, the sample in which the characteristic was most intense, and
nothing about the degree of the difference between the two samples.[280] Whenever
questions about the degree of difference must be answered, other discriminative tests
or descriptive sensory tests must be conducted.

Although the paired comparison difference test is very efficient, care must be taken
to ensure that the specific sensory characteristic of interest can indeed be specified and
that the panelists can actually perceive this specific sensory characteristic.[303]

5.4.2.1.2 3-Alternative Forced Choice (AFC) Test

The conventional balanced triangle test (Table 5.10) may be modified to the "3-
Alternative Forced Choice (3-AFC) Test."[310] This test is similar to the conventional
triangle test in that a panelist is simultaneously presented with three samples (two
samples from one product and one sample from another product), but unlike the triangle test, one product (e.g., the experimental sample) is always the odd sample and
the control sample is always the duplicate sample.[308] When this change is made, panelists are asked "which sample has the strongest stimulus,"[308] e.g., sweet flavor, rather
than "which sample is different." Therefore the 3-AFC must not be used unless the
sensory characteristic of interest can be both specified and perceived.[311]

The 3-AFC test is very suitable for the determination of absolute (detectable)
thresholds (Glossary). This is accomplished by having panelists evaluate numerous
sets of three samples (one test sample and two blanks), with the concentration of the
test sample covering a wide range.[312] The alteration of the concentration of the test

sample is quite easy, as the test sample is always the odd sample. Once all three samples are assessed, the panelist is forced to indicate (even if it is a guess) which sample has the strongest stimulus (e.g., sweet flavor). The detection threshold is the lowest concentration of those samples evaluated that results in a statistically significant difference from the blanks.[312]

Although (when used to detect thresholds) the 3-AFC test has practical advantages over the conventional triangle test, this test can measure differences between samples just as well as the conventional triangle test.[313] Although the results of the 3-AFC test indicate which product has the strongest stimulus, its results (like those of the conventional triangle test) do not indicate the degree of the perceived difference, the acceptability of each product, and which product was preferred.

5.4.2.2 Tests Using Unspecified Sensory Characteristics

Often the sensory characteristic of interest cannot be specified and/or adequately perceived by the panelists. Whenever this occurs, discriminative tests other than the paired comparison or the 3-AFC tests must be used.

5.4.2.2.1 Duo-Trio Test

One such test is the duo-trio test (Table 5.9). During this test three samples (a reference sample and two coded samples) are simultaneously presented to a panelist.[64,67,280,303] Since only one of the coded samples is similar to the reference sample, each panelist (after assessing all three samples) is forced to indicate which of the two coded samples is different from the reference sample.[64,67,280,303] Although three samples are presented to each panelist, the duo-trio test involves only two comparisons (as the reference sample is identified). Therefore, this test is most useful when it is suspected the panelists will suffer from sensory fatigue and/or memory fatigue, because the samples being as-

Table 5.9. SUGGESTED QUESTIONNAIRE FOR DUO-TRIO TEST, USED TO DETERMINE IF THERE IS A PERCEIVED SENSORY DIFFERENCE BETWEEN TWO SAMPLES

PANELIST _____   DATE _____

Assess the reference sample (**R**) and the two coded samples in the order presented (left to right) on the evaluation form. Once a sample has been assessed, please rinse your mouth with water before assessing the next sample. When all samples have been assessed, indicate which coded sample was different from **R** by placing an X underneath the coded sample that was different. **You must make a choice, even if it is a guess.**

INDICATE WHICH SAMPLE IS DIFFERENT FROM R

R   CODE _____   CODE _____

           _____   _____

sessed have a strong flavor and/or odor.[64,67,280] Since the existence of only two comparisons means each panelist has a 50% chance of guessing the correct sample, the duo-trio is less efficient than either the paired comparison difference test or the triangle test[309] and, therefore, should not be used unless there is a potential danger of sensory and/or memory fatigue. Often when this test is conducted, during half of the duo-trio tests the reference sample is the same as one coded sample, whereas during the other half of the tests the reference sample is the same as the other coded sample.[64,303] However, when one coded sample is very familiar to the panelists (such as during product development or during the determination of thresholds), then this very familiar sample should always be used as the reference.[64,303] This latter test may be referred to as the constant-reference duo-trio test.[303] Regardless of which type of duo-trio test is used, the results indicate whether there is a perceivable sensory difference between the two coded samples, but do not reveal anything about the degree of this perceived sensory difference, the acceptability of either sample, which, if any, coded sample was preferred, and whether the different panelists used different sensory characteristics to identify the correct sample.[67,280] Whenever any of these four questions need to be answered, sensory tests other than the duo-trio test must be used.

5.4.2.2 Triangle Test

The triangle test (Table 5.10), another sensory test used to determine if there is a perceived sensory difference, does not require that the specific sensory characteristic of interest can be both specified and perceived. During this test a panelist is simultaneously presented with three coded samples: two are the same and the other is different. Once all three samples have been assessed, each panelist is forced to indicate which sample is different.[64,66,67,280] The presence of three coded samples means that to correctly identify the odd sample, each panelist must make three different comparisons (A versus B, B versus C, and C versus A), which is substantially more than the two

Table 5.10. SUGGESTED QUESTIONNAIRE FOR TRIANGLE TEST
(3-ALTERNATIVE FORCED CHOICE TEST)[a], USED TO DETERMINE
IF THERE IS A PERCEIVED SENSORY DIFFERENCE BETWEEN
TWO SAMPLES

PANELIST _____   DATE _____

Assess the three coded samples in the order (left to right) presented on the evaluation. Once each sample has been assessed, rinse your mouth with water before assessing the next sample. When all samples have been assessed, indicate which coded sample was different from the other two coded samples by placing an X underneath the coded sample that was different. **You must make a choice, even if it is a guess.**

CODE _____   CODE _____   CODE _____

_____   _____   _____

[a] The difference between a triangle test and a three alternative forced choice test is described in the text.

different comparisons that are necessary with either the duo-trio test or the paired comparison test.[303] The three comparisons necessary with the triangle test means that each panelist has only a 33% chance of correctly guessing the correct sample.[280] However, this relatively large number of comparisons also means that the triangle test should be used only if the samples being assessed do not have a strong flavor and/or odor, and thus cannot cause the panelists to experience sensory and/or memory fatigue.[64,303] Since no sensory attribute is specified during the triangle test, each panelist, individually, decides which sensory characteristic(s)/sensory attribute(s) contributes to any perceived difference among the samples.[308] Whenever the triangle test is used to assess only one particular attribute, extreme care must be taken to ensure that this attribute is the only attribute that differs among the samples being evaluated.[280] Since the triangle test is believed to be free of expectation error (Table 5.2) it has been observed to be very useful in determining if seafood is tainted (Glossary).[310,312] Usually the triangle test is conducted such that 50% of the panelists receive one product as the odd sample and the other 50% of the panelists receive that product as the duplicate sample.[280] When conducted in this balanced manner, the results indicate only whether there is a difference between the two products being evaluated.[67] Questions concerning the degree of the perceived sensory difference, the acceptability of each product, which product was preferred, and which sensory attribute(s)/characteristic(s) was responsible for the perceived difference must be answered using alternate sensory tests.

5.4.2.2.3 Degree of Difference Test

Although the triangle test is extremely useful in determining if there is a perceived sensory difference between samples, at times it must be used with caution. One such instance is when the history of the samples being assessed is not known. This is particularly true when it is known that the sensory characteristics (of either type of samples) often vary during the production of those samples (i.e., either type of sample is heterogeneous). Since (under such circumstances) the triangle test easily gives false differences, the degree of difference test (Table 5.11) should therefore be used.[340] This test was developed to evaluate four samples: one sample is a reference sample, a second sample is from the same batch as the reference sample, a third sample is from a different batch than the reference sample, and a fourth sample is the test sample.[340] The degree that each of the second, third, and fourth samples differs from the reference sample is assessed (Table 5.11).

5.4.2.3 Limitations of Affective and Discriminative Sensory Tests to Measure Seafood Freshness Quality

The previously mentioned sensory methods used to determine sensory acceptance, preference, and differences may be useful in the determination of freshness quality, particularly when evaluating new products/species. In fact, discriminative testing that measures difference (of a representative sample) from a standard or a control is a recognized method of using sensory evaluation to routinely control sensory quality of foods.[287]

Table 5.11.   QUESTIONNAIRE FOR DEGREE OF DIFFERENCE TEST
(0 = NO DIFFERENCE, 5 = EXTREMELY LARGE DIFFERENCE)[a]

PANELIST _____   DATE _____

Sample X is a reference sample. The coded samples *may* or *may not* be different from sample X. You are looking at *overall flavor* difference only.

Taste Sample X first, then taste each of the coded samples, from left to right. Compare the coded samples against the X sample when making your judgment of overall flavor difference. Make your judgment on *overall flavor differences only* and not appearance or texture differences.

Difference from reference	Sample Codes
No difference	
Very slight difference	
Slight difference	
Moderate difference	
Large difference	
Extremely large difference	
Describe the overall flavor difference, if any:	

[a]   Reprinted with permission from Aust et al.[340]

One feature of using either affective or discriminative sensory methods to determine freshness quality is that the observed results can be used only indirectly to determine if a product meets the standards set by the buyer, user, and/or regulatory agency. The observed sensory results (concerning the product of interest) can be directly related only to the observed sensory results of a reference product, which was evaluated by the same sensory panel, and whose relationship to the product standards is well known.

Whenever product standards are very specific, affective sensory methods, which are subjective, should not be used to evaluate freshness quality. Under such circumstances, discriminative tests (which are objective) may be appropriate, but only if a range of consistent reference products are also available and assessed.[287,303] Some of these reference products must meet the specific product standards, whereas other reference products must fail to meet the specific product standards. Only then will the results of the discriminative test identify the actual "level" of appearance, flavor, odor, and/or texture of the product being evaluated. Specific product standards necessitate the determination of the specific "level" of any particular sensory attribute (of the product being evaluated). Otherwise the producer cannot readily decide if that product meets the buyer's and user's specific minimum expectations.

5.4.3 Descriptive Sensory Methods

Identification of the specific level of any particular sensory attribute of any particular product may also be achieved using descriptive sensory methods. Depending on the type of descriptive method used, the results will quantify and/or precisely describe the characteristics of the particular sensory attribute(s) being evaluated. Attribute rating and descriptive analysis are the two major types of descriptive sensory methods.[66]

5.4.3.1 Attribute Rating

Each different coded sample is assessed by each panelist, using a scale that consists of words and/or numbers.[66,280,315] During any particular sensory evaluation session each sensory attribute is assessed using a structured category scale, an unstructured interval scale, or magnitude estimation, which involves a ratio scale.[66,280,315] Regardless of the type of scale used, several samples are usually presented to each panelist[66] and more than one attribute of each sample may be evaluated during each session.[280] When a structured category scale or an unstructured interval scale is used the coded samples may be presented either simultaneously or sequentially.[66] Whenever magnitude estimation is used, the samples are to be presented sequently.[66]

Compared to discriminative sensory tests, the use of scales has numerous advantages because (1) they require much less time, (2) the procedure is more interesting to panelists, (3) psychologically, they have a much wider range of application, (4) they can be used with psychologically naive panelists with a minimum of training, (5) they can be used with large numbers of stimuli, and (6) they produce better aesthetic (hedonic) judgments of single samples than when comparative judgments are made.[315]

5.4.3.1.1 Structured Category Scale

A category scale (Glossary) such as the example presented in Table 5.12 consists of a limited number of different preestablished categories. Each of the different categories is described using different words, such as those shown in Table 5.12, or described using different numbers.[67] When a panelist is finished assessing the coded sample, he or she must indicate which of the predefined but described (words or numbers) categories best agrees with the panelists' perception of the attribute being evaluated. Since there is a range of categories, based on a continuous (decreasing or increasing) progression, the results of this test reveal information about the intensity of the sensory attribute being evaluated. Whenever such a scale is used, it is extremely important that the category scale be a balanced scale (Glossary) and that every panelist agree on the meaning of each term.[67,288] This means that each term must be an objective (e.g., slightly tender, moderately tender, very tender, or extremely tender) term rather than a preference (subjective) term such as slightly too tender, moderately too

Table 5.12. SUGGESTED QUESTIONNAIRE FOR A STRUCTURED CATEGORY
SCALE, USED TO ASSESS THE PERCEIVED INTENSITY (QUANTITY)
OF THE SENSORY ATTRIBUTE (E.G., THE CHEWINESS ASPECT OF
TEXTURE) BEING EVALUATED

PANELIST _____ DATE _____

Evaluate the coded samples in the order (left to right) presented on the evaluation form. While assessing
each coded sample, check the description that best describes the sensory attribute being evaluated. Once
each coded sample has been assessed, rinse your mouth with water before assessing the next coded sample.

CODE _____   CODE _____   CODE _____

___ Extremely tender   ___ Extremely tender   ___ Extremely tender
___ Very tender   ___ Very tender   ___ Very tender
___ Moderately tender   ___ Moderately tender   ___ Moderately tender
___ Slightly tender   ___ Slightly tender   ___ Slightly tender
___ Slightly tough   ___ Slightly tough   ___ Slightly tough
___ Moderately tough   ___ Moderately tough   ___ Moderately tough
___ Very tough   ___ Very tough   ___ Very tough
___ Extremely tough   ___ Extremely tough   ___ Extremely tough

tender, much too tender, or very much too tender.[67] Use of such subjective terms
makes it impossible for the sensory evaluation panel to function as an analytical device because the meaning of each term may then be unique to each panelist conducting the evaluation.[67,233] Even when objective terms are used, objectivity may not be
achieved without training all panelists[315] and/or using standards for various categories
of the scale.[67] Both of these actions should also help reduce any effect of "error of
central tendency" (Table 5.2), which is often a problem with this type of scale.[280]
When the sensory characteristic being evaluated becomes more complex, the difficulty of all panelists agreeing on the meaning of the different terms (thereby evaluating the same characteristic) usually increases,[67,288] necessitating the need for
increased training of panelists.

Although the results of category scales do reveal some information about the intensity of the sensory attribute being evaluated, these scales reveal no direct information about the acceptability or preference of the attribute being evaluated. For
example, using the category scale may reveal that a seafood product is slightly tender.
The actual acceptability or preference of that product depends entirely on individual
buyers or users and their specific desires, expectations, and wants. However, if specific product standards have been established (e.g., requiring the seafood to be
slightly tender), the results of using an appropriate category scale can be very useful.
In fact, the "in/out" method and the "quality ratings method" are recognized quality
control procedures that use category scaling to determine if production samples do indeed meet product specifications.[287]

The results of using a category scale may not reveal sufficient detailed information
about the specific degree of the intensity of the attribute being evaluated. This is be-

cause the intervals between any two different adjacent terms may not be equal.[67,280,315,316] For example, the sensory (psychological) distance between extremely tender and very tender may not be the same as the distance between very tough and extremely tough.[67,280,315,316] This means that a sample rated extremely tender (eighth category of Table 5.12) is not necessarily twice as tender as a sample rated slightly tough (fourth category of Table 5.12). A major reason for this is that category ratings are psychological rather than physical measurements.[288] Therefore, during the same evaluation panel, the same physical stimulus may not yield identical psychological responses (category ratings) in different panelists.[308,316] Similarly, with any particular panelist, the same physical stimulus may not result in the same response during different sessions.[308,316] Whenever questions concerning very specific degrees of intensity (of an attribute) must be answered, category scales should not be used. During such situations, magnitude estimation (ratio scale) should be considered.

5.4.3.1.2 Unstructured Interval Scale

An unstructured interval scale (Glossary), such as the example presented in Table 5.13, also uses words to describe the attribute being evaluated.[280,303,315] However these words describe only the two different extremes of the attribute being assessed and are placed or anchored at[315] or near[280,303] opposite ends of a horizontal line. The words reflecting the most intense aspect of the attribute should be placed at or near the right end of the line.[303] The length of the horizontal line is often 10 cm[303] or 15 cm.[280] When a panelist is finished assessing a coded sample he or she must mark the horizontal line at the point that best reflects the panelist's impression concerning the intensity of the attribute being evaluated.[280,303,315] The position of this mark is usually measured, in millimeters, from the left end of the line.[315] An unstructured interval scale that is 10 cm or 15 cm long thus produces scores of 0 to 100 or 0 to 150, respectively. Such a scale does not have the coarseness of a category scale with only eight or nine different categories.[315] Since there are no categories between the two extreme descriptions (anchors), use of this type of scale eliminates the problem of unequal intervals between categories.[280] However, since it is more difficult to remember a position on a line than to remember a number, using an unstructured interval scale makes it more difficult for panelists to be consistent.[64] This may be a major disadvantage. Unlike those of the category scale, the results of an unstructured interval scale do reveal information concerning the specific degree of intensity of the attribute being evaluated. This may be a major advantage. Whenever specific product standards have been established, the results of using an unstructured interval scale should be very useful to determine the level of an attribute that is specified in the product standards. Just like the results of a structured category scale, the results of an unstructured interval scale reveal no direct information concerning acceptability of the attribute or which sample was preferred. Also the existence of two extreme descriptions means that results (panelist's response) of an unstructured scale, like those of a category scale, are constrained and should not be interpreted as ratios.[315] During some situations (e.g., the development of new products) questions concerning the ratio (of the attribute being evaluated) are extremely important and may have to be an-

Table 5.13. SUGGESTED QUESTIONNAIRE FOR AN UNSTRUCTURED INTERVAL
SCALE, USED TO ASSESS THE PERCEIVED INTENSITY (QUANTITY)
OF THE SENSORY ATTRIBUTE (E.G., CHEWINESS ASPECT OF
TEXTURE) BEING EVALUATED

PANELIST _____   DATE _____

Evaluate the coded samples in the order, top to bottom, presented on the evaluation form. While evaluating
the chewiness (tender vs tough) of each sample, please place a vertical line on the location, of the line
scale, that best indicates your rating of chewiness of each coded sample. Once a coded sample has been assessed, please rinse your mouth with water before you assess the next coded sample.

swered. Under such situations magnitude estimation, not an unstructured interval
scale, should be conducted.

5.4.3.1.3 Magnitude Estimation

Magnitude estimation (Glossary) uses a ratio scale, such as the example presented in
Table 5.14, to measure the intensity of the attribute being evaluated.[280,303,315] Although
a descriptive method, this type of scale uses only numbers, not words, to describe the
intensity of the attribute. Regardless of the attribute being assessed, each panelist as-
signs a chosen positive number to each coded sample.[315] Negative numbers and zero
must not be used.[66] The number assigned the first sample is freely chosen. Each panelist is requested to assign any number he or she may want to the first sample.[317,318]
However, with each subsequent sample, every panelist needs to ensure that the ratio
between the number assigned that individual sample and the number assigned the
first sample equals the ratio between the intensity of the attribute being assessed that
is perceived in that individual sample and the intensity of the same attribute that is

Table 5.14.   AN EXAMPLE OF A QUESTIONNAIRE INVOLVING A RATIO SCALE
(MAGNITUDE ESTIMATION) FOR ASSESSING THE PERCEIVED
INTENSITY (QUANTITY) OF THE SENSORY ATTRIBUTE (E.G.,
CHEWINESS ASPECT OF TEXTURE) BEING EVALUATED

PANELIST _____   DATE _____

Evaluate the coded samples in the order, top to bottom, presented on the evaluation form.

When the chewiness of the first sample has been assessed, assign that sample a freely chosen number.

When evaluating all subsequent samples, the number assigned the chewiness of each sample must be proportionate (higher or lower) to the chewiness of the first sample. For example, if the chewiness of a sample is half that of the first sample the number assigned must be half that of the number assigned the first sample or if the chewiness is twice that of the first sample the number assigned must be twice that assigned the first sample.

Once a coded sample has been assessed, please rinse your mouth with water before you assess the next coded sample.

SAMPLE	ASSIGNED NUMBER
CODE _____	_____
CODE _____	_____
CODE _____	_____
CODE _____	_____

perceived in the first sample.[317,318] Since only the ratios between the numbers assigned each sample convey information, the actual numbers the panelist uses do not influence the scale.[66] Thus unlike the results of either the structured category scale or the unstructured interval scale, the results of magnitude estimation measure the ratio (between samples) of the intensity of the attribute being assessed.[317,319] This type of attribute rating is used primarily in academic studies to measure a single attribute that varies over a wide range of intensities.[64] In general, the use of magnitude estimation has been quite controversial because some sensory scientists actively claim the method has several important advantages (Table 5.15), whereas other sensory scientists strongly maintain its use has numerous, but important, disadvantages (Table 5.15). However, when all three methods of attribute rating were compared, the ability of each method to differentiate small physical differences was approximately equal,[320] but magnitude estimation may be more difficult to conduct as a test method.

Like the results of the structured category scale and the unstructured interval scale, the results of magnitude estimation do not reveal direct information concerning the acceptability of the attribute or which sample was preferred. Also, with magnitude estimation, it is only the ratios (not the actual assigned numbers themselves) that convey information. Therefore the results of magnitude estimation cannot be directly related to specific product standards.

Table 5.15. ADVANTAGES AND DISADVANTAGES OF USING MAGNITUDE
ESTIMATION (RATIO SCALING) TO ASSESS SENSORY ATTRIBUTES

Advantages[a]

1. Ratio scaling provides the ability to express the perceived intensities of samples as ratios or proportion (i.e., sample X is two-thirds as chewy as sample Y).

2. There are no end points on the scales, so panelists cannot run out of numbers to assign to extreme samples.

3. The scales are continuous, thereby allowing discrimination accuracy to be equal to that of the perceptual system.

4. The scales are simple to use and can be easily adapted for use with children and other people who may have difficulty in making numeric judgments.

5. After normalization, the data can be analyzed using parametric statistics.

6. For the purposes of studying subjective–objective correlations, the method provides ratio scale data to match the ratio scale data provided by most instrumental measurements.

Disadvantages[b]

1. Magnitude estimation is a complex task, especially for measurement of tastes, textures, and odors.

2. The task is confusing for many panelists, who revert to category scaling, invalidating the ratio scaling.

3. There is a bias against very high numbers (over 100) and very low numbers (less than 1.0). Fractions are seldom used.

4. Although it may work well in model systems with a wide range of known concentrations, difficulty arises when it is used with experimental food samples that have unknown differences and unknown ranges of concentrations.

5. There is a potential for misuse of ratios when testing "before" and "after" conditions.

6. Magnitude estimation appears to have been misused for measurement of hedonic responses that are bidirectional (like–dislike).

[a]   Printed with permission from Sawyer.[321]
[b]   Printed with permission from Pangborn.[318]

5.4.3.2 Descriptive Analysis

Attribute rating methods of sensory evaluation are generally used to assess one, some, or only a few sensory characteristics of a specific food product.[280] Sometimes it is necessary to have a thorough and complete analytical description that both verbally identifies all of the sensory characteristics of a food and measures the intensity of these characteristics, This can be achieved only using descriptive analysis.[64,66,280]

Compared to other methods of sensory evaluation, descriptive analysis (Glossary) is very sophisticated and therefore is extremely demanding.[64,303,321] The requirements for successful texture profile panelists (Table 5.16) clearly reveal the extent of the demand that may be placed on panelists who are members of descriptive analysis panels. The demand placed on individual leaders of descriptive analysis panels is even greater as he or she must also have a personality that puts panelists at ease and encourages them to put forth their best effort, leadership qualities capable of bringing the entire panel to a consensus opinion without imposing his or her ideas on them, and some scientific training and understanding of the scientific method.[322]

Table 5.16. RECOMMENDED REQUIREMENTS FOR SUCCESSFUL TEXTURE
PROFILE PANELISTS[a]

1. Ability to work cooperatively and harmoniously with a group and develop a feeling of team identity
   with it.

2. Ability to spare the time for training (2–3 hr a day for several weeks) and the regular operation of the
   panel for an indefinite period.

3. Their supervisor must approve the expenditure of time willingly, not reluctantly.

4. Panel members should be very interested in their work and dedicated to developing a team that can
   give results with the precision of a scientific instrument.

5. Panel members must have common sense and reasonable intelligence. A high I.Q. is not essential. No
   special education is necessary. For example, laboratory technicians and secretaries frequently make the
   best panel members because they can readily spare more time, they are always available, they are less
   likely to be preoccupied with other matters (as are senior scientists and administrators), and, hence, are
   able to devote their whole interest to the work at hand.

6. Panel members should be able to discuss the tests with other members of the panel and be able to reach
   a consensus. People with a domineering or bossy attitude and people who are excessively timid or cannot express an opinion are unsuited for panel work.

7. Panelists should be able to develop a professional attitude toward their work and take pride in it,.

8. Panelists should not have dentures because false teeth may restrict the perception of some texture attributes.

9. People who are deeply involved in product development should not be on the panel because they tend
   to come to the panel with preconceived ideas of the textural quality of the products to be examined.

10. It is desirable to have members of both sexes represented on the panel, although the panel can be com-
    prised predominantly of one sex.

[a] Reprinted courtesy of Civille and Szczesniak.[322]

The major methods of descriptive analysis are the flavor profile method, the texture profile method, quantitative descriptive analysis, and free choice profiling.

5.4.3.2.1 Flavor Profile Method

Flavor profile panels provide comprehensive descriptions of all the important attributes of odor and flavor or taste in a product or product group. In general, flavor profile panels rate the intensity of the amplitude (Glossary) of the aroma (Glossary), the
amplitude of the flavor or taste, each aroma character note, and each flavor or taste
character note.[323] Although this method is conducted in a facility that has "eliminated" distraction by foreign odor, appearance, and being uncomfortable, the panelists involved do not sit in individual booths and discussion among the panelists is
encouraged not discouraged.

A flavor profile (Glossary) of a particular seafood is "produced" by a panel of
four to six trained panelists that must truly function as one analytical instrument.[64,321] This "functioning as one instrument" is not easy to achieve.[321,324]
Therefore, the successful operation of a flavor profile panel can be very time consuming and expensive.[321,324,325] An examination of the aroma and flavor character
notes of cooked fish muscle (Table 5.17) that were used by a flavor profile panel

Table 5.17. AROMA AND FLAVOR CHARACTER NOTES OF COOKED FISH
            MUSCLE, DEFINED BY THE FLAVOR PROFILE PANEL OF
            PRELL AND SAWYER[a]

Aroma	Definition
Briny	The aromatics associated with the smell of clean seaweed and ocean air.
Sweet	The sweet fragrance, minus the identifying aromatics, of many products, such as cooked fresh fish.
Fresh fish	The aromatics associated with cooked fresh fish that distinctly characterize it as fish, yet fresh.
Old fish	The aromatics associated with cooked fish with an off note related to trimethylamine.
Stale fish	The aromatics associated with cooked fish that is getting "off," but is not yet old.
Sour	The aromatics associated with vinegar or lemon. Sharp indicates a nostril-irritating type of pungency. Dishrag indicates the sour aromatics of a wet, musk-stale dishrag.
Shellfish	The aromatics associated with any cooked shellfish such as lobster, clam, or scallop.
Gamey fish	The aromatics associated with the heavy gamey, characteristics of some cooked fish such as Atlantic mackerel, as opposed to a delicate aroma of fish such as sole. Analogous to the relationship of the heavy gamey characteristics of fresh cooked venison compared to fresh cooked beef, or duck to chicken.
Fish oil	The aromatics associated with fish oil, such as found in mackerel, canned sardines, or cod liver oil.
Earthy	The aromatics associated with slightly undercooked boiled potato, soil, or a slight musty note.
Nutty–buttery	The aromatics associated with the rich, full flavor of chopped nuts such as pecans and warm melted butter.
Musty	The aromatics associated with a moldy, dank cellar.
Scorched	The aromatics associated with the burnt character common to an overheated ironing board, burnt sugar, or toasted popcorn, sometimes reminiscent of tar, phenol, or creosote.

Flavor	Definition
Salty–briny	A combination of the taste sensations of sodium chloride and the other salt compounds found in ocean water.
Sour (sharp)	The taste sensation caused by acids. The taste of vinegar or lemon is a typical example. Sharp indicates a biting, stinging kind of sensation.
Sweet	The basic taste sensation of which the taste of sucrose is typical.
Fresh fish	As in aroma.
Old fish	As in aroma.
Stale fish	As in aroma
Shellfish	As in aroma.
Gamey fish	As in aroma.
Fish oil	As in aroma.
Earthy	As in aroma.
Nutty–buttery	As in aroma.
Canned salmon	The flavor associated with the salmon character in canned salmon.

Table 5.17. *Continued*

Flavor	Definition
Bitter	The taste sensation of which the taste of a solution of caffeine or quinine is a typical example.
Metallic	The taste sensation suggesting the taste of a slightly oxidized metal such as tin or iron.
Mouth drying	The sensation of dry skin surfaces of the oral cavity; dry feeling in the mouth after swallowing; astringency.
Mouth filling	The sensation of a bloom or fullness of flavor dispersing throughout the mouth. Produced by compounds such as monosodium glutamate, chicken, or beef broth.

[a] Reprinted with permission from Prell and Sawyer.[325]

during the flavor profiling of 17 species of North Atlantic fish[325] immediately causes one to appreciate the magnitude of this fundamental requirement of flavor profile panels. Consequently, meticulous screening and extremely extensive training of each flavor profile panelist are absolute necessities.[321,324,325] During this training, reference standards (Glossary), which are also called standard samples or anchors, are frequently required throughout the entire range of the character notes.[326] Depending on the variety of different foods that a flavor profile panel must assess, individual panelists may quickly be required to have a vocabulary of 300 to 500 different, but specific, character notes.[325]

During the flavor profiling of a sample, the panelists must (in the following order) (1) rate the amplitude of the aroma, (2) identify and rate the intensity of each character note of the aroma, (3) rate the amplitude of the flavor or taste, (4) identify and rate the intensity of each character note of the flavor or taste, and (5) identify each character note of the aftertaste.[323] Once each panelist has assessed a sample, the panel leader guides the discussion until the entire panel unanimously agrees on the sample's complete flavor profile.[64,323,324,327] Depending on the sample being profiled, several panel sessions may have to be conducted before a refined, but complete, flavor profile is unanimously agreed on. Since this unanimity is a core foundation of the flavor profile method, it is extremely important that none of the members (including the leader) of the flavor profile panel be overly persuasive and thereby have an undue influence on the "unanimous" profile.[64,67]

In addition to being used to characterize flavors, which includes odor, substances may be profiled for odor only. For example, an atlas of the odor character profiles of 160 different individual chemicals or mixtures has been published.[328]

Since the flavor or odor profile panel is expected to be both extremely detailed and to function as a single analytical instrument, each panel member must evaluate each sample in an identical manner. Thus, the size of the sample tasted, the number of sniffs (for aroma) or sips (for flavor), the exact time (since last swallowing) of determining aftertaste, and the exact order in which the attributes are assessed must comply with an extremely standardized procedure.[323] For example, it is important that each panelist record each rating and/or identification on a blank evaluation form.[323] Since a check list is suggestive,[323] it must not be used for it may result in either identifying character notes that are not present or excluding character notes that are actually present.

Flavor and/or odor profile panels are particularly useful during the development of new products, but may also be helpful in the quality control of both raw materials and finished products.[323] The very detailed, but unanimous, results are one of the major advantages of a flavor profile panel. The rapid speed at which trained flavor profile panels may produce results is also an advantage.[303] The major disadvantages are (1) the small number of panelists,[64] (2) possible undue influence of forceful members in achieving unanimity,[67] and (3) the data produced are not designed to be subjected to statistical analyses.[280]

5.4.3.2.2 Texture Profile Method

A texture profile (Glossary) of an individual seafood is "assembled" by a panel of six to nine panelists who also must definitely function as one analytical instrument.[66,273,329] The resulting texture profile provides a detailed sensory characterization of the mechanical, geometric, fat, and moisture aspects of the particular food being examined.[66,280] The identity, intensity, and order of appearance (between first bite, swallowing, and residual phases) of each "textural" sensory characteristic is reported.[66] In addition to being used to characterize textural properties, this method may also be used to describe nontextural properties such as color. For example, using a 10-cm unstructured interval scale appearance and texture profiles of 17 species of North Atlantic fish quantified (7-point category scale) darkness, visual flakiness, hardness, oral flakiness, chewiness, fibrousness, moistness, and oily mouthcoating[330] whereas during the texture profiling of shrimp surface roughness, hardness, friability, cohesiveness, toughness, chewing resistance, wetness, juiciness, fibrousness, and graininess were quantified.[331]

The necessity of operating as a detailed, but single, analytical instrument means that a potential texture profile panel normally requires tremendous training and practice (Table 5.16).[329] This training usually requires a large number of reference standards throughout the entire range of the texture to demonstrate the exact meaning of each descriptive term and a large amount of discussion among all of the panelists to achieve complete unanimity of agreement on each descriptive term.[280,329] In addition, the manner, order, and time of presenting the samples to the panelists must be extremely well standardized. Since the purpose of training (e.g., teaching and demonstrating) is to ensure that each panelist will uniformly recognize each sensory characteristic, a standard rating scale (e.g., a 14-point intensity scale) should be used.[329] Once this training has been completed and product testing is being conducted, the intensity of the sensory characteristics is quantified. This is achieved using a category scale, a line scale, or a ratio scale. However, no type of scale should be used if all panelists have not previously used that scale in an assortment of circumstances.[329] Depending on the specific reason for determining the texture profiles, the panelists may either have group discussion and develop an unanimous texture profile or individually assess each sample, without having a subsequent discussion, so that the data may be statistically analyzed.[329] Whenever individual assessments are required, the evaluations must be conducted within individual booths (Table 5.3).

Since commercial materials (not pure substances such as chemicals) have to be used as reference samples, texture profiling may be more difficult to conduct than flavor profiling.[324] However, texture profile panels, which are normally thorough and precise, are often useful in the development of new products.

5.4.3.2.3 Quantitative Descriptive Analysis

The general nature of the method of quantitative descriptive analysis is considerably different from both the flavor profile method and the texture profile method.[324] Once trained, flavor profile panels and texture profile panel are capable of analytically assessing the respective attribute for which they have been trained (e.g., appearance, flavor, odor, or texture, no other sensory attribute), in a wide range of products. In contrast, once trained, a quantitative descriptive analysis (QDA) panel is capable of assessing all of the sensory attributes (appearance, flavor, odor, texture, and noise, if applicable) of only one type of product,[324] for which they have been trained. Since the panel must function as an analytical device for a wide range of sensory attributes, training of a QDA panel is also extensive. However, during this training, reference samples (anchors) are normally used only at the extremities of each sensory attribute. Within these extremities, the intensity (quantity) of each attribute is normally measured using a 15-cm unstructured interval scale.[64,303,324] During the training of QDA panelists, the panel leader is not to enter into the discussion and thereby influence the panelists (who are being trained), but the leader must guide the discussion to ensure complete participation of all members.[64,324] Also, once trained, a QDA panel assesses a minimum of four to six replicate samples for each "product" being evaluated.

The "comprehensive descriptive method" is a recognized quality control procedure that utilizes a QDA panel to assess the intensity of a variety of very specific, but important, sensory attributes.[287]

5.4.3.2.4 Free Choice Profile Method

The free choice profile method (Glossary) of descriptive analysis is unique because the sensory panelists, themselves, are not required to operate as a single analytical device. During the assessment of samples, each panelist is encouraged to create and utilize his or her own evaluation form that contains as many descriptive terms as he or she desires.[64] Once they are created, each individual panelist must consistently use these descriptive terms throughout all the evaluations of that "product."[298] Since no extensive training (to ensure unanimity of the panelist's assessments) is required, the results must be analyzed using a statistical method entitled "Procrustean analysis" to make the wide range of descriptions more "unanimous."[64,298,324] However, unlike profiling methods that involve intensive training and mandatory descriptive terms, free choice profiling has been reported to be incapable of usefully describing the sensory changes that develop during the spoilage of fish.[298]

5.5 Screening, Selecting, Training, and Monitoring Panelists

Once appropriate facilities have been obtained and the appropriate evaluation method has been selected, the panelists used to properly assess the samples must be chosen. The type of assessor (panelist) required depends on the type of sensory evaluation to be conducted. Whenever affective sensory tests are to be conducted, selection of panelists is based on factors other than sensory ability, as these sensory evaluation panels are not expected to function as an analytical instrument.[67] In contrast, a fundamental principle of both discriminative sensory tests and descriptive sensory methods is that evaluation panels using these procedures must function as an analytical device.[67] Therefore, decisions concerning screening, selecting, and training cannot be adequately made until the objective of the work has been clearly specified and the sensory evaluation method to be used has been selected.

Prior to choosing any panelists, one must first decide whether to choose volunteers (from within the organization and/or building), hire people (from outside the organization and/or building) to specifically serve as panelists, or use a mixture of both. This decision can best be made by reviewing the clearly defined reason(s) for conducting the sensory evaluations and studying the practical effects (Table 5.18) of using volunteers or paid panelists. Once this has been decided, potential panelists need to be recruited, screened (Glossary), selected (Glossary), and trained.

The subsequent discussion concerning screening, selecting, and training primarily applies when either discriminative or descriptive procedures are used.

Prior to screening any person who may become a panelist, it must first be clearly established that he or she is (1) interested in becoming a panelist and should, once trained, understand the importance of sensory evaluation, (2) capable of being promptly available for the vast majority of the sessions, (3) of good health and does not have any ailment, such as an allergy or color blindness, that may affect his or her ability to perceive sensory attributes, and (4) willing to assess the type of samples that are to be evaluated.[285] Whenever descriptive analysis methods are to be used the potential panelist must also clearly exhibit good verbal and/or writing skills.[285]

5.5.1 Screening Potential Panelists

Screening consists of defining the sensory skills of each potential panelist that has met the previously mentioned basic qualifications. This evaluation of a person's actual sensory skills is achieved by subjecting that person to a series (e.g., at least 20) of realistic sensory tests. This means that during testing the type of sample, the method of preparation, and the type of sensory test used must be similar to that which will be used once the screening and training are completed.[285] One must also ensure that each potential panelist clearly understands the screening test being used. In general, one should screen at least two to three times as many people as will be needed for the selected and trained panel.[280] However, when screening for either a flavor profile panel or a texture profile panel, five to six times as many people may need to be screened.[285]

Screening of panelists for discriminative tests often involves using a series of triangle tests, which must range in at least three degrees of difficulty.[64] Since the results

Table 5.18. FACTORS TO BE CONSIDERED WHEN DECIDING TO USE VOLUNTEERS FROM WITHIN THE ORGANIZATION AS SENSORY PANELISTS OR PEOPLE FROM OUTSIDE THE ORGANIZATION WHO ARE PAID TO BE SENSORY PANELISTS[a]

Factor	Volunteers from within the Organization (Building)
1	Depending on the regular duties of the individual, the person may be more readily available.
2	Depending on the frequency of panel sessions, the use of volunteers is much less expensive.
3	Volunteers are more suitable if the results must be kept confidential.
4	Volunteers are more suitable if it is desirable to have little change, with time, of the panelists.
5	Volunteers are less suitable when acceptability of the samples is being assessed.
6	Depending on the size of the organization volunteers may have too much knowledge about the samples being assessed and lack of potential volunteers may make them very difficult to replace.

Factor	People Who Are Paid to Be Panelists
1	Depending on the community in which the organization is located, there may be a wider range of potential panelists.
2	Once hired there is normally less of a problem of the panelists objecting to the type of panel being conducted and/or sample being assessed.
3	There is no concern of offending potential panelists if they are not suitable.
4	Depending on the frequency of panel sessions, using paid panelists may become very expensive.
5	Depending on when the panelists must be available, only certain types of people (e.g., pensioners, students, or unemployed people) may be obtainable.[41]
6	There is a high risk of panelists leaving without giving much notice.

[a] Reprinted courtesy of International Standards Organization.[286]

are often used to rank the potential panelists according to their ability to discriminate the samples being evaluated,[280] the triangle test of each difficulty should be repeated several times.

The screening for either attribute rating or quantitative descriptive analysis also frequently involves using a large number of triangle tests.[285] Each potential panelist is subjected to a broad range of samples that, preferably, at each different screening session varies in only appearance, aroma, flavor, or texture. These results are then used to rank the performance of the different people being screened.

Screening for the flavor profile method consists of evaluating each person's ability to (1) distinguish among sweet, sour, salty, and bitter tastes, (2) rank the intensity of sweet, sour, salty, and bitter tastes, and (3) identify and describe both seafood aromas that occur frequently and some relevant aromas that occur infrequently.[285] Screening for the texture profile method involves assessing each person's ability to rank increasing hardness, increasing viscosity, and differences in particle size shape and/or orientation.[273] In particular, if the texture of raw fish is to be evaluated, screening for the person's ability to rank differences in resiliency may also be required.

5.5.2 Selecting Panelists

Once the appropriate screening tests have been completed, the results are used to select the people who possess the necessary sensory skills to be sensory evaluation panelists. To qualify for a discriminative panel, an attribute rating panel, or a quantitative descriptive analysis panel a person should correctly identify approximately 66% of the triangle tests.[285]

Qualifications for both flavor profile method and the texture profile method are very specific, and are clearly described by the American Society of Testing and Materials[285] and by Meilgaard et al.[64]

5.5.3 Training Panelists

Unless the panelists are trained, sensory evaluation panels using discriminative tests and particularly those panels using descriptive sensory methods may not function as an analytical instrument.

Once selected, all panelists must be trained to definitely understand the following:

1. Sensory evaluation of seafood is extremely important and must be taken seriously by all panelists.
2. During all discriminative tests and all descriptive methods, each panelist must be objective, which means ignoring his or her likes and dislikes.
3. The negative effects of not promptly arriving at the specified time.
4. Exposure to candy, cosmetics, food, gum, smoking, and other odorous materials may seriously affect sensory evaluation and must not occur within 30 min of the evaluations.[64]
5. The importance of good health and the necessity of reporting any illnesses,[285] because only then may the panelist be excused or the session cancelled.
6. The exact evaluation techniques that must be used whenever appearance, flavor, odor, or texture is being evaluated.[280]
7. The specific sensory evaluation "test" that is being used.[285]

Depending on the type of sensory evaluation being conducted and on the particular topic being taught, the training is conducted with or without practice evaluation sessions. When uncomplicated discriminative sensory tests are to be used, few (if any) practice sessions are required.[285] However, since descriptive analysis methods are often both comprehensive and detailed, the amount of training required to achieve agreement among all of the panelists may be very great.[64,285] A panelist for a texture profile panel may be trained 2–3 hr a day for several weeks (Table 5.16). Similarly panelists for a flavor profile panel were given 48 hr (8 days) of in-depth training and 126 hr (14 weeks) of practice sessions.[332] However, the exact amount of training required depends on the samples being evaluated, the panelists themselves, and the actual evaluation test being used. The length of time necessary to train replacement panelists has recently been reported to have been reduced to 50% of the time required to train the original panelists.[333] This was achieved by during the first week of training utilizing posters, music (as well as food samples), and numerical values to teach how flavor can be divided into different parts thereby becoming "untangled," during the next 2–6 weeks of training always utilizing some original panelists as cotrainers, and during the last two weeks, training the original and replacement panelists together.[333] Although the training time was reduced by 50%, the replacement panelists were smoothly combined with the original panelists, without disrupting the panel activities of the original panelists.[333]

During the training of panelists that will be evaluating samples using the flavor profile method, the texture profile method, or quantitative descriptive analysis the use of reference standards[326] and the importance of language in describing perceptions[288] cannot be overemphasized.

A reference standard (Glossary) should, if possible, be both simple and reproducible, identify only one item, and be capable of being diluted without altering its character.[326] The use of reference standards assists panelists to generate the terminology used to describe the samples by making the chore easier and the terms more accurate, helps determine intensities and anchor end points of unstructured interval scales (which are used in quantitative descriptive analysis), demonstrates the effect of specific ingredients or interaction of ingredients, and reduces the time required to train the panelists.[326]

Regardless of what it describes, proper sensory descriptive terms must differentiate between similar sensations, identify the sensation it describes, and allow recognition of the sensation once other similarly trained panelists have seen the descriptive term.[288] Fulfilling these requirements is best achieved if the descriptive terms are not redundant, clearly related to the attribute (appearance, flavor, odor, or texture) being described, based on a broad set of reference standards, precise, and comprised of primary (not integrated) terms.[288]

5.5.4 Monitoring Panelists

It cannot be assumed that once a discriminative or a descriptive sensory evaluation panel is properly screened, selected, and trained the panel will continuously function as an analytical device. To ensure this it is very important that the performance of every panelist be monitored.[286] Monitoring consists of regularly comparing the performance of each individual panelist with his or her past performance as well as with the performance of the panel "as a whole."

Computers are now often being installed in each evaluation booth.[314,334,335] The subsequent use of computerized, rather than paper, evaluation forms allows for immediate computerized storage of all results and, when desired, very rapid analysis of these results.[314,334,335] This development has greatly reduced the difficulty of regularly monitoring each panelist.[314,336,337]

Whenever the performance of panelist(s) has substantially declined, this must be corrected by regenerating the panelists' interest,[286] retraining the panelist,[286] and (when definitely necessary) removing and replacing the panelist.

5.6 Preparation and Presentation of Samples

Using improper procedures to either prepare the samples or present them to panelists can easily impair the final sensory results. Whenever this occurs a large portion of the effort undertaken to ensure the use of appropriate facilities, evaluation methods, and screening, selecting, and training may have been wasted. The techniques used to prepare and/or present the samples must ensure that the results of evaluating those samples are based entirely on each sample itself. No additional factor(s), caused by the method of preparing and/or presenting the samples, must alter the results.

5.6.1 Preparing Samples

Elimination of such additional factors during the preparation of samples cannot be achieved unless each of the factors described in Table 5.19 are always considered extremely seriously.

5.6.2 Presenting Samples

Similarly, while presenting samples to the panelists one needs to consistently remember all of the physiological factors (Table 5.1) and the psychological factors (Table 5.2) that influence the results of sensory evaluation. Serious implementation of numerous practical procedures (Table 5.20) will greatly reduce, if not eliminate, the effects of these psychological factors.

Always presenting the samples in both a randomized order (Glossary) and a balanced manner (Glossary) will reduce the effects of at least one-half of the psychological factors (Tables 5.2 and 5.20). Determining the random order may be achieved by numbering the samples and subsequently using a table of random numbers to select the actual order of presentation[64,280] or drawing sample cards out of a container.[64]

Table 5.19. IMPORTANT FACTORS TO BE CONSIDERED WHEN PREPARING SAMPLES FOR SENSORY EVALUATION

1. All samples being prepared must be representative of the specific seafood(s) being evaluated.[338]

2. Only the factor being investigated should be varied.[280] Otherwise, all samples must be prepared in an identical manner. Thus the size, shape, temperature, etc. must not vary among samples being assessed.

3. Whenever the samples are to be assessed using affective sensory methods, the method used to prepare the sample must be representative of how that product is typically consumed.[338]

4. Whenever the samples are to be assessed using discriminative sensory tests, the preparation method used must be the realistic preparation method that is least likely to mask, add to, or alter the sensory characteristic being assessed.[280]

5. During the preparation of each sample, only inert materials (e.g., glass, stainless steel) must physically contact the sample being prepared.[64]

6. Ensure that the number of samples being prepared for each panelist will not cause sensory fatigue during the evaluation of these samples.[303] This actual number depends on both the type of seafood "product" being assessed and the specific sensory evaluation method being used.

Table 5.20. PROCEDURES NECESSARY TO REDUCE PSYCHOLOGICAL FACTORS
THAT NEGATIVELY INFLUENCE SENSORY PANELISTS, AND HENCE
THE RESULTS OF SENSORY EVALUATION

Procedure to ensure reduction of factor(s)	Factor(s) reduced[a]
All sensory evaluations must be conducted in a proficient manner[64,280] and, whenever appropriate, use experienced panelists.[303]	Decreased motivation, leniency error
Ensure that each panelist is placed within a separate booth and do not allow any talking within the evaluation area.[64,280]	Mutual suggestion
Ensure that all samples are presented in a randomized order and that each panelist receives each of the conceivable combinations of samples an equal number of times (i.e., a balanced order of presentation)[64,280,303] (see Glossary).	Contrast effect, convergence effect, errors of expectation, habituation, and central tendency, pattern effect, position effect, and stimulus error
Guarantee that the level of the sensory attribute(s) of samples being presented for evaluation is varied, (if necessary use doctored samples) and if possible use experienced panelists.[64,303]	Error of habituation
Guarantee that each panelist does not have any specific knowledge about the samples being evaluated.[303]	Error of expectation
The performance during each session of all panelists must be overseen.[64] Whenever necessary each panelist must be given appropriate guidance and/or training.[64]	Capriciousness
Thoroughly examine every sample to ensure that all samples are uniform in every detail (except for the specific attribute being evaluated).[303] Whenever differences cannot be eliminated they must be masked (e.g., using colored lights to mask color differences)[64,280,303] and whenever appropriate use experienced panelists.[303]	Logical error, stimulus error
Unless it is not possible, be sure to have each attribute evaluated at a different session of the same sensory evaluation panel.[64,280]	Halo effect
When appropriate, be sure to give each panelist a report of the results after the study has been completed.[64,280]	Decreased motivation

[a] Each of these factors is clearly defined in Table 5.2.

Even if samples are numbered prior to selecting the random order, all samples that are presented to panelists must be identified using a code consisting of a three-digit random number (obtained from a table of random numbers).[280] This procedure is necessary to reduce important psychological factors, such as expectation error.

Presenting the samples in a balanced manner is very necessary and has important practical implications. For example, a small increase in the number of different products assessed at any one time greatly increases the number of different combinations that must be assessed, to achieve a balanced manner (see Section 4.2.1.2). In addition, when the triangle test is used to evaluate samples from treatment A and from treatment B, there are six possible orders (AAB, ABA, ABB, BBA, BAB, and BAA) in which the samples may be presented.[280] For the presentation to be balanced, each combination must be evaluated during the study an equal number of times. This can be achieved only if the number of panelists utilized are a multiple of six, so that each of the six different combinations may be presented one, two, three, or four times, etc.

Using experienced panelists when appropriate will also reduce the effects of several of the psychological factors (Table 5.20).

In addition to ensuring the sample being presented is representative of the "product" being evaluated, the size of the sample should allow each panelist the option of reevaluating the sample, if this is desired and allowed.[67,338]

5.7. Analysis and Interpretation of Results

Once all of the samples have been evaluated, the results must be analyzed and interpreted.

5.7.1 Analyzing Results

There are many statistical method(s) that are used to analyze such results. The sensory test that was used is a major factor that determines which statistical method to use.

With the paired comparison test for difference, the paired comparison test for preference, and the duo-trio and triangle tests the results are compared to an appropriate table of minimum numbers necessary to achieve a specified probability level (i.e., level of significance) (Tables 5.21, 5.22, and 5.23).[280] Alternatively, to know the exact probability of the results that were obtained, the reader may readily refer to such published tables.[335]

Whenever Tables 5.21 to 5.23 are to be utilized, it is extremely important to specify, before the evaluations begin, the number of samples that are to be evaluated. Regardless of the significance level of the observed results, additional tests must not be conducted (to try to achieve a higher level of significance).[297]

The results of the duo-trio test must be compared to the minimum numbers tabulated in Table 5.21, whereas the results of the triangle test must be compared to the minimum numbers presented in Table 5.22. However, the specific table used to analyze the results of either the paired comparison test for difference or the paired comparison test for preference depends on the reason for conducting the test (type of results that are expected).[280,335] If the reason is to verify that "product" A is preferred to "product" B or that "product" A is firmer than "product" B, the results must be compared to the minimum numbers presented in Table 5.21 because it is a "one-tailed" test.[64] However, if the reason is to determine which of the two products (A or B) is preferred or which of the two products is firmer, the results must be compared to the minimum numbers listed in Table 5.23, as it is a two-tailed test.[64,280,335]

Whenever the results of the 3-AFC test (particularly when it is used for the determination of thresholds) needs to be analyzed and interpreted, the reader is referred to the American Society of Testing and Materials (ASTM) Publication E679.[312]

Table 5.21.   MINIMUM NUMBER OF CORRECT JUDGMENTS TO ESTABLISH SIGNIFICANCE AT NUMEROUS PROBABILITY LEVELS FOR THE DUO-TRIO TEST, THE ONE-TAILED PAIRED DIFFERENCE TEST, AND THE ONE-TAILED PAIRED PREFERENCE TEST (ONE-TAILED, $p = 1/2$)

Number of trials (n)	Probability Levels						
	0.150	0.100	0.050	0.030	0.010	0.005	0.001
7	6	6	7	7	7	—	—
8	6	7	7	8	8	8	—
9	7	7	8	8	9	9	—
10	8	8	9	9	10	10	10
11	8	9	9	10	10	11	11
12	9	9	10	10	11	11	12
13	9	10	10	11	12	12	13
14	10	10	11	11	12	13	13
15	11	11	12	12	13	13	14
16	11	12	12	13	14	14	15
17	12	12	13	13	14	15	16
18	12	13	13	14	15	15	16
19	13	13	14	15	15	16	17
20	13	14	15	15	16	17	18
21	14	14	15	16	17	17	18
22	14	15	16	16	17	18	19
23	15	16	16	17	18	19	20
24	16	16	17	18	19	19	20
25	16	17	18	18	19	20	21
26	17	17	18	19	20	20	22
27	17	18	19	19	20	21	22
28	18	18	19	20	21	22	23
29	18	19	20	21	22	22	24
30	19	20	20	21	22	23	24
31	19	20	21	22	23	24	25
32	20	21	22	22	24	24	26
33	20	21	22	23	24	25	26
34	21	22	23	23	25	25	27
35	22	22	23	24	25	26	27
36	22	23	24	25	26	27	28
37	23	23	24	25	27	27	29
38	23	24	25	26	27	28	29
39	24	24	26	26	28	28	30
40	24	25	26	27	28	29	31
41	25	26	27	27	29	30	31
42	25	26	27	28	29	30	32
43	26	27	28	29	30	31	32
44	26	27	28	29	31	31	33
45	27	28	29	30	31	32	34
46	28	28	30	30	32	33	34
47	28	29	30	31	32	33	35
48	29	29	31	31	33	34	36
49	29	30	31	32	34	34	36
50	30	31	32	33	34	35	37

(*Continued*)

Table 5.21. *Continued*

Number of trials (n)	Probability Levels						
	0.150	0.100	0.050	0.030	0.010	0.005	0.0051
51	30	31	32	33	35	36	37
52	31	32	33	34	35	36	38
53	31	32	33	34	36	37	39
54	32	33	34	35	36	37	39
55	32	33	35	35	37	38	40
56	33	34	35	36	38	39	40
57	33	34	36	37	38	39	41
58	34	35	36	37	39	40	42
59	34	35	37	38	39	40	42
60	35	36	37	38	40	41	43
61	36	37	38	39	41	41	43
62	36	37	38	39	41	42	44
63	37	38	39	40	42	43	45
64	37	38	40	40	42	43	45
65	38	39	40	41	43	44	46
66	38	39	41	42	43	44	46
67	39	40	41	42	44	45	47
68	39	40	42	43	45	46	48
69	40	41	42	43	45	46	48
70	40	41	43	44	46	47	49
71	41	42	43	44	46	47	49
72	41	42	44	45	47	48	50
73	42	43	45	46	47	48	51
74	42	44	45	46	48	49	51
75	43	44	46	47	49	50	52
76	44	45	46	47	49	50	52
77	44	45	47	48	50	51	53
78	45	46	47	48	50	51	54
79	45	46	48	49	51	52	54
80	46	47	48	49	51	52	55
82	47	48	49	50	52	54	56
84	48	49	51	52	54	55	57
86	49	50	52	53	55	56	58
88	50	51	53	54	56	57	59
90	51	52	54	55	57	58	61
92	52	53	55	56	58	59	62
94	53	54	56	57	59	60	63
96	54	55	57	58	60	62	64
98	55	56	58	59	61	63	65
100	56	57	59	60	63	64	66

Although the degree of difference test is a discriminative sensory test, its results are subjected to analysis of variance to determine if the sensory characteristics of the test sample are significantly different from that of the reference sample.[314]

Similarly, analysis of variance is frequently used to analyze the results of attribute assessment that utilized hedonic scale, structured category scale, unstructured scale

Table 5.22. MINIMUM NUMBER OF CORRECT JUDGMENTS TO ESTABLISH SIGNIFICANCE AT NUMEROUS PROBABILITY LEVELS FOR THE TRIANGLE TEST (ONE-TAILED, $p = 1/3$)

Number of trials (n)	Probability Levels						
	0.150	0.100	0.050	0.030	0.010	0.005	0.001
5	4	4	4	5	5	5	—
6	4	5	5	5	6	6	—
7	5	5	5	6	6	7	—
8	5	5	6	6	7	7	—
9	5	6	6	7	7	8	8
10	6	6	7	7	8	8	9
11	6	7	7	8	8	9	10
12	7	7	8	8	9	9	10
13	7	8	8	9	9	10	11
14	7	8	9	9	10	10	11
15	8	8	9	10	10	11	12
16	8	9	9	10	11	11	12
17	9	9	10	10	11	12	13
18	9	10	10	11	12	12	13
19	9	10	11	11	12	13	14
20	10	10	11	12	13	13	14
21	10	11	12	12	13	14	15
22	11	11	12	13	14	14	15
23	11	12	12	13	14	15	16
24	11	12	13	13	15	15	16
25	12	12	13	14	15	16	17
26	12	13	14	14	15	16	17
27	13	13	14	15	16	17	18
28	13	14	15	15	16	17	18
29	13	14	15	16	17	17	19
30	14	14	15	16	17	18	19
31	14	15	16	16	18	18	20
32	14	15	16	17	18	19	20
33	15	15	17	17	18	19	21
34	15	16	17	18	19	20	21
35	16	16	17	18	19	20	22
36	16	17	18	18	20	20	22
37	16	17	18	19	20	21	22
38	17	17	19	19	21	21	23
39	17	18	19	20	21	22	23
40	17	18	19	20	21	22	24
41	18	19	20	20	22	23	24
42	18	19	20	21	22	23	25
43	19	19	20	21	23	24	25
44	19	20	21	22	23	24	26
45	19	20	21	22	24	24	26
46	20	20	22	22	24	25	27
47	20	21	22	23	24	25	27
48	20	21	22	23	25	26	27
49	21	22	23	24	25	26	28

(*Continued*)

Table 5.22. *Continued*

Number of trials (n)	Probability Levels						
	0.150	0.100	0.050	0.030	0.010	0.005	0.001
50	21	22	23	24	26	26	28
51	21	22	24	24	26	27	29
52	22	23	24	25	26	27	29
53	22	23	24	25	27	28	30
54	23	23	25	26	27	28	30
55	23	24	25	26	28	29	30
56	23	24	26	26	28	29	31
57	24	25	26	27	28	29	31
58	24	25	26	27	29	30	32
59	24	25	27	28	29	30	32
60	25	26	27	28	30	31	33
61	25	26	27	28	30	31	33
62	26	26	28	29	30	31	33
63	26	27	28	29	31	32	34
64	26	27	29	30	31	32	34
65	27	28	29	30	32	33	35
66	27	28	29	30	32	33	35
67	27	28	30	31	33	34	36
68	28	29	30	31	33	34	36
69	28	29	31	31	33	34	36
70	28	29	31	32	34	35	37
71	29	30	31	32	34	35	37
72	29	30	32	33	34	36	38
73	30	31	32	33	35	36	38
74	30	31	32	33	35	36	39
75	30	31	33	34	36	37	39
76	31	32	33	34	36	37	39
77	31	32	34	35	36	38	40
78	31	32	34	35	37	38	40
79	32	33	34	35	37	38	41
80	32	33	35	36	38	39	41
82	33	34	35	36	38	40	42
84	33	35	36	37	39	40	43
86	34	35	37	38	40	41	44
88	35	36	38	39	41	42	44
90	36	37	38	40	42	43	45
92	36	37	39	40	42	44	46
94	37	38	40	41	43	44	47
96	38	39	41	42	44	45	48
98	39	40	41	43	45	46	48
100	39	40	42	43	46	47	49

interval scale, magnitude estimation (ratio scale), and quantitative descriptive analysis.[280] However, the results of these sensory tests often do not meet the underlying assumptions necessary to conduct analysis of variance.[296–298] Therefore, depending on the actual results obtained, a statistical method other than analysis of variance may

Table 5.23. MINIMUM NUMBER OF CORRECT JUDGMENTS TO ESTABLISH SIGNIFICANCE AT VARIOUS PROBABILITY LEVELS FOR THE TWO-TAILED PAIRED DIFFERENCE TEST AND THE TWO-TAILED PAIRED PREFERENCE TEST (TWO-TAILED, $p = 1/2$)

Number of trials (n)	Probability Levels						
	0.150	0.100	0.050	0.030	0.010	0.005	0.001
6	6	6	6	—	—	—	—
7	6	7	7	7	—	—	—
8	7	7	8	8	8	—	—
9	8	8	8	9	9	9	—
10	8	9	9	9	10	10	11
11	9	9	10	10	11	11	11
12	9	10	10	11	11	12	12
13	10	10	11	11	12	12	13
14	11	11	12	12	13	13	14
15	11	12	12	13	13	14	14
16	12	12	13	13	14	14	15
17	12	13	13	14	15	15	16
18	13	13	14	15	15	16	17
19	14	14	15	15	16	16	17
20	14	15	15	16	17	17	18
21	15	15	16	16	17	18	19
22	15	16	17	17	18	18	19
23	16	16	17	18	19	19	20
24	17	17	18	18	19	20	21
25	17	18	18	19	20	20	21
26	18	18	19	19	20	21	22
27	18	19	20	20	21	22	23
28	19	19	20	21	22	22	23
29	19	20	21	21	22	23	24
30	20	20	21	22	23	24	25
31	20	21	22	22	24	24	25
32	21	22	23	23	24	25	26
33	22	22	23	24	25	25	27
34	22	23	24	24	25	26	27
35	23	23	24	25	26	27	28
36	23	24	25	25	27	27	29
37	24	24	25	26	27	28	29
38	24	25	26	27	28	29	30
39	25	26	27	27	28	29	31
40	26	26	27	28	29	30	31
41	26	27	28	28	30	30	32
42	27	27	28	29	30	31	32
43	27	28	29	30	31	32	33
44	28	28	29	30	31	32	34
45	28	29	30	31	32	33	34
46	29	30	31	31	33	33	35
47	29	30	31	32	33	34	36
48	30	31	32	32	34	35	36
49	31	31	32	33	34	35	37

(Continued)

Table 5.23. *Continued*

Number of trials (n)	Probability Levels						
	0.150	0.100	0.050	0.030	0.010	0.005	0.001
50	31	32	33	34	35	36	37
51	32	32	33	34	36	36	38
52	32	33	34	35	36	37	39
53	33	33	35	35	37	38	39
54	33	34	35	36	37	38	40
55	34	35	36	37	38	39	41
56	34	35	36	37	39	39	41
57	35	36	37	38	39	40	42
58	35	36	37	38	40	41	42
59	36	37	38	39	40	41	43
60	37	37	39	39	41	42	44
61	37	38	39	40	41	42	44
62	38	38	40	41	42	43	45
63	38	39	40	41	43	44	45
64	39	40	41	42	43	44	46
65	39	40	41	42	44	45	47
66	40	41	42	43	44	45	47
67	40	41	42	43	45	46	48
68	41	42	43	44	46	46	48
69	41	42	44	44	46	47	49
70	42	43	44	45	47	48	50
71	43	43	45	46	47	48	50
72	43	44	45	46	48	49	51
73	44	45	46	47	48	49	51
74	44	45	46	47	49	50	52
75	45	46	47	48	50	51	53
76	45	46	48	48	50	51	53
77	46	47	48	49	51	52	54
78	46	47	49	50	51	52	54
79	47	48	49	50	52	53	55
80	47	48	50	51	52	53	56
82	49	49	51	52	54	55	57
84	50	51	52	53	55	56	58
86	51	52	53	54	56	57	59
88	52	53	54	55	57	58	60
90	53	54	55	56	58	59	61
92	54	55	56	57	59	60	63
94	55	56	57	58	60	62	64
96	56	57	59	60	62	63	65
98	57	58	60	61	63	64	66
100	58	59	61	62	64	65	67

need to be used to determine if the sensory characteristics of the different products were, statistically, significant.[296-298]

Comparing the observed results to minimum numbers in an appropriate table or conducting analysis of variance analyzes the variability of the results and, thereby, indicates the specific probability level at which the results could have occurred by "chance alone." In addition, the results must be summarized by calculating the mean, standard deviation, median, mode, and frequency table (graph) of the observed results.[299] These summary statistics are used to assess the size of the difference of the sensory attribute between the different "products."

The large number of sensory evaluation methods that may be utilized to assess a sensory attribute(s) does not make the task of selecting the appropriate statistical methods an easy one. However, it is a very serious task as the use of inappropriate statistical methods may readily lead to incorrect conclusions. Therefore the reader is encouraged to study specific statistical references concerning sensory evaluation.[297,298,339]

5.7.2 Interpreting Results

It is essentially impossible to interpret sensory evaluation results without conducting some type of statistical analysis. However, interpretation of sensory evaluation results also involves serious consideration of a large number of other factors.

The clearly defined reasons for conducting the attribute assessments must be carefully reviewed. Similarly, all of the procedures (that were utilized), such as type of sampling, number of samples assessed, type of facilities used, type of sensory test used, methods of screening, selecting, training, and monitoring panelists, number of panelists utilized, manner of preparing and presenting samples, and methods of statistically analyzing the results, must be very critically reviewed to determine if any of these procedures would have negatively affected the validity of the observed results. Once completed, the conclusions of the review must be critically compared to the clearly defined objectives (reasons) why freshness quality was evaluated, using attribute assessment. Whenever the conclusions (concerning the procedures that were used) do not definitely allow the clearly defined objective(s) to be achieved, the interpretation of the results must be affected accordingly. This type of interpretation helps ensure that a valid conclusion is made. This is extremely important, as only valid conclusions will ensure that expectations of the buyers, users, and regulatory agencies are being met.

CHAPTER
6

Conclusion

Freshness quality is neither a distinct object nor a specified actuality. Instead, it is a concept and, therefore, is seriously affected by what impresses a person. Thus the specific meaning of seafood freshness quality depends on the particular buyer, user, or regulatory agency that is buying, using, or regulating the seafood. Consequently, it is not surprising that no single method of evaluating freshness quality has been observed to be suitable for measuring the freshness quality of all types of seafood products and species.

Before evaluating freshness quality it is extremely important to have very clearly defined written reasons why the freshness quality of that particular seafood product needs to be evaluated. These reasons must include the specific definition of freshness quality, for that particular product, buyer, user, or regulatory agency. Once this is achieved, each of the four different methods (chemical methods, physical methods, freshness quality grading, and attribute assessment) described in Chapters 2, 3, 4, and 5 can be critically reviewed (i.e., compared to these written reasons) so that the most appropriate method for that specific situation can be realistically selected.

Regardless of which of the four methods is used to determine freshness quality, it is extremely important that (1) a sufficient number of samples to be evaluated be randomly selected, (2) the collected samples be handled, stored, and prepared (to be evaluated) in a manner that does not substantially affect the freshness quality of the samples, (3) the specific method used to evaluate the samples be conducted using scientifically sound procedures, as described in the appropriate chapter, (4) the specific method that is utilized be monitored to ensure that it is indeed accurately measuring that specific freshness quality, (5) the collected results be analyzed using statistically

145

sound procedures, and (6) when interpreting of the results all factors (other than the samples themselves) that may have seriously affected the observed results be very seriously considered. Following these principles will enhance the accuracy of the observed results and, thereby, enable the processor to ensure that the expectations of buyers and users are being met, thus encouraging them to purchase the product again.

Glossary

Absolute threshold   *See* detection threshold.[64]

Acceptance   "The act of a given individual or population of finding that a product answers satisfactorily to his/her/its expectations."[272]

Accuracy   "The extent to which the results of a calculation or the readings of an instrument approach the true values of the calculated or measured quantities, and are free from error."[341]

Adenosine triphosphate (ATP)   "Compound which, in living tissue, is involved in the transfer of energy (movement of muscle); breaks down after death to compounds such as inosine monophosphate, inosine, and hypoxanthine."[52]

Adhesiveness   "Mechanical textural attribute relating to the force required to remove material that adheres to the mouth or to a substrate. The terms sticky, tacky, and gooey/gluey represent low, moderate, and high levels of adhesiveness, respectively."[272]

Affective sensory tests   "Sensory tests used to assess the personal response (preference and/or acceptance) by current or potential customers."[64]

Aftertaste   "The experience that, under certain conditions, follows the removal of the taste stimulus."[47] "During flavor profiling, panelists note and record aftertastes at a predetermined time after completion of tasting."[323]

Algae   "Chlorophyll-bearing plants that are primarily aquatic; subclassified as green, blue-green, red, and brown.[342]

Amplitude   "Is a measure of the degree to which all aspects of an aroma or flavor are blended together to form a whole."[323] When involved in the flavor-profile method, panelists have to rate amplitude before they assess each character note.[323] "In the flavor-profile method, a combination of qualitative and quantitative evaluation of a product; overall judgment."[47]

Appearance "All visible attributes of a substance or object."[272] This includes size, shape, color, and conformation."[47]

Aroma "The fragrance or odor of food, perceived by the nose by sniffing."[47]

Assessment "A judgment or an evaluation."[47]

Bacteria "Microscopic unicellular organisms that do not contain chlorophyll and which multiply rapidly by simple fission; largely responsible for the later stages of fish (seafood) spoilage and for food poisoning."[52]

Balanced manner During presentation of samples, "each of the possible combinations is presented an equal number of times."[64]

Balanced sensory scales "Sensory scales that have an equal number of positive and negative categories and have steps of equal size."[64]

Belly burn "Damage to belly wall, especially in pelagic fish, through digestion by gut enzymes, making the weakened belly susceptible to abrasion, and resulting eventually in a *burst belly*."[52]

Biogenic amines Amines formed by the microbial decarboxylation of amino acids or other biogenic amines. Agmatine, cadaverine, histamine, phenethylamine, putrescine, tryptamine, and tyramine are formed from the amino acids arginine, lysine, histidine, phenylalanine, arginine, tryptophan, and tyrosine, respectively. Spermidine and spermine are formed from the biogenic amines putrescine and spermidine, respectively. Agmatine, cadaverine, histamine, putrescine, spermidine, and spermine are diamines, whereas phenethylamine, tryptamine, and tyramine are monoamines.

Biosensor "A device or system that uses an immobilized biological material to detect and measure a chemical compound."[343]

Bruising "Physically damaging a fish soon after capture by the striking of a blow that causes contusion and the formation of a *bruise* or *blood mark*."[52]

Burst belly "Belly wall, especially of pelagic fish, ruptured by severe belly burn."[52]

Category scale See "ordinal scale"[303] for complete definition. It may also be called a "structured scale."[280]

Character notes "Individual components of aroma and flavor."[323] "In the Flavor Profile Method, each product category has an associated glossary of terms with which all panelists are familiar."[323]

Chewiness "Mechanical textural attribute related to cohesiveness and to the length of time or number of chews required to masticate a solid food into a state ready for swallowing. The terms tender, chewy, and tough represent low, moderate, and high levels of chewiness, respectively."[272]

Clot (also called blood clot) "Defect in the form of a semisolid lump of coagulated blood."[52]

Cohesiveness   "A mechanical textural attribute relating to the degree to which a substance can be deformed before it breaks. It includes the properties of fracturability, chewiness, and gumminess."[272]

Color   "(1) Sensation induced by the stimulation of the retina by light rays of various wavelenghts. (2) Attribute of products inducing the color sensation."[272]

Compression   "Reduction in the volume of a substance due to pressure."[341]

Confounded   "Of or related to the sources of an experiment that is not designed so that the effect of two or more competing sources of variation in the results can be distinguished."[343]

Contamination   "Direct or indirect transmission of harmful or objectionable matter to food, especially during handling and processing."[52]

Convenience   "Ease, simplicity of use."[2]

Crustaceans   "Members of the phylum Arthropoda, which also includes insects, spiders, centipedes, and millipedes. Among the 26,000 known species of crustaceans are some of the most popular and valuable seafood products: crabs, shrimp, and lobsters."[344]

Decomposed   "Fish that has an offensive or objectionable odor, flavor, color, texture, or substance associated with spoilage."[55]

Descriptive sensory analysis   "A sensory methodology that provides quantative descriptions of products, based on the perceptions of a group of qualified subjects. It is a total sensory description, taking into account all sensations that are perceived when the product is evaluated."[303]

Detection threshold   "Minimum value of a sensory stimulus needed to give rise to a sensation."[272] "The sensation need not be identified."[272]

Difference threshold   "The extent of change in the stimulus necessary to produce a noticeable difference."[64] "Value of the smallest perceptible difference in the physical intensity of a stimulus."[272]

Discriminative sensory tests   "These tests are used to measure the perception of difference between two or more objects in respect to certain characteristics."[47]

Enzyme sensor   This sensor is a biosensor comprised, specifically, of an enzyme rather another type of biologically sensitive material, such an antibody, membrane component organelle bacteria, whole slices of tissue.[345]

Expectation   "The result of assessors obtaining information about the samples being evaluated, causing them to have expectations concerning the results."[64,303]

Expert assessor   "Selected assessor with a high degree of sensory sensitivity and experience of sensory methodology, who is able to make consistent and repeatable sensory assessments of various products."[272]

Fibrous   "Stringy textural property."[47]

Fibrousness   "The perceived degree (number × size) of fibers evident during mastication."[206]

Flaky   "Textural property consisting of loose layers that separate easily"[47] (e.g., "the perceived degree of separation of the sample into individual flakes when manipulated with the tongue against the palate"[330]).

Flavor   "A mingled but unitary experience which includes sensations of taste, smell, pressure, and other cutaneous sensations such as warmth, cold, mild pain."[47]

Flavor profile   "The description of the flavor and aroma of a food product. The description names the perceptible factors, the intensity of each, the order in which the factors are perceived, the aftertaste, and the overall impression."[67]

Fractureability   "Mechanical textural attribute related to cohesiveness and to the force necessary to break a product into crumbs or pieces."[272]

Freshness quality   The degree of excellence to which a seafood meets the characteristics concerning appearance, flavor, odor, and/or texture that the buyer, user, and regulatory agency normally associates with a particular seafood product/species when that particular seafood product species is (1) caught at the best time of year, (2) caught in the best location, (3) caught by the best method, and (4) handled, processed, prepared, and served in the best manner. Defined in Chapter 1 of this book.

Fungi   "A group of plants which contain no chlorophyll."[342]

Gaping   "Having gaps between flakes of muscle that spoil the appearance of a fillet or split fish."[52]

Grading   "Sorting into defined categories of quality, such as freshness quality."[52]

Groundfish   "Those species that feed on the bottom, referred to as demersal organisms, because they live close to the bottom of a body of water that is limited by the contental shelf."[346]

Gumminess   "Mechanical textural attribute related to the cohesiveness of a tender product. In the mouth it is related to the effort required to disintegrate the product to the state ready for swallowing."[272]

Hardness   "Mechanical textural attribute related to the force required to achieve a given deformation or penetration of a product. The terms soft, firm, and hard represent low, moderate, and high levels of hardness, respectively."[272]

Hazard   "An organism, substance, or condition having the potential to cause disease."[6]

Hue   "That attribute of color which corresponds to variation in wavelegths."[272]

Integrity   "The product is what the supplier claims it is in terms of net weight, count, species, ingredients, origin, etc."[30] Integrity also includes consistency of the product: is the quality of the product similar to what it was the previous time(s) it was purchased or consumed?

Intensity   "The magnitude of the perceived sensation"[272] or "The magnitude of the stimulus causing the perceived sensation."[272]

Interval data   See interval scale.

Interval scale   "A scale where numbers are chosen in such a way that equal numerical intervals are assumed to correspond to equal differences in sensory perception."[272] A line scale (also called a graphic scale) is a type of interval scale used during sensory evaluation.[303] This type of scale may also be called an unstructured scale.[280]

Intrinsic quality "Quality as reflected by composition, physiological condition, and other attributes at time of capture; dependent largely on age, size, maturity, season, nutrition, disease, and pollution."[52]

Kamaboko "All products made from surimi are generally called kamaboko, but strictly speaking, kamaboko are those mounted on a wood plate and steamed and/or broiled."[225]

Magnitude estimation "Process of assigning values to the intensities of an attribute in such a way that the ratio of the value assigned and the assessor's perception are the same."[272] A ratio scale is used, by the panelists, to estimate the magnitude of an attribute.

Mean "It is commonly called an average."[296]

Median "The middle number of a set of numbers arranged in order."[296]

Microorganism "This term includes bacteria, viruses, fungi, algae, protozoans, and yeasts."[52] Also called microscopic organism.

Minced fish "Mechanically separated flesh that has not been washed and does not have a good freeze storability."[225]

Mode "The most frequently occurring value."[296]

Moistness "The perceived degree of oil and/or water in the sample during chewing."[330]

Mollusks "The mollusks fishery is based primarily on the harvest of bi-valves (two-shelled mollusks) such as clams or oysters, but gastropods such as abalone or conchs, and cephalopods such as squid or octopus are also harvested."[347]

Neutral "Describes a product without any distinct characteristic."[272]

Neutral color "Describes a color without any distinct characteristic"[272] (e.g., white, cream, and gray).

Nominal data *See* nomial scale.

Nominal scale "The items examined are placed in two or more groups which differ in name but do not obey any particular order nor any quantitative relationship; example, the numbers carried by football players."[64]

Nutrients "Those elements and substances the body requires to function and cannot make itself."[24]

Nutrition "The partnership between your body and its diet, with each helping the other."[24]

Nutritional quality "Total contribution that a food can make, in measurable terms, to the nutritive requirements of the consumer."[52] Also called nutritive value.

Objective method "Any method in which the effects of personal opinions are minimized."[272]

Odor "That which is smelled."[47] "Odor may refer to the stimulus or to the sensation resulting from the stimulation of olfactory receptors in the nasal cavity."[47]

Oily "The perceived degree of oil left on the teeth, mouthcoating tongue, and palate after swallowing."[206]

Opaque "Describes an object not allowing the passage of light."[272]

Ordinal data *See* ordinal scale.

Ordinal scale "Scale where points are arranged according to a pre-established or continuous progression."[272] "Panelists place the items examined into two or more groups which belong to an ordered series; example: slight, moderate, strong."[64] It may also be called a category scale and/or a structured scale.[280]

Parasite "Organism that lives in or on another and derives nutriment from it: fish infested by parasites may be of poor appearance or eating quality, may be more difficult to process, and occasionally more harmful to eat."[52]

Pathogen "An organism (especially a microorganism) capable of causing disease or injury to health, especially of man."[52]

Pelagic fish "Generally means those species adapted to living not far from the ocean surface. The pelagic fish of commercial interest may be found from top surface water to depths as great as 200 m, or more."[184]

Peritoneum "Bellwall lining."[52]

Peroxide value "The quantity of those substances in the sample, expressed in terms of milli-equivalents of active oxygen per kilogram, which oxidize potassium iodide under defined conditions."[349]

Personal threshold "The concentration the observer can detect 50% of the time."[64]

Pest "In food processing, any animal, bird, or insect that can damage or contaminate the product; pests are also called vermin."[52]

Pesticides "This term refers to a group of chemicals which are designed to control or inhibit undesirable life forms (i.e., pests). Thus by definition these chemicals are toxic and therefore present health and environmental risks."[350]

Physiology "A branch of biology dealing with the functions of living organisms or their parts."[343]

Preference "Expression of the emotional state of reaction of an assessor which leads him/her to find one product better than one or several others."[272]

Probability "The likelihood of an event taking place."[342] (e.g., 10%).

Protozoan "Single cellular animal organisms that are often parasitic and can infest fish often causing softening and milkiness of the flesh, especially in hake, halibut, and swordfish."[52,342]

Psychology "The scientific study of mind and behavior."[343]

Quality The degree of excellence to which a product meets all of the attributes, characteristics, or features of the product that the buyer or user of the product desires, expects, or wants. Defined in Chapter 1 of this book. Also see Table 1.1 of Chapter 1.

Rancid "Smelling or tasting like stale fat or linseed oil, pungent, acrid, bitter."[52]

Rancidity "Of fish, the state of having a rancid odor and flavor, as a result of oxidation of unsaturated fat, or hydrolysis of fat."[52]

Randomized "The order in which the selected combinations appear was chosen according to the laws of chance."[64]

Range "The absolute difference between the largest and smallest value in the data."[296]

Ratio data *See* ratio scale.

Ratio scale "Scale where numbers are chosen in such a way that equal numerical ratios are assumed to correspond to equal sensory perception ratios."[272] A ratio scale is used during magnitude estimation.

Recognition threshold "Minimum value of a sensory stimulus permitting identification of the sensation perceived."[272]

Reference standard "Any chemical, spice, ingredient, or product which can be used to characterize or identify an attribute or attribute intensity found in whatever class of products is being evaluated by the trained panel."[272]

Resilience "The ability of a strained material to recover its size and shape, after being deformed."[343]

Risk "Probability that a person will become ill from a hazard."[6]

Safety "Probability that harm will not occur under specified conditions (the reciprocal of risk)."[6]

Scale "A graded arrangement, used in reporting assessments: it is divided into successive values, which may be graph, descriptive, or numerical."[315]

Scombroid poisoning "Seafood poisoning, rarely fatal, associated mainly with the consumption of tuna, mackerel, and related species. It is an allergic-type reaction, with symptoms of headache, dizziness, and nausea and it is associated with bacterial spoilage. The presence of plentiful amounts of histamine in spoiled fish of these species is often an indicator and may be related to the cause."[52]

Screening "Preliminary selection procedure."[272]

Selected assessor "Assessor chosen for his/her ability to carry out a sensory test."[272]

Selected panelist "A panelist chosen for his/her ability to perform a sensory test."[272]

Shellfish "Mollusks and crustaceans."[344,347]

Specialized expert assessor "Expert assessor who has additional experience as a specialist in the product and/or the process and/or marketing, who is able to perform sensory analysis of the product and to evaluate or predict effects of variations relating to raw materials, recipes, processing, storage, ageing, etc."[272]

Spoilage "Seafood spoilage is a change in seafood making it unsafe, less acceptable, or unacceptable to the consumer for its original purpose."[351]

Springiness "Mechanical textural attribute relating to (a) the rapid recovery from a deforming force, and (b) the degree to which a deformed material returns to its undeformed condition after the deforming force is removed. The terms plastic, malleable, and elastic/springy/rubbery represent low, moderate, and high levels of springiness, respectively."[272]

Standard *See* reference standard sample.

Structured scale Also referred to as a "category scale"[280] or as an "ordinal scale."[303]

Subjective "Any method in which the personal opinions are taken into consideration."[272]

Surimi "A Japanese term for mechanically deboned; fish flesh that has been washed with water and mixed with cryoprotectants for a good frozen storage life. It is used as an intermediate product for a variety of fabricated seafoods, such as crab legs and flakes."[225]

Taint "Undesirable odor or flavor picked up by a food from another or from its surroundings during storage."[52] "Undesirable odor or flavor transmitted to the flesh from the diet or the environment of a living animal or fish, for example, fishy pig or poultry meat, oil-polluted fish."[52]

Tainted fish "Fish that is rancid or has an abnormal odor or flavor."[55]

Tainting threshold "The concentration of the chemical in water that will, after exposure of an organism to the water, cause a change in the flavor of the organism that can be detected by 50% of a population of panelists."[40]

Terminal threshold "Minimum value of an intense sensory stimulus above which no difference in intensity can be perceived."[272]

Texture "All mechanical, geometrical, and surface attributes of a product perceptible by means of mechanical, tactile and where appropriate, visual and auditory receptors. The **mechanical attributes** (hardness, cohesiveness, viscosity, springiness, and adhesiveness) are those related to the reaction of the product to stress. The **geometrical attributes** are those related to the size, shape, and arrangements within a product. The **surface attributes** are those related to the sensations produced by moisture and/or fat content. In the mouth they are also related to the way in which these constituents are released."[272]

Texture profile "The description of the textural characteristics perceived in a food product, the intensity of each, and the order in which they are perceived. Mechanical characteristics are described qualitatively and quantitatively, and geometric characteristics are described qualitatively and semi-quantitatively."[67]

Thiobarbituric acid (TBA) value The intensity of a red pigment, caused by the reaction of lipid oxidation products with thiobarbituric (TBA) acid, "This intensity is proportional to the degree of oxidation."[349]

Total volatile basic nitrogen (TVB-N) "Amount of nitrogen in the volatile bases present in fish, being the usual way of expressing the value of total volatile bases as an index of spoilage, typically in mg TVB-N/100 g fish. Also called total basic nitrogen and total volatile nitrogen."[52]

Tough   High level of chewiness.[272]

Toxin   "Poisonous substance produced by a living organism."[52]

Translucent   "Describes an object allowing light to pass but which does not allow images to be distinguished."[272]

Transparent   "Describes an object allowing light to pass and distinct images to appear."[272]

Trimethylamine oxide (TMAO)   "Odorous chemical component of fish present in variable amounts in all marine species, but absent in almost all freshwater fish, which is broken down to trimethylamine during storage."[52]

Trimethylamine (TMA)   "A volatile base produced in marine fishes by the breakdown of trimethylamine oxide (TMAO) during spoilage, which produces an offensive odor. Measurement of the quantity of TMA present, usually by a method involving the formation of the picrate salt or by gas chromatography, can be used as a chemical test for spoilage."[52]

Unstructured scale   *See* interval scale.

Unwholesome   "Fish that has in or upon it bacteria of public health significance or substances toxic or aesthetically offensive to man."[55]

Virus   "A parasitic type of infectious agent composed of proteins and nucleic acids. They are not actual organisms, as they do not metabolize nutrients or utilize oxygen."[342]

Viscosity   "Mechanical textural attribute relating to resistance to flow. It corresponds to the force required to draw a liquid from a spoon over the tongue, or to spread it over a substrate. The terms fluid, thin, and viscous represent low, moderate, and high levels of viscosity, respectively."[272]

Volatile bases   "Volatile odorous compounds such as ammonia, the lower amines, and other related compounds that are produced in fish as a result of spoilage."[52]

Wholesome   "Uncontaminated and safe to eat; free from harmful or objectionable matter. The term does not normally relate to freshness."[52]

Yeasts   "In general terms yeasts can be described as microfungi that exist as single cells during some part of their life cycle. They are widely distributed in nature, are not motile, usually reproduce vegetatively by budding or fusion, and have no photosynthetic ability."[352]

References

1. McNutt K. Consumer attitudes and the quality control function. *Food Technol* 1988; 42(12):97–98, 103.

2. Freeman LK. The quest for quality. *Food Eng* 1990; 62(1):62–71.

3. Straus K. Seafood standards. In: Straus K, ed. *The Seafood Handbook: Seafood Standards*. Rockland, ME: Seafood Business Magazine, 1991: 7–17.

4. Ward DR, Hackney C. *Microbiology of Marine Food Products*. New York: AVI, Van Nostrand Reinhold, 1991: 450p.

5. Liston J. Microbial hazards of seafood consumption. *Food Technol* 1990; 44(12):56, 58–62.

6. Ahmed FE (ed). *Seafood Safety*. Washington, D.C.: National Academic Press, 1991: 432p.

7. Perkins C (ed). *The Advanced Seafood Handbook*. Rockland, ME: Seafood Business Magazine, 1992: 136p.

8. Huss HH. Development and use of the HACCP concept in fish processing. *Int J Food Microbiol* 1992; 15:33–44.

9. Huss HH. Microbiological quality assurance in the fish industry. *Infofish Int* 1989; 89/5:36–37.

10. White DRL, Noseworthy JEP. The Canadian quality management program. In: Huss HH, Jakobsen M, Liston J, eds. *Quality Assurance in the Fish Industry*. Amsterdam: Elsevier Science Publishing, 1992: 509–513.

11. McEachern V, McGuinness P. QMP in the Canadian fish processing industry. *INFOFISH Int* 1992; 4(92):58–62.

12. McMeekin TA, Ross T, Olley J. Application of predictive microbiology to assure the quality and safety of fish and fish products. *Int J Food Microbiol* 1992; 15:13–32.

13. Beard TD, III. HACCP and the home: The need for consumer education. *Food Technol* 1991; 45(6):123–124.

14. Siewicki TC, Balthrop JE. Marine toxins. In: Hui YH, ed. *Encyclopedia of Food Science and Technology*. New York: John Wiley, 1991: 1653–1657.

15. Huss HH. Development and use of the HACCP concept in fish processing. In: Huss HH, Jakobsen M, Liston J, eds. *Quality Assurance in the Fish Industry*. Amsterdam: Elsevier Science Publishing, 1992: 489–500.

16. Hudak-Roos M, Garrett ES. Monitoring, corrective action and record keeping in HACCP. In: Huss HH, Jakobsen M, Liston J, eds. *Quality Assurance in the Fish Industry*. Amsterdam: Elsevier Science Publishing, 1992: 521–531.

17. International Commission on Microbiological Specifications for Foods (ICMSF). *Application of the Hazard Analysis Critical Control Point (HACCP) System to Ensure Microbiological Safety and Quality*. London.: Blackwell Scientific Publications, 1988.

18. National Advisory Committee on Microbiological Criteria for Foods. Hazard analysis and critical control point system. *Int J Food Microbiol* 1992; 16:1–23.

19. Anonymous. Microbial and parasitic exposure and health effects. In: Ahmed FE, ed. *Seafood Safety*. Washington, D.C.: National Academy Press, 1991: 30–86.

20. Anonymous. Naturally occurring fish and shellfish poisons. In: Ahmed FE, ed. *Seafood Safety*. Washington, D.C.: National Academy Press, 1991: 87–110.

21. Hotchkiss JH, Pesticide residue controls to ensure food safety. *Crit Rev in Food Sci Nutr* 1992; 31(3):191–203.

22. Tricker AR. Nitrosamines. In: Hui YH, ed. *Encyclopedia of Food Science and Technology*. New York: John Wiley, 1991: 1871–1879.

23. Hui YH. Nutrition. In: Hui YH, ed. *Encyclopedia of Food Science and Technology*. New York: John Wiley, 1991: 1883–1887.

24. Nettleton JA. *Seafood Nutrition*. New York: Van Nostrand Reinhold (an Osprey Book), 1985: 280p.

25. Kinsella JE. Food components with potential therapeutic benefits: The n-3 polyunsaturated fatty acids of fish oils. *Food Technol* 1989; 40(2):89–97, 146.

26. Lands WEM. Fish and human health: A story unfolding. *World Aquaculture* 1989; 20(1):59–62

27. Piggot GM, Tucker BW. *Seafood: Effect of Technology on Nutrition*. New York: Marcel Dekker, 1990: 362p.

28. Krzynowek J. Effects of handling, processing and storage of fish and shellfish. In: Karmas E, Harris RS, eds. *Nutritional Evaluation of Food Processing*, 3rd ed. New York: Van Nostrand Reinhold, 1988: 245–265.

29. Pedraja RR. Role of quality assurance in the food industry: New concepts. *Food Technol* 1988; 42 (12):92–93.

30. Martin R. Contaminants in relation to quality of seafood. *Food Technol* 1988; 42(12):104, 108.

31. Lund D. QA is no dead end. *Food Eng* 1990; 62(10):66–67.

32. Jones TP. Marketing seafood: When the consumer talks we need to listen. *Seafood Business* 1992; 11(1):192–193.

33. Cannon-Bonventure K. Marketing seafood: You can still come out on top. *Seafood Business* 1992; 11(3):32–36.

34. Anonymous. Investigation into consumer perceptions and reactions to promotional tools with respect to fish. *Canada Market Res Report* 3677, 1991.

35. Tillotson JE. Too much looking back at the 60's. *Food Eng* 1990; 62(1) 64.

36. Connell JJ. *Control of Fish Quality*, 3rd ed. London: Fishing News Books, 1990: 227p.

37. Kramer D, Crapo C. Timing the harvest for top quality. *Pacific Fishing*, 1992; XIII(11):69.

38. Sorensen NK. Physical and instrumental methods for assessing seafood quality. In: Huss HH, Jakobsen M, Liston J, eds. *Quality Assurance in the Fish Industry*. Amsterdam: Elsevier Science Publishers, 1992: 321–332.

39. Sakaguchi M, Koike A. Freshness assessment of fish fillets using the Torrymeter and K-values. In: Huss HH, Jakobsen M, Liston J, eds. *Quality Assurance in the Fish Industry*. Amsterdam: Elsevier Science Publishers, 1992: 333–338.

40. Howgate PF. Quality assessment and quality control. In: Aitken A, Mackie M, Merritt JH, Windsor ML, eds. *Fish Handling and Processing*. Edinburgh: Her Majesty's Stationery Office, 1982: 177–186.

41. Piggott GM. Fish and shellfish products. In: Hui YH, ed. *Encyclopedia of Food Science and Technology*. New York: John Wiley, 1991: 882–907.

42. Nettleton JA. Seafood nutrition in the 1990's: Issues for the consumer, In: Bligh EG, ed. *Seafood Science and Technology*. London: Fishing News Books, 1992: 32–39.

43. Holub BJ. Potential benefits of the omega-3 fatty acids in fish. In: Bligh EG, ed. *Seafood Science and Technology*. London: Fishing News Books, 1992: 40–45.

44. Mermelstein NH. A new era in food labelling. *Food Technol* 1993; 47(2):81–86,94, 96.

45. Wekell JC, Barnett HJ. Seafoods: Flavor and quality. In: Hui YH, ed. *Encyclopedia of Food Science and Technology*. New York: John Wiley, 1991: 2300–2323.

46. Alli I. Fundamental aspect of food quality assurance. *Can Inst Food Sci Technol J* 1988; 21(1): AT33–AT38.

47. Amerine MA, Pangborn RM, Roessler EB. *Principles of Sensory Evaluation of Food*. New York: Academic Press, 1965: 602p.

48. Crosby PB. *Quality Is Free*. New York: McGraw-Hill, 1979: 309p.

49. Fiskken D. Sensory quality and the consumer viewpoints and directions. *J Sensory Studies* 1990; 5:203–209.

50. Gavin DA. Competing on the eight dimensions of quality. *Harvard Business Rev* 1987; 65(6):101–109.

51. Gould WA. *Food Quality Assurance*. Westport, CT: AVI, 1977: 314p.

52. Waterman JJ. *Composition and Quality of Fish: A Dictionary*. U.K. Ministry of Agriculture, Fisheries and Food, Torry Research Station, Torrey Advisory Note No. 87. Edinburgh: Her Majesty's Stationery Office, 1982: 28p.

53. Dore I. *Fish and Shellfish Quality Assessment*. New York: Van Nostrand Reinhold, 1991: 112p.

54. Gould E, Peters JA. *On Testing the Freshness of Frozen Fish*. London: Fishing News (Books) Ltd., 1971: 80p.

55. Canada Department of Fisheries and Oceans. *Fish Inspection Regulations amended February 25, 1992*. Ottawa, Canada: Government of Canada, 1992: 45p.

56. Karmas E. Biogenic amines as indicators of seafood freshness. *Lebensmittel-Wissenschraft Technol* 1981; 14:273–275.

57. Regenstein JM, Regenstein CE. *Introduction to Fish Technology*. New York: Van Nostrand Reinhold (an Osprey Book) 1991: 269p.

58. Wheaton FW, Lawson TB. *Processing Aquatic Food Products*. New York: John Wiley, 1985: 225.

59. Eber W. A chemical measure for putrefaction, *Zeit Fleish Milchhygiene* 1891; 1:118.

60. Gill TA. Objective analysis of seafood quality. *Food Rev Int* 1990; 6(4):681–714.

61. Gill TA. Biochemical and chemical indices of seafood quality. In: Huss HH, Jakobsen M, Liston J, eds, *Quality Assurance in the Fish Industry*. Amsterdam: Elsevier Science Publishers, 1992: 377–388.

62. Gill TA, Thompson TW, Gould S, Sherwood D. Characterization of quality deterioration in yellowfin tuna. *J Food Sci* 1987; 52:580–583.

63. Connell JJ, Howgate PF, Fish and fish products. In: Herschdoerfer SM, ed. *Quality Control in the Food Industry*, Vol 2. London: Academic Press, 1986: 347–405.

64. Meilgaard M, Civille GV, Carr BT. *Sensory Evaluation Techniques*. Boca Raton, FL.: CRC Press, 1991: 354p.

65. Jellinek G. *Sensory Evaluation of Food: Theory and Practice*. Chichester, U.K.: Ellis Horwood Ltd., 1993: 429p.

66. Sensory Evaluation Division of the Institute of Food Technologists. Sensory evaluation guide for testing food and beverage products. *Food Technol* 1981; 35(11):50–59.

67. Larmond E. Sensory evaluation can be objective. In: Kapsalis JK, ed. *Objective Methods in Food Quality Assessment*. Boca Raton, FL: CRC Press, 1986: 3–14.

68. Pangborn RM. The evolution of sensory science and its interaction with IFT. *Food Technol* 1989; 43(9):248–250, 252, 254, 256, 307.

69. Trant AS, Pangborn RM, Little, AC. Potential fallacy of correlating hedonic responses with physical and chemical measurements. *J Food Sci* 1981; 46:583–588.

70. Powers JJ. Sensory science: sSandardization and instrumentation. In: Hui YH, ed. *Encyclopedia of Food Science and Technology*. New York: John Wiley, 1991: 2354–2370.

71. Piggott JR. Relating sensory and chemical data to understand flavor. *J Sensory Studies* 1990; 4:261–271.

72. Yantis, JE, ed. *The Role of Sensory Analysis in Quality Control*. Philadelphia: American Society of Testing and Materials (ASTM), 1992; ASTM Manual Series: MNL 14:51p.

73. Antonacopoulos N, Vyncke W. Determination of volatile basic nitrogen in fish: A third collaborative study by the Western European Fish Technologists' Association (WEFTA). *Z Lebensm Unters Forsch* 1989; 189:309–316.

74. Botta JR, Lauder JT, Jewer MA. Effect of methodology on total volatile basic nitrogen (TVB-N) determination as an index of quality of fresh Atlantic cod (*Gadus morhua*). *J Food Sci* 1984; 49:734–736, 750.

75. Perez-Villarreal B, Howgate P. Spoilage of european hake (Merluccius merluccius) in ice. *J Sci Food Agric* 1987; 41:335–350.

76. Aitken A. TVB—a quality index? *INFOFISH Int* 1988; 3(88):43.

77. Vyncke W, Luten J, Brunner K, Moermans R. Determination of total volatile bases in fish: A collaborative study by the Western European Fish Technologist's Association (WEFTA). *Z Lebensm Unters Forch* 1987; 184:110–114.

78. Storey RM, Davis, HK, Owen D, Moore L. Rapid approximate estimation of volitle amines in fish. *J Food Technol* 1984; 19:1–10.

79. Hebard CE, Flick GJ, Martin RE. Occurrence and significance of trimethylamine oxide and its derivatves in fish and shellfish. In: Martin RE, Flick GJ, Ward DR, eds. *Chemistry and Biochemistry of Marine Food Products*. Westport, CT: AVI, 1982: 149–304.

80. Pedrosa-Menabrito A, Regenstein JM, Shelf-life extension of fresh fish—A review. Part III—Fish quality and methods of assessment. *J Food Quality* 1990; 13:209–223.

81. Oehlenschlager J. Evaluation of some well established and some underrated indices for the determination of freshness and/or spoilage of ice stored wet fish. In: Huss HH, Jakobsen M, Liston J, eds. *Quality Assurance in the Fish Industry*. Amsterdam: Elsevier Science Publishers, 1992: 339–350.

82. Martin RE, Gray RJH, Pierson MD. Quality asssessment of fresh fish and the role of the naturally occurring microflora. *Food Technol* 1978; 32(5):188–192.

83. Laycock RA, Regier L. Trimethylamine-producing bacteria on haddock (*Melanogrammus aeglefinus*) fillets during refrigerated storage. *J Fish Res Board Can* 1971; 28:305–309.

84. Castell CH, Neal WE, Dale J, Comparison of changes in trimethylamine, dimethylamine, and extractable protein in iced and frozen gadoid fillets. *J Fish Res Board Can* 1973; 30:1246–1248.

85. Gill TA, Paulson AT. Localization, characterization and partial purification of TMAO-ase, *Comp Biochem Physiol* 1982; 71B:49–56.

86. Tokunaga T. Trimethylamine oxide and its decomposition in the bloody muscle of fish-II: Formation of DMA and TMA during storage. *Bull Jpn Soc Sci Fish* 1970; 36:510–515.

87. Castell CH, Smith B, Dyer WJ. Simultaneous measurements of trimethylamine and dimethylamine in fish, and their use for estimating quality of frozen-stored gadoid fillets. *J Fish Res Board Can* 1974; 31:383–389.

88. Lundstrom RC, Raciot LD. Gas chromatographic determination of dimethylamine and trimethylamine in seafoods. *J Assoc Off Anal Chem* 1983; 66:1158–1163.

89. Gill TA, Thompson JW. Rapid, automated analysis of amines in seafood by ion-moderated partition HPLC. *J Food Sci* 1984; 49:603–606.

90. Branch AC, Vail AMA, Bring fish inspection into the computer age. *Food Technol Aust* 1985; 37(8):352–355.

91. Wong K, Barlett F, Gill TA. A diagnostic strip for the semiquantitative determination of trimethylamine in fish. *J Food Sci* 1988; 53:1653–1655.

92. Krzymien ME, Elias L. Feasibility study on the determination of fish freshness by trimethyamine headspace analysis. *J Food Sci* 1990; 55:1228–1232.

93. Krzymien M, Elias L, Sim PG. Development of an instrumental approach to assessing fish freshness by headspace analysis for trimethylamine. In: Bligh EG, ed. *Seafood Science and Technology*. London: Fishing News Books, 1992: 216–224.

94. Kennish JM, Kramer DE. A review of high-pressure liquid chromatographic methods for measuring nucleotide degradation in fish muscle. In: Kramer DE, Liston J, eds. *Seafood Quality Determination*. Amsterdam: Elsevier Science Publishers, 1987: 209–219.

95. Hiltz DF, Dyer WJ, Nowlan S, Dingle JR, Hollingworth TA, Jr, Throm HR. Correlation of ethanol concentration with sensory classification of decomposition in canned salmon. *J Food Sci* 1982; 47:1315–1317.

96. Jones NR. Hypoxanthine and other purine-containing fractions in fish muscle as indices of freshness. In: Kreuzer R, ed. *The Technology of Fish Utilization*. London: Fishing News (Books) Ltd., 1965: 179–183.

97 Chiba A, Hamaguchi M, Kosaka M, Tokuno T, Asai T, Chichibu S. Quality evaluation of fish meat by [31]phosphorus-nuclear magnetic resonance. *J Food Sci* 1991; 56:660–664.

98. Surette M, Gill TA, LeBlanc PJ. Biochemical basis of postmortem nucleotide catabolism in cod (*Gadus morhua*) and its relationship to spoilage. *J Agric Food Chem* 1988; 36:19–22.

99. Ehira S, Uchiyama H. Determination of fish freshness using the K value and comments on some other biochemical changes in relation to freshness. In: Kramer DE, Liston J, eds. *Seafood Quality Determination.* Amsterdam: Elsevier Science Publishers, 1987: 185–207.

100. Jacober LF, Rand AGJ. Biochemical evaluation of seafood. In: Martin RE, Flick GJ, Hebard CE, Ward DR, eds. *Chemistry and Biochemistry of Marine Food Products.* Westport, CT: AVI, 1982: 347–366.

101. Huss HH. *Fresh Fish: Quality and Quality Changes.* Rome: Food and Agriculture Organization (FAO) of the United Nations, 1988: 132p.

102. Murata M, Sakaguchi M. Storage of yellowtail (*Seriola quinqueradiata*) white and dark muscles in ice: Changes in content of adenine nucleotides and related compounds, *J Food Sci* 1986; 51:321–326.

103. Watabe S, Kamal M, Hashimoto K. Postmortem changes in ATP, creatine phosphate and latate in sardine muscle. *J Food Sci* 1991; 56:151–153.

104. Perez-Villarreal B, Pozo R. Chemical composition and ice spoilage of albacore (*Thunnus alalunga*). *J Food Sci* 1990; 55:678–682.

105. Price RJ, Melvin EF, Bell JW. Postmortem changes in chilled round, bled and dressed albacore, *J Food Sci* 1991; 56:318–321.

106. Smith G, Hole M, Hanson SW. Assessment of lipid oxidation in Indonesian salted-dried marine catfish (*Arius thalassinus*). *J Sci Food Agric* 1990; 51:193–205.

107. Fletcher GC, Scott DN, Seelye RJ, Summers G, Hogg-Stec MG. Retail shelf-life of fillets from fresh orange roughy. *New Zealand Department of Scientific and Industrial Research, Fish Processing Bulletin,* 1988; 10:32p.

108. Fatima R, Farooqui B, Qadri RB. Inosine monophosphate and hypoxanthine as indices of quality of shrimp (*Penaeus merguensis*). *J Food Sci* 1981; 46:1125–1131.

109. Karube I, Matsuoka H, Sufzuki S, Watanabe E, Toyama K. Determination of fish freshness with an enzyme sensor system. *J Agric Food Chem* 1984; 32:314–319.

110. Luong JHT, Male KB, Masson C, Nguyen AL. Hypoxanthine ratio determination in fish extract using capillary electrophoresis and immobilized enzymes. *J Food Sci* 1992; 57:77–81.

111. Burns GB, Ke PJ, Irvine BB. Objective procedure for fish freshness evaluation based on nucleotide changes using a HPLC system. *Canadian Technical Report of Fisheries and Aquatic Science* 1985; 1373: 35p.

112. Saito T, Arai K, Mutsuyoshi M. A new method for estimating the freshness of fish. *Bull Jpn Soc Sci Fish* 1959; 24:749–750.

113. Brenner HA. A convenient easy-to-use system for estimating the quality of chilled seafoods. *Fish Processing Bull* 1985; 7:59–70.

114. Greene DH, Bernatt-Byrne EI. Adenosine triphosphate catabolites as flavor compounds and freshness indicators in Pacific cod (*Gadus macrocephalus*) and pollock (*Theragra chalcogamma*). *J Food Sci* 1990; 55:257–258.

115. Luong JHT, Male KB, Huynh MD. Applications of polarography for assessment of fish freshness. *J Food Sci* 1991; 56:335–340.

116. Straus K. Seafood standards. In: Straus K, ed. *The Seafood Handbook: Seafood Standards.* Rockland, ME: Seafood Business Magazine, 1991: 7–17.

117. Greene DH, Babbitt JK, Reppond KD. Patterns of nucleotide catabolism as freshness indicators in flat fish from the Gulf of Alaska. *J Food Sci* 1990; 55:1236–1238.

118. Burns BG, Ke PJ. Liquid chromatographic determination of hypoxanthine content in fish muscle. *J Assoc Off Anal Chem* 1985; 68(3):444–448.

119. Ryder JM. Determination of adenosine triphosphate and its breakdown products in fish muscle by high performance liquid chromatography. *J Agric Food Chem* 1985; 33:678–680.

120. Mcdowell RD. Laboratory automation and laboratory management systems. In: Kiceniuk JW, Ray S, eds., *Analysis of Contaminants in Edible Aquatic Resources*, Vol I. New York: VCH, 1994: 59–90.

121. Jahns FD, Howe JL, Coduri RJ, Jr, Rand AG, Jr. A rapid visual enzyme test to assess fish freshness. *Food Technol* 1976; 30(7):27–30.

122. Negishi S, Karube I. An enzymatic assay method for IMP determination and an application of the principle to a test parer method. *Nippon Suisan Gakkaishi* 1989; 55 (11):1591–1597.

123. Lowe CR. An introduction to the concepts and technology of biosensors. *Biosensors* 1985; 1:3–16.

124. Kim JM, Suzuki M, Schnid RD. A novel amplified enzyme assay method for hypoxanthine. *Biocatalysis* 1990; 3:269–275.

125. Morin JF. Determination of K value by biosensor. In: Voigt MN, Botta JR, eds. *Advances in Fisheries Technology and Biotechnology for Increased Profitability*. Lancaster, PA: Technomic Publishing Co., 1990: 481–485.

126. Mulchandani A, Luong JHT, Male KB. Development and application of a biosensor for hypoxanthine in fish extracts. *Anal Chim Acta* 1989; 221:215–222.

127. Mulchandani A, Maassayle KB, Luong JHT. Development of a biosensor for assaying postmortem nucleotide degradation in fish tissues. *Biotechnol Bioeng* 1990; 35:739.

128. Suzuki M, Suzuki H, Karube I, Schmid D. A disposable hypoxanthine sensor based on a micro oxygen electrode. *Anal Lett* 1989; 22(15):2915–2927.

129. Watanabe E, Toyama K, Karube I, Matsuoka H, Suzuki S, Enzyme sensor for hypoxanthine and inosine determination in edible fish. *Appl Microbiol Biotechnol* 1984; 19:18–22.

130. Watanabe E, Toyama K, Karube I, Mutsuoka H, Suzuki S. Determination of inosine-5-monophosphate in fish tissue with an enzyme sensor. *J Food Sci* 1984; 49:114–116.

131. Nguyen A, Luong JHT, Masson C. Determination of nucleotides in fish tissue using capillary electropheresis, *Anal Chem* 1990; 62:2490–2493.

132. Finne G. Enzymatic ammonia production in penaied shrimp held on ice. In: Martin RE, Flick GJ, Ward DR, eds. *Chemistry and Biochemistry of Marine Food Products*. Westport, CT: AVI, 1982: 323–331.

133. Halland H, Njaa LR. Ammonia (NH_3) and total volatile nitrogen in preserved and unpreserved stored whole fish. *J Sci Food Agric* 1988; 44:335–342.

134. Meitz JL, Karmas E. Polyamine and histamine content of rockfish, salmon, lobster, and shrimp as an indicator of decomposition. *J Assoc Off Anal Chem* 1978; 61(1):139–145.

135. Vyncke W. Determination of the ammonia content of fish as an objective quality assessment method. *Mededelingen Van De Faculteit Landbouwwetenschappen, Rijksuniversiteit Gent* 1970; 35:1033–1046.

136. Vyncke W. An accelerated microdiffusion method for the determination of ammonia in cartilaginous fish. *Fish News Int* 1968; 7(7):49–51.

137. Farn G, Sims GG. Chemical indices of decomposition in tuna. In: Kramer DE, Liston J, eds. *Seafood Quality Determination*. Amsterdam: Elsevier Science Publishers, 1987: 175–184.

138. Yamanaka H, Shiomi K, Kikuchi T. Agmatine as a potential index for freshness of common squid (*Todarodes pacificus*). *J Food Sci* 1988; 52:936–938.

139. Yamanaka H, Shimakura K, Shiomi K, Kikuchi T. Changes in nonvolatile amine contents of meats of sardine and saury pike, during storage. *Bull Jpn Soc Sci Fish* 1986; 52:127.

140. Sims GG, Farn G, York RK. Quality indices for canned skipjack tuna: Correlation of sensory attributes with chemical indices. *J Food Sci* 1992; 57:1112–1115.

141. Madere R, Behrens WA. Malonaldehyde determination in foods by ion-pairing high-performance liquid chromatography. *Food Res Int* 1992; 25:37–40.

142. Yen GC, Hsieh CL. Simultaneous analysis of biogenic amines in canned fish by HPLC. *J Food Sci* 1991; 56:158–160.

143. Noggle FT, Jr. Enhanced detectability and chromatography of some amines by high pressure liquid chromatography. *J Assoc Off Anal Chem* 1980; 63(4):702–706.

144. Hollingworth TA, Jr, Throm HR. Correlation of ethanol concentration with sensory classification of decomposition in canned salmon. *J Food Sci* 1982; 47:1315–1317.

145. Iida H, Tokubnaga T, Nakamura K. Usefulness of ethanol as a quality index of fish and fish products–I: The relationship between the sensory judgment of canned albacore and its ethanol content. *Bull Tokai Reg Fish Res Lab* 1981; 104:77–82.

146. Kelleher SD, Zall RR. Ethanol accumulation in muscle tissue as a chemical indicator of fish spoilage. *J Food Biochem* 1983; 7:87–92.

147. Iida H, Tokunaga T, Nakamura K, Ota Y. Usefulness of ethanol as a quality index of fish and fish products—II: Changes of ethanol contents in raw fish during storage. *Bull Tokai Reg Fish Res Lab* 1981; 104:83–90.

148. Hollingworth TA, Jr., Throm HR. A headspace gas chromatographic method for the rapid analysis of ethanol in canned salmon. *J Food Sci* 1983; 48:290–291.

149. Hollingworth TA, Jr., Throm HR, Wekell ME, Trager WF, O'Donnell MW, Jr. Headspace chromatographic method for determination of ethanol in canned salmon: Collaborative study. *J Assoc Off Anal Chem* 1986; 69(3):524–526.

150. Chang O, Cheuk WL, Nickelson R, Martin R, Finne G. Indole in shrimp: Effect of fresh storage temperature, freezing and boiling. *J Food Sci* 1983; 48:813–816.

151. Chambers TL. Modification of AOAC gas-liquid chromatographic method for indole in shrimp: Collaborative study. *J Assoc Off Anal Chem* 1982; 65:842–845.

152. Matches JR. Effects of temperature on the decomposition of Pacific coast shrimp (*Pandalus jordani*). *J Food Sci* 1982; 47:1044–1047, 1069.

153. Shamshad SI, Kher-Un-Nisa, Riaz M, Suberi R, Qadri RB. Shelf life of shrimp (*Penaeus merguiensis*) stored at different temperatures. *J Food Sci* 1990; 55:1201–1205, 1242.

154. Chambers TL, Staruszkiewicz WFJ, High pressure liquid chromatographic method for indole in shrimp: Development of method and collaborative study. *J Assoc Off Anal Chem* 1981; 64:592–602.

155. Chambers TL, Staruszkiewicz WF, Jr. Ultraviolet detection procedure for liquid chromatographic determination of indole in shrimp. *J Assoc Off Anal Chem* 1981; 64:603–606.

156. Cheuk W, Finne, G. Modified colorimetric method for determining indole in shrimp. *J Assoc Off Anal Chem* 1981; 64: 783–785.

157. Gutterridge JMC. Aspects to consider when detecting and measuring lipid peroxidation, *Free Rad Res Comm* 1986; 1(3):173–184.

158. Khayat A, Schwall D. Lipid oxidation in seafood. *Food Technol* 1983; 37(7):130–140.

159. Hoyland DV, Taylor AJ. A review of the methodology of the 2-thiobarbituric acid test. *Food Chem* 1991; 40:271–291.

160. Ladikos D, Lougovois V. Lipid oxidation in muscle foods: A review. *Food Chem* 1990; 35:295–314.

161. Melton S. Methodology for following lipid oxidation in muscle foods. *Food Technol* 1983; 37(7):105–111, 116.

162. Pearson AM, Gray JI, Wolzak AM, Horenstein NA. Safety implications of oxidized lipids in muscle foods. *Food Technol* 1983; 37(7):121–129.

163. Rossell JB. Measurement of rancidity. In: Allen JC, Hamilton RJ, eds. *Rancidity in Foods*. New York: Elsevier Science Publishers, 1989: 23–52.

164. Aubourg SP. Review: Interaction of malondialdehyde with biological molluscs—new trends about reactivity and significance. *Int J Food Sci Technol* 1993; 28:313–335.

165. Kolakowska A, Deutry J. Some comments on the usefulness of 2-thiobarbituric acid (TBA) test for evaluation of rancidity in frozen fish. *Nahrung* 1983; 27:513–518.

166. Coxon D. Measurement of lipid oxidation. *Food Sci Technol Today* 1987; 1:164–166.

167. Smith G, Hole M. Browning of salted sun-dried fish. *J Sci Food Agric* 1991; 55:291–301.

168. Maruf FW, Ledward DA, Neale RJ, Poulter RG. Chemical and nutritional quality of Indonesian dried-salted mackerel (*Rastrelliger kanagurta*). *Int J Food Sci Technol* 1990; 25:66–77.

169. Lubis Z, Buckle KA. Rancidity and lipid oxidation of dried salted sardines. *Int J Food Sci Technol* 1990; 25:295–303.

170. Hasegawa K, Endo Y, Fujimoto K. Oxidative deterioration in dried fish model systems assessed by solid sample fluorescence spectrophotometry. *J Food Sci* 1992; 57:1123–1126.

171. Erickson MC. Compositional parameters and their relationship to oxidative stability of channel catfish. *J Agric Food Chem* 1993; 41:1213–1218.

172. Freeman DW, Hearnberger JO. An instrumental method for determining rancidity in frozen catfish fillets. *J Aquatic Food Product Technol* 1993; 2(1):35–50.

173. Botta JR, Shaw DH. Chemical and sensory analysis of roughhead grenadier (*Macrourus berglax*) stored in ice. *J Food Sci* 1975; 40:1249–1252.

174. Ryder JM, Fletcher GC, Stec MG, Seelye RJ. Sensory, microbial and chemical changes in hoki stored in ice. *Int Food Sci Technol* 1993; 28:169–180.

175. Botta JR, Shaw DH. Chemical and sensory analyses of roundnose grenadier (*Coryphaenoides rupestris*) stored in ice. *J Food Sci* 1976; 41:1285–1288.

176. Spinelli J. Degradation of nucleotides in ice-stored halibut. *J Food Sci* 1967; 30:1063–1067.

177. Dingle J, Hines JA. Degradation of inosine 5′-monophosphate in the skeletal muscle of several North Atlantic fishes. *J Fish Res Board Can* 1971; 28:1125–1131.

178. Scott DN, Fletcher GC, Hogg MG, Ryder JM. Comparison of whole with headed and gutted orange roughy stored in ice: Sensory, microbiology and chemical assessment. *J Food Sci* 1986; 51:79–83.

179. Hattula T, Kiesvaara M. Patterns of adenosine tripolyphosphate catabolism as freshness indicators in fish species from the Baltic Sea. *J Sci Food Agric* 1992; 58:485–488.

180. Wong K, Gill TA. Enzymatic determination of trimethylamine and its relationship to fish quality. *J Food Sci* 1987; 52:1–3, 6.

181. Barile LE, Milla AD, Reilly A, Villadsen A. Spoilage patterns of mackerel (*Rastrelliger faughni Matsui*): 1. Delays in icing. *ASEAN Food J* 1985; 1(2):70–77.

182. Suwejta IK. Comparative study on freshness and ATP breakdown products in fish and marine invertebrates, *J Faculty Applied Biological Sci, Hiroshima University* 1990; 28(1–2):113–114.

183. Veciana-Nogues MT, Vidal-Carou MC, Marine-Font A. Histamine and tyramine during spoilage of anchovie (*Engraulis encrasicholus*): Relationships with other fish spoilage indicators. *J Food Sci* 1990; 55:1992–1995.

184. Kaylor JD, Learson RJ, Martin RE, Flick GJ. Pelagic fish. In: Martin RE, Flick GJ, eds. *The Seafood Industry*. New York: Van Nostrand Reinhold (an Osprey Book), 1990: 67–76.

185. Erickson MC. Ability of chemical measurements to differentiate oxidative stabilities of frozen minced muscle from farm-raised striped bass and hybrid striped bass. *Food Chem* 1993; 48:381–385.

186. Gallardo JM, Perez-Martin RI, Franco JM, Aubourg S, Sotelo CG. Changes in volatile bases and trimethylamine oxide during the canning of albacore (*Thunnus alalunga*). *Int J Food Sci Technol* 1990; 25:78–81.

187. Reilly A, Bernarte MA, Dangla E. Storage stability of brackishwater prawns during processing for export. *Food Technol Aust* 1984; 36(6):283–286.

188. Ogawa M, Meneses ACS, Perdigao NB, Kozima T. Influence of storage conditions and quality evaluation of discolored spiny lobster tails. *Bull Jpn Soc Sci Fish* 1983; 49:975–982.

189. Ohashi E, Okamoto M, Ozawa A, Fujita T. Characterization of common squid using several freshness indicators. *J Food Sci* 1991; 56:161–163, 174.

190. Licciardello JJ, Ravesi EM, Gerow SM, D'Entremont D. Storage characteristics of iced whole logigo squid. In: *Proceedings of the International Institute Refrigeration Conference on Storage lives of Chilled and Frozen Fish and Fish Food*. Aberdeen, Scotland: 1985: 249–257.

191. Fatima R, Qadri RB. Quality changes in lobster (*Panulirus polyphagus*) muscle during storage in ice. *J Agric Food Chem* 1985; 33:117–122.

192. Perez-Martin RI, Franco JM, Molist P, Gallardo JM. Gas chromatographic method for the determination of volitile amines in seafood. *Int J Food Sci Technol* 1987; 22:509–514.

193. Dyer WJ. Amines in fish muscle I. colormetric determination of trimethylamine as the picrate salt. *J Fish Res Board Can* 1945; 6:351–358.

194. Tozawa H, Enokihara K, Amano K. Proposed modification to Dyer's method for trimethylamine determinine in cod fish. In: Kreuzer R, ed. *Fish Inspection and Quality Control*. London: Fishing News (Books) Ltd., 1971: 187–190.

195. Dyer WJ, Mounsey YA. Amines in fish muscle II. Development of trimethylamine and other amines. *J Fish Res Board Can* 1945; 6:359–367.

196. Boeri RL, Amandos ME, Ciarlo AS, Giannini DH. Formaldehyde instead of dimethylamine determination as a measure of total formaldehyde formed in frozen Argenine hake (*Merluccius hubbsi*). *Int J Food Sci Technol* 1993; 28:289–292.

197. Castell CH, Smith B. Measurement of formaldehyde in fish muscle using TCA extraction and the Nash reagent. *J Fish Res Board Can* 1973; 30:91–98.

198. LeBlanc EL, Leblanc RJ, Irvin DM. Comparison of three methods of formaldehyde determination on frozen sole, pollock, haddock and cod fillets. *J Food Biochem* 1988; 12:79–95.

199. Watanabe E, Endo H, Takeuchi N, Hayashi T, Toyama K. Determination of fish freshness with a multielectrode enzyme sensor. *Bull Jpn Soc Sci Fish* 1986; 52:489–495.

200. Bligh EG, Dyer WJ. A rapid method of total lipid extraction and purification. *Can J Biochem Physiol* 1959; 37:911–917.

201. Association of Official Analytical Chemists (AOAC). *Official Methods of Analysis*. Arlington, VA: Association of Official Analytical Chemists, 1990: 1298p.

202. Young CT, Hovis ARA. A method for rapid analysis of headspace volatiles of raw and roasted peanuts. *J Food Sci* 1990; 55:279–280.

203. Pivarnik LF, Kazantzis D, Karakoltsidis PA, Constantinides S, Jhaveri SN, Rand AG, Jr. Freshness assessment of six New England fish species using the Torrymeter. *J Food Sci* 1990; 55:79–82.

204. Valdimarsson G. Developments in fish processing—technological aspects of quality. In: Huss HH, Jakobsen M, Liston J, eds. *Quality Assurance in the Fish Industry*. Amsterdam: Elsevier Science Publishers, 1992: 169–184.

205. Johnson EA, Peleg M, Sawyer FM. Mechanical methods of measuring textural properties of fish flesh, *Refrigeration Sci Technol* 1981; 4:93–102.

206. Sawyer FM, Cardello AV, Prell PA, Johnson EA, Segars RA, Maller D, Kapsalis J. Sensory and instrumental evaluation of snapper and rockfish species. *J Food Sci* 1984; 49:727–733.

207. Botta JR, Bonnell G, Squires BE. Effect of method of catching and time of season on sensory quality of fresh raw Atlantic cod (*Gadus Morhua*). *J Food Sci* 1987; 52:928–939.

208. Gill TA, Kieth RA, Smith-Lall B. Textural deterioration of red hake and haddock muscle in frozen storage as related to chemical parameters and changes in myofibrillar proteins. *J Food Sci* 1979; 44:661–667.

209. Kramer DE, Peters MD. Effect of pH and prefreezing treatment on the texture of yellowtail rockfish (*Sebastes flavidus*) as measured by the Ottawa Texture System. *J Food Technol* 1981; 16:493–504.

210. LeBlanc E, Leblanc RJ, Blum IE. Prediction of quality in frozen cod (*Gadus morhua*) fillets. *J Food Sci* 1988; 53:328–340.

211. Bilinski E, Lau YC, Jonas REE. Objective measurement and control of firmness of canned herring. Canada Department of Fisheries and Environment, Fisheries and Marine Service, 1977; Technical Report No. 727: 23p.

212. Godber JS, Wang J, Cole MT, Marshell GA. Textural attributes of mechanically and cryogenically frozen whole crayfish (*Procambarus clarkii*). *J Food Sci* 1989; 54:564–566.

213. Krivchenia M, Fennema O. Effect of cryoprotectants on frozen whitefish fillets. *J Food Sci* 1994; 53:999–1003.

214. Krueger DJ, Fennema OR. Effect of chemical additives on toughening of fillets of frozen Alaska pollock (*Theragra chalcograma*). *J Food Sci* 1989; 54:1101–1106.

215. Marshell GA, Moody MW, Hackney CR, Godber JS. Effect of blanch time on the development of mushiness in ice-stored crawfish packed with adhering hepatopancreas. *J Food Sci* 1987; 52:1504–1505.

216. Hamann DD, Lanier TC. Instrumental methods for predicting seafood sensory texture quality. In: Kramer DE, Liston J, eds. *Seafood Quality Determination*. Amsterdam: Elsevier Science Publishers, 1994: 123–136.

217. Botta JR, Instrument for nondestructive texture measurement of raw Atlantic cod (*Gadus morhua*). *J Food Sci* 1991; 65:962–968.

218. Borderias AJ, Lamua M, Tejada M. Texture analysis of fish fillets and minced fish by both sensory and instrumental methods. *J Food Technol* 1983; 18:85–95.

219. Azam K, Mackie IM, Smith J. The effect of slaughter method of rainbow trout (*Salmo gairdneri*) during storage on ice. *Int J Food Sci Technol* 1989; 24:69–79.

220. Golovin AN, Slavin AV. Some data on changes in elastic and plastic properties of fish tissues during storage. *Trudy Vses N-I Instut Morskogo Rybngo Khozyaistvai Okeanografi* 1974; 95:27–32.

221. Tauti M, Hirose I, Wada M. A physical method of testing the freshness of raw fish. *J Imperial Fisheries Inst (Jpn)* 1931; 26:59.

222. Miller RJ, O'Keefe PJ. Seasonal and depth distribution size, and molt cycle of spider crabs (*Chionecetes opilio, Hyas araneus* and *Hyas coarctatus*) in a Newfoundland Bay. Canadian Technical Report of Fisheries and Aquatic Science 1981; 1003: 18p.

223. Foyle TP, Hurley GV, Taylor DM. Field testing shell hardness gauges for the snow crab fishery. *Canadian Industry Report of Fisheries and Aquatic Sciences* 1994; 193: 36p.

224. Botta JR, Brothers G. Soft shell crab assessment. Canada Department of Fisheries and Oceans, Newfoundland Region 1990; Atlantic Fisheries Development Project Summary No. 21: 4p.

225. Lee CM. Surimi process technology. *Food Technol* 1984; 38(11):69–80.

226. Hamann DD. Surimi, a building block for formulated foods. In: *Proceedings of the Meeting of Commission C2, Chilling and Freezing of New Fish Products*. Paris: International Institute of Refrigeration, 1990: 19–26.

227. Lee CM. Surimi manufacturing and fabrication of surimi-based products. *Food Technol* 1986; 40(3):115–124.

228. Lanier TC. Functional properties of surimi. *Food Technol* 1986; 40(3):107–114.

229. Lanier TC, Hart K, Martin RE. *A Manuel of Standard Methods for Measuring and Specifying the Properties of Surimi*. Raleigh, NC: Univ. North Carolina Sea Grant Program, 1991: 61p.

230. MacDougall DB. Colour vision and appearance measurement. In: Piggott JR, ed. *Sensory Analysis of Foods*, 2nd ed. London: Elsevier Applied Science Publishers, 1994: 103–130.

231. Anonymous. Chemical and health risk assessment—critique of existing practices and suggestions for improvements. In: Ahmed FE, ed. *Seafood Safety*. Washington, D.C.: National Academy Press, 1991: 172–266.

232. Tisler JM. The Food and Drug Administration's perspective on HACCP. *Food Technol* 1991; 45(6):125–127.

233. Francis FJ. Color measurement and interpretation. In: Fung DYC, Matthews, eds. *Instrumental Methods for Quality Assurance in Foods*. New York: Marcel Dekker, 1991: 189–209.

234. Bengoetxea K. Optical properties of fish classes. In: Pau LF, Olafsson R, eds. *Fish Quality Control by Computer Vision*. New York: Marcel Dekker, 1991: 71–78.

235. Botta JR, Bonnell G. Causes of reduced quality of fresh Atlantic cod (*Gadus morhua*) caught by Otter trawl. In: *Proceedings of the World Symposium on Fishing Gear and Vessel Design. St. John's, NF, Canada: Marine Institute*, 1988: 340–344.

236. Botta JR, Squires BE, Johnson J. Effect of bleeding/gutting procedures on the sensory quality of fresh raw Atlantic cod (*Gadus morhua*). *Can Inst Food Sci Technol J* 1986; 19(4):186–190.

237. Alaska Seafood Marketing Institute. *Color Evaluation Guide for Pacific Salmon (Coho and Chum)*. Juneau AK: Alaska Seafood Marketing Institute, 1993: 8p.

238. Alaska Seafood Marketing Institute. *Color Evaluation Guide for Pacific Salmon II (Pink and Sockeye)*. Juneau AK: Alaska Seafood Marketing Institute, 1993: 8p.

239. Bolton RS, Mann JH, Gushue W. Use of standardized color surfaces in the grading of canned salmon for colour. *J Fish Res Board Can* 1967; 24:1613–1621.

240. Dymond D. Electronic sorting of shrimp. *INFOFISH Int* 1988; 1(88):46–47.

241. Francis FJ, Clydesdale FM. *Food Colorimetry Theory and Applications*. Westport, CT: AVI, 1975: 477p.

242. Ochiai Y, Chow CJ, Watabe S, Hashimoto K. Evaluation of tuna meat discoloration by Hunter color difference scale. *Bull Jpn Soc Sci Fish* 1988; 54(4):649–653.

243. Skrede G. Instrumental colour analysis of salmonids. In: *Rapid Analysis in Food Processing and Food Control*, Vol 2. Proc Eur Food Chem IV. Leon Norvay: 1987: 470–474.

244. Skrede G, Storebakken T. Characteristics of color in raw baked and smoked wild and pen-reared Atlantic salmon. *J Food Sci* 1986; 51:804–808.

245. Skrede G, Storebakken T. Instrumental color analysis of farmed and wild Atlantic salmon when raw baked and smoked. *Aquaculture* 1986; 53:279–286.

246. Dziezak JD. Meetings reports: Color and appearance seminar. *Food Technol* 1989; 43(4):156–157.

247. Marshell GA, Moody MW, Hackney CR. Differences in color, texture and flavour of processed meats from red swamp crawfish (*Procambrus clarki*) and white river crawfish (*P. acutus acutus*). *J Food Sci* 1988; 53:280–281.

248. Young KW, Whittle KJ. Colour measurement of fish minces using Hunter L, a, b values. *J Sci Food Agric* 1985; 36:383–392.

249. No HK, Storebakken T. Color stability of rainbow trout fillets during frozen storage. *J Food Sci* 1991; 56:969–972, 984.

250. Gates KW, Parker AH. Characterization of minced meat extracted from blue crab picking plant by-products. *J Food Sci* 1992; 57:267–270, 292.

251. Wassen OH, Reppond KD, Kandianis TM. Antioxidants to preserve rockfish colour. *J Food Sci* 1991; 56:1564–1566.

252. Spencer KE, Tung MA. Surimi processing of fatty fish. In: Shahidi F, Botta JR, eds. *Seafood: Chemistry Processing Technology and Quality*. London: Chapman and Hall, 1994: 288–319.

253. Gullett EA. Color and food. In: Hui, YH, ed. *Encyclopedia of Food Science and Technology*. New York: John Wiley, 1992: 452–460.

254. Skrede G, Risvik E, Huber M, Enersen G, Bluumlein L. Developing a color card for raw flesh of astanthin-fed salmon. *J Food Sci* 1990; 55:361–363.

255. McCallum IM, Cheng KM, March BE. Carotenoid pigmentation in two strains of chinook salmon (*Oncorhynchus tshawytscha*) and their crosses. *Aquaculture* 1987; 67:291–300.

256. Arnarson H. Fish and fish product sorting. In: Pau LF, Olafsson R, eds. *Fish Quality Control By Computer Vision*. New York: Marcel Dekker, 1991: 245–261.

257. Arnarson H, Bengoetxea K, Pau LF. Vision applications in the fishing and fish product industries. In: Pau LF, Olafsson R, eds. *Fish Quality Control by Computer Vision*. New York: Marcel Dekker, 1991: 21–41.

258. Pau LF, Olafsson R. Advanced vision methods and technologies for the fishing and fish product industries. In: Pau LF, Olafsson R, eds. *Fish Quality Control by Computer Vision*. New York: Marcel Dekker, 1991: 283–290.

259. Strachan NJC, Murray CK. Image analysis in the fish and food industries. In: Pau LF, Olafsson R, eds. *Fish Quality by Computer Vision*. New York: Marcel Dekker, 1991: 209–223.

260. Sarkar NR. Machine vision for quality in the food industry. In: Fung DYC, Matthews RF, eds. *Instrumental Methods for Quality Assurance in Foods*. New York: Marcel Dekker, 1991:167–187.

261. Scudder B. Improving product yield. *Seafood Process Packaging Int*, 1993; Autumn: xvii–xix.

262. Botta JR, Kiceniuk JW, White DRL. Rapid non-destructive method of determining if snow crab (*Chionoecetes opilio*) are alive. In: Huss HH, Jakobsen M, Liston J, eds. *Quality Assurance in the Fish Industry*. Amsterdam: Elsevier Science Publishers, 1992: 369–375.

263. Botta JR, Kiceniuk JW. Quality control of various shellfish using electrical stimulation. *INFOFISH Int* 1993; 6(93):26–28.

264. Kaneps M, Boothroyd F. Evaluation of response of post-mortem, uncooked lobsters to electrical stimulation over time and correlation with cooked meat quality. Clarke's Harbour, N.S., Canada: Cleawater Fine Foods, 1991; Technical Memorandum: 8p.

265. Anonymous. Speedy shrimp grading. *INFOFISH Int* 1993; 5(93):12.

266. Emsholm H, Neilsen J, Borresen T. Automatic detection of fish fillets. In: *Rapid Analysis in Food Processing and Food Control*, Vol 2. Proc. Eur Chem IV. Leon, Norway: 1987: 450–454.

267. Anonymous. Excellent year and excellent prospects for Marel. *World Fishing* 1992; January: 30–31.

268. Anonymous. The computer revolution: An automatic quality control system for salted fish. *Fiskifrettir* 1991; 23(9):8.

269. Jason AC, Lees A. *Estimation of Fish Freshness by Dielectric Measurement*. Aberdeen, Scotland: Dept. of Trade and Industry, Torrey Research Station, 1971: 49p.

270. Martinsdottir E, Atnason A. Redfish, Kapittel 4, Sluttraport. In: *Nordic Industrial Fund, Quality Standards for Fish: Final Report Phase II* 1992: 21–35.

271. Lees A, Smith GL. Assessment of the freshness of fillets by the GR Torrymeter. In: Connell JJ, ed. *Anvances in Fish Science and Technology*. London: Fishing News Books Ltd, 1980: 400–403.

272. International Standards Organization (ISO). *International Standard: Sensory Analysis—Vocabulary*, ISO Reference number ISO 5492. Geneva, Switzerland: International Standards Organization, 1992: 22p.

273. Bourne MC. *Food Texture and Viscosity: Concept and Measurement*. New York: Academic Press, 1982: 325p.

274. Lee CM. Surimi processing from lean fish. In: Shahidi F, Botta JR, eds. *Seafood: Chemistry, Processing Technology and Quality*. London: Chapman & Hall, 1994: 263–287.

275. Lee CM, Chung KH. Analysis of surimi gel properties by compression and penetration tests. *J Texture Studies* 1989; 20:363–377.

276. Chung KH, Lee CM. Relationships between physiochemical properties of nonfish protein and textural properties of protein-incorporated surimi gel. *J Food Sci* 1990; 55:972–988.

277. Nielsen J, Reines JH, Jespersen CM. Quality assurance in the fishing industry with emphasis on the future use of vision techniques. In: Pau LF, Olafsson R, eds. *Fish Quality Control by Computer Vision*. New York: Marcel Dekker, 1994: 3–20.

278. York RK. Canadian fish products—fish inspection and sensory evaluation. *Can Inst Food Sci Technol J* 1989; 22(5):AT441–444.

279. International Standards Organization (ISO). *Sensory Analysis—General Guidance for the Selection, Training and Monitoring of Assessors, Part II: Experts, Draft International Standard*. Geneva Switzerland: ISO, 1991: 12p.

280. Poste LM, Mackie DA, Butler G, Larmond E. *Laboratory Methods for Sensory Analysis of Food*, Agriculture Canada, Research Branch, Ottawa, Ont., Canada, Publication 1864/E, 1991: 90p.

281. Codex Alimentarius Commission. *Draft Report of the Twentieth Session of the Codex Committee on Fish and Fish Products*. Bergen, Norway, 1992.

282. Howgate P. Review of inspection procedures (sensoric evaluation) for fish and shellfish. Joint FAO/WHO FOOD Standards Programme, Codex Alimentarius Commission, Committee on Fish and Fishery Products. Bergen, Norway, 1992: 33p.

283. Bjarnasson J. Past, present and future of the Icelandic fresh fish inspection. In: Moller A, ed. *Fifty Years of Fisheries Research in Iceland*. Iceland: Icelandic Fisheries Laboratories Reykjavik, 1984: 23–31.

284. Martinsdottir E, Stafansson G. Development of a new grading system for fresh fish. In: Moller A, ed. *Fifty Years of Fisheries Research in Iceland*. Reykjavik, Iceland: Icelandic Fisheries Laboratories, 1984: 45–59.

285. American Society of Testing and Materials (ASTM). *Guidelines for the Seletion and Training of Sensory Panel Members*. Philadelphia: ASTM Special Technical Publication, 1981, 758: 35p.

286. International Standards Organization (ISO). *Sensory Analysis—General Guidance for the Selection, Training, and Monitoring of Assessors*, Part I *SelectedAssessors*. Geneva, Switzerland: ISO, 1991, 15p.

287. Munoz A, Civille GV, Carr BT. *Sensory Evaluation in Quality Control*. New York: Van Nostrand Reinhold, 1992: 240p.

288. Civille GV, Lawless HT. The importance of language in describing perceptions. *J Sensory Studies* 1986; 1: 203–215.

289. Larsen E, Heldbo J, Jespersen CM, Nielsen J. Development of a method for quality assessment of fish for human consumption based on sensory evaluation. In: Huss HH, Jakobsen M, Liston J, eds. *Quality Assurance in the Fish Industry*. Amsterdam: Elsevier Science Publishing, 1992: 351–358.

290. Nielsen J, Hansen TK, Jonsdottir S, Larson EP. Development of methods for quality index of fresh fish. FAR Meeting, Noordwijkkerhort, Netherlands, 1992.

291. Brenner HA, Olley J, Vail AMA. Estimating time-temperature effects by a rapid systemic sensory method. In: Kramer DE, Liston J, eds. *Seafood Quality Determination*. Amsterdam: Elsevier Science Publishers, 1987: 413–435.

292. Jonsdottir S. Kvalitetsnomer pa sild, Slutrapport. In: *Nordic Industrial Fund, Quality Standards for Fish: Final Report Phase II*. 1992: 36–59.

293. Rahman HA, Olley J. Assessment of sensory techniques for quality assessment of Australian fish. *CSIRO Tasmanian Regional Laboratory Occasional Paper No. 8*, 1993: 55p.

294. Kudu G, Okada M, Miyauchi D. Gel-forming capacity of washed and unwashed flesh of some Pacific coast species of fish. *Marine Fish Rev* 1973; 35(12):10–15.

295. Montgomery DC. *Introduction to Statistical Quality Control*. New York: John Wiley, 1993: 674p.

296. O'Mahony M. *Sensory Evaluation of Food: Statistical Methods and Procedures*. New York: Marcel Dekker, 1986: 487p.

297. O'Mahony M. Some assumptions and difficulties with common statistics for sensory analysis. *Food Technol* 1982; 36(11): 75–82.

298. Gacula M, Jr. Some issues in the design and analysis of sensory data: Revisited. *J Sensory Studies* 1987; 2:169–185.

299. Smith GL. Statistical analysis of sensory data. In: Piggott JR, ed. *Sensory Analysis of Foods*. New York: Elsevier Science Publishers, 1988: 335–379.

300. Valdimarsson G, Einarsson H, King FJ. Detection of parasites in fish muscle by candling technique. *J Assoc Off Anal Chem* 1985; 68(3):549–551.

301. Howgate P, Johnston A, Whittle A (eds). *Multilingual Guide to EC Freshness Grades for Fishery Products*. Aberdeen, Scotland: Torry Research Station, Food Safety Directorate, Ministry of Agriculture Fisheries and Food, 1992: 32p.

302. Lupin HM, Gainninni DG, Soule CD, Davidovitch LA, Boreri L. Storage life of chilled Patagonian hake (*Merluccius hubbsi*). *J Food Technol* 1980; 15:285–300.

303. Stone H, Sidel JL. *Sensory Evaluation Practices*. New York: Academic Press, 1993: 338p.

304. Eggert J, Zook K. *Physical Requirement Guidelines for Sensory Evaluation Laboratories*. Philadephia: American Society for Testing and Materials (ASTM), Special Publication No. 913, 1986: 54p.

305. Meiselman HL. Consumer studies of food habits. In: Piggott JR, ed. *Sensory Analysis of Foods*. New York: Elsevier Science Publishers, 1988: 267–334.

306. Brandt FI, Arnold RG. Sensory difference tests in food product development. *Food Product Development* 1977; 11(8):56.

307. Muller HG. Sensory quality control: Report on a survey. In: Symons HW, Wren JJ, eds. *Sensory Quality Control: Practical Approaches in Food and Drink Production*. London: Institute of Food Science and Technology and Society of Chemical Industry, 1993.

308. Frijters JER. Sensory difference testing and measurement of sensory discriminability. In: Piggott JR, ed. *Sensory Analysis of Foods*. New York: Elsevier Science Publishers, 1988: 131–154.

309. Francois P, Sauvageot F. Comparison of the efficiency of pair, duo-trio and triangle tests. *J Sensory Studies* 1988; 3:81–94.

310. Howgate P. Measurement of tainting in seafoods. In: Kramer DE, Liston J, eds. *Seafood Quality Determination*. Amsterdam: Elsevier Science Publishers, 1987: 63–72.

311. Ennis DM. Relative power of difference testing methods in sensory evaluation. *Food Technol* 1990; 44(4):114, 116–117.

312. American Society for Testing and Materials (ASTM). *Standard Practice for the Determination of Odor and Taste Thresholds by a Forced-Choice Ascending Concentration Series Method of Limits*. Philadelphia: ASTM Publication E679, 1979: 513–519.

313. Frijters JER. Three stimulus procedures in olfactory psychophysics: An experimental comparison of Thurstone-Ura and 3-alternative force choice models of signal detection theory. *Perception Psychophys* 1980; 28:390–397.

314. Aust LB. Computers as an aid in discrimination testing. *Food Technol* 1984; 38(9):71–73.

315. Land DG, Shepherd R. Scaling and ranking methods. In: Piggott JR, ed. *Sensory Analysis of Foods*. New York: Elsevier Science Publishers, 1988: 155–185.

316. Riskey DR. Use and abuses of category scales in sensory measurement. *J Sensory Studies* 1986; 1:217–236.

317. Moskowitz HR, Jacobs BE. Magnitude estimation: Scientific background and use in sensory analysis. In: Moskowitz HR, ed. *Applied Sensory Analysis of Foods*. Vol I. Boca Raton, FL: CRC Press, 1988: 193–223.

318. Pangborn RM. Physiological and psychological misadventures in sensory measurement or the crocodiles are coming. In: Johnston RM, ed. *Sensory Methods for the Practising Food Technologist, IFT Shortcourse*. Chicago: Institute of Food Technologists, 1979: 3-1–3-21.

319. Cardello AV, Maller O. Psychophysical bases for the assessment of food quality. In: Kapsalis JG, ed. *Objective Methods in Food Quality Assessment*. Boca Raton, FL: CRC Press, 1987: 61–125.

320. Lawless HT, Malone GJ. A comparison of rating scales: Sensitivity, replicates and relative measurement, *J Sensory Studies* 1986; 1:155–174.

321. Sawyer FM. Sensory methodology for estimating quality attributes of seafoods. In: Kramer DE, Liston J, eds. *Seafood Quality Determination*. Amsterdam: Elsevier Science Publishers, 1987: 89–97.

322. Civille GV, Szczesniak AS. Guidelines to training a texture profile panel. *J Texture Studies* 1973; 4:204–223.

323. Nielson AJ, Ferguson VB, Kendall DA. Profile methods: Flavor profile and profile attribute analysis. In: Moskowitz HR, ed. *Applied Sensory Analysis of Foods*, Vol I. Boca Raton, FL: CRC Press, 1988: 21–41.

324. Powers JJ. Current practices and application of descriptive methods. In: Piggott JR, ed. *Sensory Analysis of Foods*, 2nd ed. New York: Elsevier Science Publishers, 1988: 187–266.

325. Prell PA, Sawyer FM. Flavor profiles of 17 species of North Atlantic fish. *J Food Sci* 1988; 53:1036–1042.

326. Rainey BA. Importance of reference standards in training panelists. *J Sensory Studies* 1986; 1:149–154.

327. Pangborn RMV. Sensory techniques of food analysis. In: Gruenwedel OW, Whitaker JR, eds. *Food Analysis: Principles and Techniques*, Vol 1, *Physical Characterization*. New York: Marcel Dekker, 1984: 37–93.

328. Dravnieks A. *Atlas of Odor Character Profiles*. Philadelphia: American Society of Testing and Materials (ASTM), Data Series 61, ASTM, 1985: 354p.

329. Skinner EZ. The texture profile method. In: Moskowitz H, ed. *Applied Sensory Analysis of Foods*. Boca Raton, FL: CRC Press, 1988: 89–107.

330. Cardello AV, Sawyer FM, Maller O, Digman L. Sensory evaluation of the texture and appearance of 17 species of North Atlantic fish. *J Food Sci* 1982; 47:1818–1823.

331. Solberg T, Tidemann E, Martens M. Sensory profiling of cooked, peeled and individually frozen shrimps (*Pandalus borealis*) and investigation of sensory changes during frozen storage. In: Kramer DE, Liston J, eds. *Seafood Quality Determination*. Amsterdam: Elsevier Science Publishers, 1987: 109–121.

332. Rutledge KP, Hudson JM. Sensory evaluation: Method for establishing and training a descriptive flavor analysis panel. *Food Technol* 1990; 44(12):78–84.

333. Rutledge KP. Accelerated training of sensory descriptive flavor analysis panelists. *Food Technol* 1992; 46(11):114–118.

334. Billmeyer BA, Wyman G. Computerized sensory evaluation system. *Food Technol* 1991; 45(7):100–101.

335. Roessler EB, Pangborn RM, Sidel JL, Stone H. Expanded statistical tables for estimating significance in paired-preference, paired difference, duo-trio and triangle tests. *J Food Sci* 1978; 43:940–943, 947.

336. Savoca MR. Computer applications in descriptive testing. *Food Technol* 1984; 38(9):74–77.

337. Findlay CJ, Gullett EA, Genner D. Integrated computerized sensory analysis. *J Sensory Studies* 1986; 1:307–314.

338. McGill LA. Sample preparation/presentation. In: Johnston RM, ed. *Sensory Methods for the Practicing Food Technologist, IFT Short Course*. Chicago: Institute of Food Technologists, 1979: 8-1–8-7.

339. Gacula MC, Jr, Singh J. *Statistical Methods in Food and Consumer Research*. New York: Academic Press, 1984: 505p.

340. Aust LB, Gacula MCJ, Beard SA, Washam RWI. Degree of difference test method in sensory evaluation of heterogeneous product types. *J Food Sci* 1985; 50:511–513.

341. Parker SB, ed. *McGraw-Hill Dictionary of Scientific Terms*, 3rd ed. New York: McGraw-Hill, 1984: 1781p.

342. Ockerman, HW, ed. *Source Book for Food Scientists*. Westport, CT: AVI, 1978: 925p.

343. Morris, C, ed. *Academic Press Dictionary of Science and Technology*. San Diego, CA: Academic Press, 1992: 2432p.

344. Oesterling MJ. Shellfish-crustaceans. In: Martin RE, Flick GJ, eds. *The Seafood Industry*. New York: Van Nostrand Reinhold (an Osprey Book), 1990: 88–102.

345. Datta AK. Sensors and food processing operations. In: Hui YH, ed. *Encyclopedia of Food Science and Technology*. New York: John Wiley, 1991: 2327–2333.

346. Flick GJ, Hong G, Hwang JW, Arganosa GC. Groundfish. In: Martin RE, Flick GJ, eds. *The Seafood Industry*. New York: Van Nostrand Reinhold (an Osprey Book), 1990: 32–66.

347. Castagna M. Shellfish-mollusks. In: Martin RE, Flick GJ, eds. *The Seafood Industry*. New York: Van Nostrand Reinhold (an Osprey Book), 1990: 77–87.

348. Anonymous. Occurrence of chemical contaminants in seafood and variability of contaminated levels. In: Ahmed FE, ed. *Seafood Safety*. Washington, D.C.: National Academy Press, 1991: 111–171.

349. Wong R, Fletcher G, Ryder J. *Manuel of Analytical Methods for Seafood Research*. New Zealand Department of Scientific and Industrial Research, DSIR Crop Research, Private Bag, Christchurch, New Zealand, Seafood Report No. 2, 1991; 79p.

350. Corlett DA, Jr. Regulatory verification of industrial HACCP systems. *Food Technol* 1991; 45(4):144–146.

351. Harrigan WF, Park RWA. *Making Safe Food: A Management Guide for Microbiological Quality*. London: Academic Press, 1991: 178p.

352. Nagodawithana T. Yeasts. In: Hui YH, ed. *Encyclopedia of Food Science and Technology*. New York: John Wiley, 1991: 2877–2905.

Index